Modelling Nation-state Information Warfare and Cyber-operations

Edited by

Brett Van Niekerk, Trishana Ramluckan and
Neal Kushwaha

Modelling Nation-state Information Warfare and Cyber-operations

ISBN: 978-1-914587-38-2 (print)

ISBN: 978-1-914587-39-9 (PDF)

Published by: Academic Conferences and Publishing International Limited, Reading, RG4 9AY, United Kingdom, info@academic-publishing.org

Available from www.academic-bookshop.com

Contents

i

About the Editors

 **Dr Brett van Niekerk** is a senior lecturer in IT at the Durban University of Technology. He serves as chair for the International Federation of Information Processing Working Group on ICT in Peace and War, and the co-Editor-in-Chief of the International Journal of Cyber Warfare and Terrorism. He has numerous years of information/cyber-security experience in both academia and industry, and has contributed to the ISO/IEC information security standards. In 2012 he graduated with his PhD focusing on information operations and critical infrastructure protection. He is also holds a MSC in electronic engineering and is CISM certified.

 Dr Trishana Ramluckan is the Research Manager at Educor Holdings and an Honorary Research Fellow at the University of KwaZulu-Natal's School of Law. Prior to this she was Postdoctoral Researcher in the School of Law and an Adjunct Lecturer in the Graduate School of Business at the University of KwaZulu-Natal. She is a member of the IFIP working group on ICT Uses in Peace and War and is an Academic Advocate for ISACA. She is also the Editor-in- Chief of the Educor Multidisciplinary Journal (EMJ). In 2017 she graduated with a Doctor of Administration specialising in IT and Public Governance and in 2020 she was listed as in the Top 50 Women in Cybersecurity in Africa. Her current research areas include Cyber Law and Information Technology Governance.

 Neal Kushwaha is a recipient of the 2019 Royal Humane Silver Medal of Bravery and 2020 commendation from the Governor General of Canada. Neal is an international bilingual speaker, a guest lecturer at Stellenbosch University, and a motivational speaker. He is the founder of a Canadian consulting company, IMPENDO Inc., specifically serving public sector clients. His research and consulting falls within the cross-section of cyberspace, security, and law. Neal has publications at various venues on topics ranging from policy and doctrine to technical matters. Aligned with his PhD research, he supports nations with their cyber programmes. While he is a prominent speaker at cyber conferences on the global stage, it is his climbing that generates the most interest. He is an accomplished mountaineer with over 28 years of climbing experience and climbs under the banner of Big Climbs, including Everest.

List of Contributing Authors

Shadi Alshdaifat
University of Sharjah, UAE

Leigh Armistead
ArmisteadTEC LLC, Virginia Beach, USA

Shaden Baradie,
German Research Center for Artificial Intelligence, Intelligent Network Research Group, Kaiserslautern, Germany

Jan Herbst
German Research Center for Artificial Intelligence, Intelligent Network Research Group, Kaiserslautern, Germany

Eduardo Izycki
King's College, London, United Kingdom and Universidade de Brasília, Brasília, Brazil

Eleni Kapsokoli
Department of International & European Studies, University of Piraeus, Greece

Andrew N. Liaropoulos
University of Piraeus, School of Economics, Business and International Studies, Greece

Christoph Lipps
German Research Center for Artificial Intelligence, Intelligent Network Research Group, Kaiserslautern, Germany

Trishana Ramluckan
University of KwaZulu-Natal and Educor Holdings, South Africa

Hans Dieter Schotten
German Research Center for Artificial Intelligence, Intelligent Network Research Group, Kaiserslautern and University of Kaiserslautern, Division of Wireless Communication and Radio Positioning, Kaiserslautern, Germany

Joshua Sipper
Air Force Cyber College, Air University, Montgomery, USA

Abderrahmane Sokri
DRDC CORA, Ottawa, Canada

Brett van Niekerk
University of KwaZulu-Natal and Durban University of Technology, South Africa

Samuel Wairimu
Karlstad University, Karlstad, Sweden

Editorial Preface

1 Introduction

Cyber operations have been increasing in complexity and number since the first publicised incident of a cyber-incident having direct physical consequences, which was the Stuxnet infection of the Natanz nuclear facility that spread beyond is apparent target and consequently became public. More nations are investing in cyber-capabilities in order to compete in the emerging digital conflict zone. Two quotes below, four years apart, illustrate the rapid rise of information and cyber in international power and conflict.

> *Coercive cyber capabilities are becoming a new instrument of state power, as countries seek to strengthen national security and exercise political influence. Military capabilities are being upgraded to monitor the constantly changing cyber domain and to launch, and to defend against, cyber attacks. (IISS, 2014: 19).*

> *Cyber capability should now be seen as a key aspect of some states' coercive power, giving them the chance to wage covert digital campaigns. This might be an adjunct to military power, or employed in its place, in order to accomplish traditional objectives. This has driven some European states to re-examine their industrial, political, social and economic vulnerabilities, influence operations and information warfare, as well as more traditional areas of military power. (IISS, 2018: 6)*

Major cyber-incidents such as WannaCry, NotPetya, Solarwinds and Hafnium, as wells as attempts at foreign election interference, were attributed to state actors (Greenberg, 2018; Hern, 2021; Mangan and Fazzini, 2018; Palmer, 2021; Schmitt, 2021b). The World Economic Forum *Global Risks Report* lists cyber-attacks in the top 10 risks for both likelihood and impact in 2020, and in the top 20 for likelihood in 2021 (WEF, 2020; WEF2021). Cyberattacks were listed in the top 5 risks by likelihood in 2012, 2014, 2018 and 2019, with 'data fraud or theft' also listed in the top 5 for 2017 to 2019 (WEF, 2021). Mimecast's *Confronting the New Wave of Cyberattacks: The State of Email Security 2022* report claims that "2021 appears to be the worst year on record for cybersecurity" (Mimecast, 2022: 3).

In 2020 the COVID-19 pandemic resulted in a rapid shift to working from home, with many organisations having to introduce additional security measures to cater for the new mode of working, and there was a rise in the use of web-based video conferencing; both of these attracted attention from both cyber criminals as well as state-actors (Palmer, 2020; Walcott, 2020). Espionage against research facilities was detected, as was the use of computational propaganda (Allen-Ebrahimian, 2020; Cimpanu, 2020). In addition to scams related to the pandemic, healthcare facilities in a number of countries were affected by ransomware (Duguin, 2021; Interpol, 2020); this latter development exploiting the crisis and the healthcare sector which was already under severe strain raised a number of ethical concerns. This led to a global virtual discussion series on "Protecting the Healthcare Sector from Cyber Harm", organised by the CyberPeace Institute, Microsoft and the Czech government (CyberPeace Institute, 2021).

Ransomware was also seen to affect the operations of critical infrastructure more: in addition to the healthcare incidents above, a major pipeline on the US East coast was affected, as was South Africa's major freight logistics company, Transnet (Gallagher and Burkhardt, 2021; Turton and Mehrotra, 2021). Compared to previous critical infrastructure cybersecurity incidents such as Stuxnet (Zetter, 2014) and the BlackEnergy attacks on the Ukrainian power grids in 2015 and 2016 (Zetter, 2017), these ransomware attacks appeared to have a far greater societal impact. The Colonial Pipeline incident resulted in panic buying of petrol on the US East Coast and three states declaring a state of emergency (BBC, 2021). The 2015 disruption of the Ukrainian power grid affected approximately 230 000 customers and lasted for 6 hours (Zetter, 2017). Similarly, the reported Israeli cyber-operation against an Iranian port was "limited in scope…but causing no substantial or lasting damage" (Bergman and Halbfinger, 2020), whereas the ransomware incident affecting the South African freight transportation resulted in much longer disruptions and forcing Transnet to declare *force majeure* for a week for some of its operations (Diphoko, 2021; Ginindza, 2021; Naidoo, 2021). Such incidents indicate that nations may use cyber-operations sparingly as a form of signalling, whereas ransomware groups need to inflict as much disruption as possible in order to coerce organisations to pay for the decryption keys.

From an international law and cyber-diplomacy perspective, there is still no universally accepted view on the details of how international law applies to cyber-operations. There has been some progress, with a number of initiatives through the United Nations and by other nations and organisations. The UN processes started with the establishment of the Group of Governments Experts (GGE) in 2004-2005 by the UN General Assembly (UNGA) to investigate the "developments in the field of information and Telecommunications in the context of international security" (Digital Watch,

Editorial Preface

2021; UNGA, 2003), of which five subsequent GGEs have been concluded in 2009-2010, 2012-2013, 2014-2015, 2016-2017, and 2019-2021 (Digital Watch, 2021; UNGA, 2005; UNGA, 2011; UNGA, 2014; UNGA, 2015b). Four reports were produced in 2010, 2013, 2015, and 2021, with the 2016-2017 GGE failing to reach consensus and produce a report (Digital Watch, 2021; Schmitt, 2021a). Key outcomes include the confirmation that international law does apply to operations in Cyberspace, and the proposal of norms for responsible behaviours of nations in Cyberspace (UNGA, 2013; UNGA 2015a).

The Open-Ended Working Group was instituted by the UNGA in 2018 to continue the work of the GGEs with particular emphasis on the implementation and further development of norms for responsible state behaviour in Cyberspace (Digital Watch, 2021; UNGA, 2018), which produced its final report in 2021, and a second OEWG was established to run from 2021-2025 (Digital Watch, 2021; UNGA, 2021). Key differences between the GGEs and OEWGs is that the GGE had at most 25 states represented (by selection), whereas the OEWG was open to all UN member states and also included supporting multi-stakeholder sessions to complement the formal discussions by the nations (Digital Watch, 2021; Let's Talk Cyber, 2021).

Another state-driven process is the Paris Call for Trust and Security in Cyberspace, which was implemented at the Paris Peace Forum in November 2018, and proposes 9 principles. In 2021, a number of working groups were held to further enhance the impact of the call, the results of which were presented at the Paris Peace Forum that year (Paris Call, 2021). Industry led initiatives include the European Cyber Agora (2021) and the CyberTech Accord (2021), with the other non-government and academia led initiatives such as the Oxford Process on International Law Protections in Cyberspace (2021) and the Global Commission for Cyber Stability, the latter which produced a report in 2019 also proposing a number of norms (GCSC, 2019).

In addition to the concept of a 'cyber-attack', the growth of apparent foreign interference in elections and online influence operations brings another dimension to state operations in Cyberspace. The most recognisable is the reported interference in the 2016 US Presidential Elections and the 2016 Brexit referendum, but also in Ukraine and European elections (Ramluckan and van Niekerk, 2019; Rid, 2021). The use of artificial intelligence and bots to generate propaganda has given rise to the field of computational propaganda (DAlessio, 2021), and example is the above-mentioned use of bots during the pandemic by nations (Allen-Ebrahimian, 2020).

3

At the time of writing, increasing tensions around Ukraine and cyber-incidents related to these tensions, such as the defacement of Ukrainian websites and increasing malware activity attributed to state-sponsored actors (Goodwin, 2022; Nardelli, Kuznetsov, and Choursina, 2022), raising the spectre of a 'cyber-war', with the potential for "collateral damage" being felt around the world (Janofsky, 2022). While these events were not foreseen at the time of embarking on the book project, they further illustrate the need for further research in the area of state-backed operations in Cyberspace.

With the growing prevalence of state operations in cyberspace and the increasing cyber diplomacy efforts, there is a need to begin collating related academic research to aid in modelling state activity in Cyberspace, whether it is their views in international law, the use of disinformation and online propaganda, or modelling trends of cyber incidents. This book is intended to contribute to the academic discussion and help fill the gap regarding state operations in Cyberspace. It is a follow-on initiative from a mini-track at the 20th *European Conference on Cyber Warfare and Security* in 2021. Given the background discussed above, the themes proposed for the submissions included:

- Models of national cyber-power;
- Mathematical, statistical and technical models of national cyber-operations and information warfare;
- International law frameworks applied to national cyber-security, cyber-warfare, cyber-espionage, information warfare, and influence operations;
- International relations models applied to information warfare, influence operations, cyber security, cyber-warfare, cyber-espionage, information warfare, and influence operations;
- Command and control and intelligence models for cyber-operations and information warfare;
- Modelling of nation-state and state-sponsored threat actors;
- Case studies of international cyber-security incidents and cyber-attacks;
- Wargaming of strategic cyber-operations, information warfare and influence operations; and,
- Closing the gap between technical and policy perspectives.

The following sections describe the chapter selection process and provide an overview of the chapters.

2 Processes for chapter selection

Chapters were solicited through an open call, of which some researchers were invited to contribute chapters based on their previous published research that was relevant to the book's themes. Twenty-one chapter proposals were received. All submitted chapters underwent a blind peer-review process, and nine chapters were selected for publication in the book.

Fourteen authors contributed to the 9 chapters, representing 11 institutions and 9 countries. Three chapters were co-authored, two of which has international collaboration. No country or institution contributed to more than 23% of the chapters, a breakdown of the national contributions to chapter is provided in Table 1 below. The values will not add to 100% due to international collaboration and some authors having dual international affiliations.

Table 1: International Representation of Chapters

Country	No. of Chapters
Brazil	1 (11%)
Canada	1 (11%)
Germany	1 (11%)
Greece	2 (22%)
South Africa	2 (22%)
Sweden	1 (11%)
UAE	1 (11%)
UK	1 (11%)
USA	2 (22%)

3 Overview of chapters

A total of nine chapters were selected after the per-review process. The first four are related to cyber in geopolitics and international law. Chapter 1, "Sanctions in Cyberspace: A Comparative Approach of the EU and US", is authored by Eleni Kapsokoli. In particular, she considers the effectiveness or symbolic nature to the two sanctions approaches. In Chapter 2 Andrew Liaropoulos discusses "The EU in the Era of Digital Geopolitics and the Challenge of Digital Sovereignty", where the challenges the EU faces in protecting its values, data and infrastructure amidst the technology race between the US and China.

Where the first two chapters focus on the European perspectives, the next two provide global considerations to cybersecurity and cyber governance. Brett van Niekerk, Shadi Alshdaifat, and Trishana Ramluckan propose a framework to foster cooperation in Cyberspace based on the cybersecurity incidents and the relevance, application, and limitations of international law to cyber-incidents in global commons in Chapter 3, "Towards an International Framework for Cyber Cooperation based on Global Commons". Chapter 4, "Cyber Power Diffusion: Global, Regional and Local Implications", is authored by Eduardo Izycki. He analyses a range of documents, notable technical reports of incidents and export controls to identify states that exhibit state-backed offensive cyber-operation capabilities and those that show evidence of acquiring capacity for offensive cyber-operations.

The next two chapters focus on cyber and information warfare related to healthcare and the pandemic. In Chapter 5, "Imaginable Cyberwar: Weaponization and Cyberespionage of e-Health Data", Samuel Wairimu considers the increasing trend of state-actors targeting the healthcare sector, the attack vectors used and the objectives of such cyber-operations, with some proposals for mitigating attacks. Chapter 6, "Pandemic Information Warfare: Cyberattacks, Disinformation, and Privacy during the COVID-19 Pandemic" authored by Brett van Niekerk and Trishana Ramluckan, investigates the malicious use of cyberoperations and disinformation by non-state and state actors during the early months of the pandemic, and the human rights implications of national measures to contain both the pandemic and accompanying 'infodemic' of misinformation.

The remaining three chapters are more technical in nature. Joshua Sipper continues the information warfare theme in Chapter 7, "Joint All-Domain Command and Control and Information Warfare: A Conceptual Model of Warfighting", where he proposes a combined model for information warfare (IW) and command and control in joint multi-domain operations, by considering the combined effects of four IW functions and how they can support multi-domain operations. Chapter 8, "Mathematical Modelling in Cyberspace", is authored by Abderrahmane Sokri, who considers a risk assessment and game-theoretical approaches to modelling cybersecurity, in particular to aid in cyber resource allocation. Finally, but not least, Christoph Lipps, Shaden Baradie, Jan Herbst, Leigh Armistead and Hans Dieter Schotten use the Colonial Pipeline incident as a case to discuss cybersecurity implications for industrial control systems and proposed some security solutions to protect critical infrastructure in Chapter 9, "Cybersecurity in Industrial Automation and Control Systems: The Recent Attack of the Colonial Pipeline".

Table 2 shows the alignment of the chapters with key themes of the book. As is evident, there is an even spread across the themes, with a mix of technical and non-technical aspects. This further highlights the importance of multi-disciplinary views and studies on cyber-operations and information warfare.

Table 2: Alignment of chapters to book themes

Chapter	Title	Cybersecurity in geopolitics	International law and cybersecurity	Cyberpower	Nation-state cyber-operations	Nation-state influence operations	Case studies of international cyber-	Modelling cyber-operations and IW	Critical infrastructure protection
1	Sanctions in Cyberspace: A Comparative Approach of the EU and US	x	x						
2	The EU in the Era of Digital Geopolitics and the Challenge of Digital Sovereignty	x	x						
3	Towards an International Framework for Cyber Cooperation based on Global Commons	x	x		x				
4	Cyber Power Diffusion: Global, Regional and Local Implications			x	x				
5	Imaginable Cyberwar: Weaponization and Cyberespionage of e-Health Data						x	x	x
6	Pandemic Information Warfare: Cyberattacks, Disinformation, and Privacy during the COVID-19 Pandemic				x	x			

Chapter	Title	Cybersecurity in geopolitics	International law and cybersecurity	Cyberpower	Nation-state cyber-operations	Nation-state influence operations	Case studies of international cyber-	Modelling cyber-operations and IW	Critical infrastructure protection
7	Joint All-Domain Command and Control and Information Warfare: A Conceptual Model of Warfighting				x	x		x	
8	Mathematical Modelling in Cyberspace							x	
9	Cybersecurity in Industrial Automation and Control Systems: The Recent Attack of the Colonial Pipeline						x		x
	Total	3	3	1	4	2	2	3	2

References

Allen-Ebrahimian, B., (2020) Bots boost Chinese propaganda hashtags in Italy, Axios, 1 April, [online], https://www.axios.com/bots-chinese-propaganda-hashtags-italy-cf92c5a3-cdcb-4a08-b8c1-2061ca4254e2.html

BBC, (2021) "US petrol supplies tighten after Colonial Pipeline hack", 12 May, [online], accessed 12 May 2021, https://www.bbc.com/news/business-57081386

Bergman, R., and Halbfinger, D.M., (2020) "Israel Hack of Iran Port Is Latest Salvo in Exchange of Cyberattacks", *The New York Times*, 19 May, [online], accessed 20 May 2020, https://www.nytimes.com/2020/05/19/world/middleeast/israel-iran-cyberattacks.html

Cimpanu, C., (2020) US formally accuses China of hacking US entities working on COVID-19 research, *Zero Day*, 13 May, [online], https://www.zdnet.com/article/us-formally-accuses-china-of-hacking-us-entities-working-on-covid-19-research/

CyberPeace Institute., (2021) *First, do no harm: A global dialogue on protecting healthcare from cyberattacks*, 22 September, [online], accessed 26 September 2021, https://cyberpeaceinstitute.org/news/global-dialogue-on-protecting-healthcare-from-cyberattacks/

CyberTech Accord (2021), [online], accessed 17 December 2021,
https://cybertechaccord.org/

DAlessio, F., (2021), "Computational Propaganda: Challenges and Responses", E-International Relations, 3 November, [online], accessed 6 November 2021,
https://www.e-ir.info/2021/11/03/computational-propaganda-challenges-and-responses/

Digital Watch (2021) "UN OEWG and GGE", [online], accessed 17 December 2021.

Diphoko, W., (2021) "Transnet website still down and chaos gets worse", *IOL*, 27 July, [online], accessed 27 July 2021,
https://www.iol.co.za/technology/software-and-internet/transnet-website-still-down-and-chaos-gets-worse-7a3fe743-5994-4c5e-aa96-900c7733e8f0

Duguin, S., (2021) "If healthcare doesn't strengthen its cybersecurity, it could soon be in critical condition", World Economic Forum, 8 November, [online], accessed 10 November 2021,
https://www.weforum.org/agenda/2021/11/healthcare-cybersecurity/

European Cyber Agora, (2021), [online], accessed 6 October 2021,
https://www.microsoft.com/en-eu/cyber-agora/

Gallagher, R., and Burkhardt, P., (2021) "'Death Kitty' Ransomware Linked to South African Port Attack", *Bloomberg*, 29 July, [online], accessed 30 July 2021, https://www.bloomberg.com/news/articles/2021-07-29/-death-kitty-ransomware-linked-to-attack-on-south-african-ports

Ginindza, B., (2021) "Transnet 'cyber attack' causes logistics logjam from road to freight and ports", IOL, 23 July, [online], accessed 23 July 2021,
https://www.iol.co.za/business-report/economy/transnet-cyber-attack-causes-logistics-logjam-from-road-to-freight-and-ports-56f6bd97-c5ef-4d65-90d6-c41d0fe290e2

Global Commission for the Stability of Cyberspace, (2019), *Advancing Cyberstability Final Report*, November, [online], accessed 1 December 2020,
https://cyberstability.org/report/

Goodwin, B., (2022) "'Russian-backed' hackers defaced Ukrainian websites as cover for dangerous malware attack", Computer Weekly, 18 January, [online], accessed 20 January 2022,
https://www.computerweekly.com/news/252512087/Russian-backed-hackers-defaced-Ukrainian-websites-as-cover-for-dangerous-malware-attack

Greenberg, A., (2018) "The White House Blames Russia for NotPetya, the 'Most Costly Cyberattack In History'", *Wired*, 15 February, [online], accessed 17 February 2018, https://www.wired.com/story/white-house-russia-notpetya-attribution/

Hern, A., (2021) "What is the Hafnium Microsoft hack and why has the UK linked it to China?" *The Guardian*, 19 July, [online], accessed 24 July 2021,
https://www.theguardian.com/world/2021/jul/19/what-is-the-hafnium-microsoft-hack-and-why-has-the-uk-linked-it-to-china

Interpol (2020) Cybercriminals targeting critical healthcare institutions with ransomware, [online], 4 April, https://www.interpol.int/en/News-and-

Events/News/2020/Cybercriminals-targeting-critical-healthcare-institutions-with-ransomware

Janofsky, A., (2022) "New Zealand warns of digital collateral damage from Russia-Ukraine crisis", *The Record*, 18 February, [online], accessed 20 February 2022, https://therecord.media/new-zealand-warns-of-digital-collateral-damage-from-russia-ukraine-crisis/

Let's Talk Cyber, (2021), [online], accessed 17 December 2021, https://letstalkcyber.org/

The International Institute for Strategic Studies, (2014) "Editor's Introduction: Financial and Strategic Rebalances Challenge Defence Planners," *The Military Balance*, vol. 114, pp. 5-8.

The International Institute for Strategic Studies, (2018) "Editor's Introduction: Western technology edge erodes further," The Military Balance, 118(1), pp. 5-6.

Mangan, D., and Fazzini, K., (2018) "North Korean hackers sanctioned, facing charges for Sony hack, Wannacry ransomware attack", CNBC, 6 September, [online], accessed 8 September 2018, https://www.cnbc.com/2018/09/06/north-korean-hackers-will-be-charged-for-sony-pictures-wannacry-ransomware-attacks.html

Mimecast, (2022) *Confronting the New Wave of Cyberattacks: The State of Email Security 2022*, [online], accessed 3 March 2022, https://www.mimecast.com/resources/ebooks/the-state-of-email-security-2022/

Naidoo, S., (2021) "Data 'has not been compromised' in Transnet cyber attack, says Gordhan's department", Moneyweb, 29 July, [online], accessed 29 July 2021, https://www.moneyweb.co.za/news/economy/data-has-not-been-compromised-in-transnet-cyber-attack-says-gordhans-department/

Nardelli, A., Kuznetsov, V., and Choursina, K., (2022) "Cyberattack Hits Ukrainian Websites as Russia Tensions Mount", *Bloomberg*, 14 January, [online], accessed 20 January 2022, https://www.bloomberg.com/news/articles/2022-01-14/several-ukraine-ministry-websites-struck-by-likely-cyberattack

Oxford Process on International Law Protections in Cyberspace, (2021), [online], accessed 17 December 2021, https://www.elac.ox.ac.uk/the-oxford-process/

Palmer, D., (2020), "Cyber criminals are trying to exploit Zoom's popularity to promote their phishing scams", *ZDNet*, 2 April, [online], accessed 18 April 2021, https://www.zdnet.com/article/cyber-criminals-are-trying-to-exploit-zooms-popularity-to-promote-their-phishing-scams/

Palmer, D., (2021), "SolarWinds: US and UK blame Russian intelligence service hackers for major cyberattack", *ZDNet*, 15 April, [online], accessed 18 April 2021, https://www.zdnet.com/article/solarwinds-us-and-uk-blame-russian-intelligence-service-hackers-for-major-cyber-attack/

Paris Call, (2021), [online], accessed 17 December 2021, https://pariscall.international/en/

Ramluckan, T., and van Niekerk, B., (2019) "International Humanitarian Law and Cyber-Influence Operations", *Journal of Information Warfare* 18(3), 67-82.

Rid, T., (2020) Active Measures: The Secret History of Disinformation and Political Warfare, Farrar, Straus and Giroux: New York.

Schmitt, M., (2021a) "The Sixth United Nations GGE and International Law in Cyberspace", Just Security, 10 June, [online], accessed June 15 2021, https://www.justsecurity.org/76864/the-sixth-united-nations-gge-and-international-law-in-cyberspace/

Schmitt, M.N., (2021b) "Foreign Cyber Interference in Elections", *International Law Studies*, vol 97, 739-764.

The World Economic Forum, (2020), *The Global Risks Report 2020*, 15 January, [online], accessed 20 January 2020, https://www.weforum.org/reports/the-global-risks-report-2020

The World Economic Forum, (2020), *The Global Risks Report 2021*, 19 January, [online], accessed 31 January 2021, https://www.weforum.org/reports/the-global-risks-report-2021

Turton, W., and Mehrotra, K., (2021) "Hackers Breached Colonial Pipeline Using Compromised Password", *Bloomberg*, 4 June, [online], accessed 6 June, https://www.bloomberg.com/news/articles/2021-06-04/hackers-breached-colonial-pipeline-using-compromised-password

United Nations General Assembly, (2003) A/RES/58/32 Developments in the field of information and telecommunications in the context of international security, 18 December.

United Nations General Assembly, (2005) A/RES/60/45 Developments in the field of information and telecommunications in the context of international security, 6 January.

United Nations General Assembly, (2011) A/RES/66/24 Developments in the field of information and telecommunications in the context of international security, 13 December.

United Nations General Assembly, (2013) A/68/98* Group of Governmental Experts on Developments in the Field of Information and Telecommunications in the Context of International Security, 24 June.

United Nations General Assembly, (2014) A/RES/68/243 Developments in the field of information and telecommunications in the context of international security, 9 January.

United Nations General Assembly, (2015a) A/70/174 Group of Governmental Experts on Developments in the Field of Information and Telecommunications in the Context of International Security, 22 July.

United Nations General Assembly, (2015b) A/RES/70/237 Developments in the field of information and telecommunications in the context of international security, 30 December.

United Nations General Assembly, (2018) A/RES/73/27 Developments in the field of information and telecommunications in the context of international security, 11 December.

United Nations General Assembly, (2019) A/RES/73/266 Advancing responsible State behaviour in cyberspace in the context of international security, 2 January.

United Nations General Assembly, (2021) A/RES/75/240 Developments in the field of information and telecommunications in the context of international security, 4 January.

Walcott, J. (2020) Foreign Spies Are Targeting Americans on Zoom and Other Video Chat Platforms, U.S. Intel Officials Say, *Time*, 9 April, [online], https://time.com/5818851/spies-target-americans-zoom-others/

Zetter, K. (2014) "An Unprecedented Look at Stuxnet, the World's First Digital Weapon", *Wired*, 3 November, [online] https://www.wired.com/2014/11/countdown-to-zero-day-stuxnet/

Zetter, K. (2017) "The Ukrainian Power Grid Was Hacked Again", *Vice*, 10 January, [online], accessed 12 January 2017, https://www.vice.com/en/article/bmvkn4/ukrainian-power-station-hacking-december-2016-report

Chapter One

Sanctions in Cyberspace: A Comparative Approach of the EU and US

Eleni Kapsokoli

Department of International & European Studies, University of Piraeus, Greece

ekapsokoli@unipi.gr

Abstract: Over the past years, both the EU and the US have faced numerous cybersecurity challenges that range from cyberattacks to the critical infrastructure to cases of ransomware and electoral interference. In order to cope with these security challenges, both actors have developed policies and institutions, including the policy option of sanctions. The purpose of this chapter is to review the cyber sanctions regimes imposed by these two actors. First, it briefly analyses the context of sanctions theory. In a latter phase, it relates the implementation of cyber sanctions with the technical, political and judicial parameters of cyber attribution. Having established a clear theoretical framework on cyber sanctions, it reviews the empirical evidence, which involves the sanctions imposed by Washington and Brussels. The end goal is to reach a conclusion on whether cyber sanctions are of symbolic nature or can be considered as an effective policy instrument. By comparing how two great powers used this policy instrument, broader conclusions about the uses and limits of the cyber sanctions regime can be reached.

Keywords: sanctions, cybersecurity, cyber sanctions, attribution, EU, US

1 Introduction

Cyberspace is a domain where norms and international regulations are gradually defining what is permissible and what is not. The increasing number of cyber incidents over the past decade demonstrates how state and non-state actors have developed a wide range of malicious cyber activities that include among others cyberattacks against the critical infrastructure, the dissemination of fake news and propaganda and the use of malware, to achieve their political goals. Malicious activities in cyberspace have become a growing threat and, therefore, the European Union (EU) and the United

States (US) have developed several institutions and policies in order to secure cyberspace and its users.

For almost a decade, the US has incorporated sanctions policy into its broader cybersecurity strategy. Since 2012, the US has imposed cyber sanctions to counter cyberattacks, cybercrime, cyber-espionage and disinformation campaigns. The US has attributed the above security issues to China, Russia, North Korea and Iran. On the other hand, the EU adopted the Cyber Diplomacy Toolbox which contains a number of diplomatic and operational measures, including the use of sanctions. In particular, the Council Regulation 2019/796 and the Council Decision 2019/797 established cyber sanctions regime. The cyber sanctions regime is a joint action of the EU which aims to secure an open and safe cyberspace based on norms and international law. Apart from the US, the EU is the only international actor that has proposed and applied cyber sanctions as a policy option in order to deal with cybersecurity issues.

Bearing in mind that cyberspace affects every facet of politics and security, it is critical to investigate how the concept of sanctions applies in this domain. Thus, this chapter aims to evaluate the utility of the cyber sanctions regime. In order to do that, it first reviews the concept of sanctions. Having established a solid understanding of sanctions, it analyses both the EU and the US policies and institutions that relate to the establishment of cyber sanctions regimes. The empirical evidence from the sanctions imposed to several cyber actors, enable us to reach safer conclusions about the utility of this strategic tool.

2   On sanctions

The term sanction is one of the most complicated and confusing terms in international politics. The international community is using sanctions to change the behaviour of a country or regime, in cases where that country or regime is violating human rights, waging war or endangering international peace and security (Baldwin, 1985). Sanctions are a tool for the policymakers to impose specific norms and behaviour to another actor. They can be of economic nature, but also include restrictions like travel bans and arms embargoes. Sanctions are defined as "an economic instrument which is employed by one or more international actors against another, ostensibly with a view to influencing that entity's foreign and/or security policy behaviour" (Taylor, 2010, 12). International actors use sanctions not only to shape or influence a state or generally an actor's behaviour or to disregard publicly or to put pressure to other state or non-state actors, but also to influence other actors' behaviour in order to support their policies and strategies.

For some scholars and practitioners, sanctions are mainly symbolic, they encapsulate the desire to act, but are not always effective in terms of shaping or influencing the behaviour of the targeted actors. In many cases, sanctions are imposed as a result of external pressure. In addition, there are also difficulties in applying such restrictive measures, since some countries are unwilling to participate. Furthermore, the targeted actors can diversify their policies regarding the sectors that are targeted (e.g. diversify their production, import from other sources, etc.) and thereby become more independent and minimise the impact of sanctions. Thus, sanctions are perceived as symbolic actions - when other diplomatic tools have failed or are unavailable - that facilitate the international or domestic pressure for responsible behaviour (Taylor, 2010, 19-20). Finally, the imposition of sanctions can have collateral damages not only for the targeted state or non-state actors, but also for the actors operating in the perpetrator's native environment (Pawlak & Biersteker, 2019, 7).

Sanctions enable policymakers to impose specific norms and behaviour to another actor which are related to their main political goals and objectives. The change of the behaviour will be successful if the senders and the targets share same interests and are likeminded, otherwise it will be ineffective or partially effective. The UN Security Council considers sanctions as a primary tool of peace enforcement, and of encountering different threats to the peace, breach of the peace or act of aggression (Charter of the United Nations, Article 39, 40 & 41). Sanctions are designed to change or influence a behaviour, to limit access to resources needed to conduct malicious activities and to stigmatize the perpetrators (Van den Herik, 2014, 433).

In general, it is difficult to value the effectiveness of sanctions. Although there have been cases in the past, where sanctions have proved to be unsuccessful, this does not exclude the possibility that they may be more useful in the future. There are two points that we should consider when applying sanctions. First, their efficiency must be seen in terms of the alternative solutions available to the policy maker at any given situation. In many cases where sanctions were imposed, they were not one of the many available options, but rather the only option. Second, sanctions have proved to be successful when they are multilateral and proportional to the goal to be achieved. Unless these conditions are met, sanctions will be counterproductive and weaken the credibility of those who impose this policy.

3   Cyber sanctions and attribution

Cyber sanctions aim to deter and respond to malicious activities following the process of attribution. Attribution is when a state or a company accuses publicly another actor for an attack. In order to attribute a cyberattack effectively, one must reveal the computer and network systems that were responsible for the attack and also identify the individuals that were responsible for these systems (Ivan, 2019, 8). The cyber sanctions are difficult to be imposed because the collection of the necessary intelligence to attribute a cyberattack is a challenging task.

Cyber attackers use crypto links, zombie routers and other ways to safeguard their anonymity and their location. The use of IP addresses as evidence of a cyberattack is not sufficient, because the attacker can alter or hide the location of the IP address. Thus, locating the origin of the attacker is a major security issue. The cyber attackers cover their affiliation with state actors to protect their source and act as a proxy via false-flag operations. The rise and spread of information and communication technologies (ICTs) and the emergence of smart cities facilitate the purposes of future perpetrators. Hard evidence on attribution requires information exchanges regarding the nature of the attacks, their actors and the vulnerabilities of the critical infrastructures. Posing sanctions based on inaccurate evidence could cause a diplomatic and political incident. There are two main obstacles regarding the attribution and response to cyberattacks. First, the ambiguity of the malicious cyber operations and second, the complexity of interconnectedness. As a result, states selects weak strategic tools such as sanctions or no response at all.

In the context of deterrence, states impose costs in the form of sanctions and indictments. They also aim to gain access to information systems in order to conduct offensive operations. The deterrence of threats in cyberspace is a complex procedure which combines actions of prevention, improvement of cyber defence capabilities and enhancement of the network systems' resilience. There are also challenges, such as the counterattack with cyber or physical means, political escalation and inefficient attribution (Libicki 2017). The supporters of cyber sanctions regime believe that imposition of these measure will be effective, because they will publicly expose and shame the perpetrators, making them afraid of more sanctions.

An inevitable question raised is whether cyber sanctions will be an effective tool to deter and respond to threats and attacks in cyberspace. Till now, the record is rather poor, since the policy option of cyber sanctions has rarely been used. The US government was the first country who imposed cyber sanctions against North Korea in 2015 as a response to the cyberattack on

Sony Pictures Entertainment (Liaropoulos, 2018, 265). Bearing in mind the relative effectiveness of sanctions in general, the difficulties in attributing cyberattacks and the broader policy options that are available, the following section reviews the cyber sanctions regime established by the EU and the US.

4 EU sanctions in cyberspace

The EU is no stranger to sanctions as a policy instrument. Sanctions involve the preventive measures (capacity building, awareness raising), the cooperative measures (dialogues, demarches), the stabilizing measures (statements, council conclusions, demarches, dialogues), the restrictive measures (diplomatic, individual: asset freeze and travel restrictions, economical: freeze of economic relations, assistance or cooperation) and the supportive measures (lawful responses with the use of article 51 or 42 paragraph 7 of the EU) (European Union External Action Service, 2016). As part of the Common Foreign and Security Policy (CFSP), sanctions include interruption of diplomatic relations, recall of diplomatic representatives, arms embargoes, restrictions on admission (travel bans), freezing of assets and economic sanctions or restrictions on imports and exports (European Commission, 2021). Over the past years, the EU has imposed 36 sanctions regimes. Some of these cases include the countering of terrorism in Libya in 1999, the case of Al Qaeda, the support of democracy, human rights and the law in the case of Belarus in 2006, and conflict management in the cases of Libya and Syria since 2011 (Moret & Pawlak, 2017, 2). The use of sanctions in the above cases was the desirable tool by policymakers when diplomacy seemed as a less effective strategy.

The EU imposes sanctions to implement the objectives of the CFSP, which are the promotion of international peace and security, prevention of conflicts, support of democracy, the rule of law and human rights and the defending of international law (European Commission, 2021). There are cases where the EU's member-states and institutions are hesitant to publish essential information to the Court of Justice, relating to the process of attribution. The above actors are reluctant to share critical intelligence, due to the fact that they do not wish to reveal their security breaches and therefore lose their prestige.

In terms of cybersecurity, the EU has developed over the last years a number of policies, strategies and institutions in order to safeguard its member-states in cyberspace. The EU aims to strengthen resilience in cyberspace, to build trust, to prevent conflicts, to protect human rights and freedoms and to promote multilateralism, but also to provide an open, safe and secure cyberspace to its citizens. To achieve the above, the EU needs to develop the necessary capabilities and technical know-how, to promote relevant norms and to engage both the civil society and the private sector in governing cyberspace (Kapsokoli, 2020).

In February 2015 the European Council mentioned for the first time the possibility of a joint EU diplomatic response to cyber threats (Council of the European Union, 2015). In 2016 the Presidency of Netherlands published a non-paper on "Developing a joint EU diplomatic response against coercive cyber operations", which pointed out that there is a need to mention the consequences of malicious activities in order to influence the behaviour of possible invaders and the need to develop a toolbox which the EU can use to respond to such cyber activities (Council of the European Union, 19 May, 2016).

In 2017, the EU stated that restrictive measures are the most suitable strategic tool of its foreign policy in order to minimize cyber threats and influence the behaviour of perpetrators. The EU restrictive measures apply only to EU based entities. The Framework on a Joint EU Diplomatic Response to Malicious Cyber Activities, the Cyber Diplomacy Toolbox refers that the restrictive measures should be adopted depending on scope, scale, duration, intensity, complexity, sophistication and impact of the malicious activity in cyberspace. It also includes confidence building measures, awareness raising on EU policies, EU cyber capacity building in third countries, negotiations, dialogues and demarches, as well as sanctions (Council of the European Union, 7 June 2017). This toolbox enables the EU to contribute to conflict prevention, to strengthen the rules based order in cyberspace, including the application of international law and the norms of responsible state behaviour, but also to raise awareness among the public and the decision makers.

On 16 April 2018 the European Council adopted conclusions on malicious cyber activities which pointed out the importance of a global, open, stable and secure cyberspace and it also mentioned the threat of malicious activities in cyberspace (Council of the European Union, 16 April 2018). The European Council stressed the need to enhance the process of attribution on cyberattacks through the use of the Cyber Diplomacy Toolbox and the cyber resilience in order to have effective cybersecurity (Council of the European Union, 28 June 2018). Later that year, the European Council requested from the member-states to develop their cyber capabilities in order to respond and deter attacks and threats through cyberspace (Council of the European Union, 18 October 2018).

Likewise, on 12 April 2019, the High Representative declared the need of promoting an open, stable and secure cyberspace, the respect of human rights, freedom and rule of law, the urging of actors to stop using cyberspace for malicious activities in order to facilitate their actions and the need for strengthening national and international cooperation (Council of the European Union, 30 July 2020). Both the Council Decision 2019/797 and the Council Regulation 2019/796 enlisted six types of cyberattacks which could lead to the imposition of sanctions. This list includes attacks against the critical infrastructure, the essential services, the critical state functions, the storage or processing of classified information, the government emergency response teams and the EU institutions and Common Security and Defence Policy missions and operations. These attacks should have a significant effect, including attempted cyberattacks which constitute an external threat to the EU or its member-states according to Article 1 of the Council Decision. Moreover, the Council Decision 2019/797 stresses that member-states could adopt measures to prevent the entry into or transit through their territories of individuals who are responsible for cyberattacks or the support to attempt cyberattacks. The EU points out that sanctions are not a measure of attribution of responsibility to a state actor, because a major number of cyberattacks (Stuxnet, WannaCry 2.0 and NotPetya) were designed by state actors and were operated by non-state actors. It is also not clear which are the criteria to characterize a cyberattack as a significant effect. The list of criteria was provided by the European Council regarding the cyberattack's impact, for example the scope, the impact or the severity of disruption caused, the number of natural or legal persons, entities or bodies that are affected, the amount of economic loss, the amount or nature of data stolen (Official Journal of the European Union, 2019a; Official Journal of the European Union, 2019b).

The EU sanctions regime is a sophisticated and complex set of measures which enables the member-states to choose between a number of possible instruments that can be used in combination with other important EU documents and legally binding decisions (Moret & Pawlak, 2017, 2). The EU's cyber sanctions regime could trigger other likeminded nations to respond in a similar manner and thereby bolster emergent norms or reinforce existing ones (Pawlak & Biersteker, 2019, 5). The EU is adopting a more active role in order to secure cyberspace based on the international norms, laws and rules of behaviour. Now, the EU is a key cyber player in the international "cyber-chessboard" due to the autonomous cyber sanctions regime, which functions as a tool to deal with malicious state or non-state actors.

However, sanctions regime is not so autonomous because it is subject to judicial decision by the Court of Justice of EU (Abazi, & Eckes, 2018, 753–

782). The EU cannot be sure how precise and accurate are the data which are used as evidence for the technical and political attribution of perpetrators in order to characterize a malicious cyber activity as a cyberattack and proceed with the imposition of relative sanctions. The evidence that is based on the data collected from the intelligence services may often be false due to human error.

Even though the inclusion of sanctions as a policy option in the EU Cyber Diplomacy Toolbox points to the right direction, we have to bear in mind the following constraints. First, the EU seems to navigate in uncharted waters, since there is no previous example of cyber sanctions regimes. Second, and despite the progress in harmonizing national cyber policies and legislations, there is still lack of consensus within the Union regarding definitions and approaches to cybersecurity. In particular, member-states differentiate on what constitutes a cyberattack and what evidence is needed in order to attribute it. Third, not all member-states have the technical ability and necessary intelligence to attribute a cyberattack, coordinate intelligence collection efforts and intelligence sharing. Fourth, and in direct relation to the above point, the sanctions regime is not an entirely autonomous mechanism, since it is subject to judicial decision by the Court of Justice of the EU. Actually, there are many cases of cyber sanctions which have been lost to the European Court of Justice due to insufficient proof by the EU Council. Fifth, cyber sanctions are not a panacea, but rather one more policy instrument. Thus, cyber sanctions must be combined with other policy instruments such as diplomacy, law enforcement, dialogue and cooperation with other likeminded countries and institutions. Sixth, cyber sanctions might influence state and state sponsored actors, but will have limited effect on non-state actors that are not dependent on their governments. Seventh, the member-states through the process of public attribution are taking the risk to expose important information and cyber capabilities. The cyber attackers can take advantage of this information for their activities to become more effective. The above happened in the NotPetya case, where the perpetrators utilized the public information regarding the WannaCry 2.0. The sharing of intelligence and cyber capabilities publicly should be in a more secure environment with limited access by non-competent actors. Getting back to the thorny issue of reliable attribution, the effectiveness of the cyber sanctions regime is highly depended on the ability to attribute a cyberattack. Apart from the technical parameters of identifying the source of an attack, attributing an attack to a specific actor, country, company or individual, is after all a political decision.

Bearing in mind the above constraints of cyber sanctions regime, the EU has adopted the following two sanctions packages. On 17 May 2019 the Council Decision 2019/796 established a framework for restrictive measures to deter and respond to threats through cyberspace (Official Journal of the European Union, 17 May 2019a). Through this framework, the EU managed to impose targeted restrictive measures so as to deter and respond to attacks through cyberspace against the EU or its member-states. The cyber sanctions will be imposed to cyberattacks that originate or are carried out from outside the EU, or use infrastructure outside the EU, or are carried out by persons or entities established or operating outside the EU, or are carried out with the support of person or entities operating outside the EU. Specifically, the above framework permits the EU to impose for the first time sanctions against persons or entities who are responsible for cyberattacks or malicious activities. The sanctions include, among others, travel bans on persons travelling in and out of the EU, the prohibition of raising funds and the freeze of assets (Official Journal of the European Union, 17 May 2019b, 2).

On 30 July 2020, within the framework of the CFSP, the European Council announced a regime of cyber sanctions which included travel bans and asset freezes against six individuals and three entities or bodies who were involved in a series of cyberattacks against the EU or its member-states, public and private sector. These persons and entities or bodies are responsible for the following cyberattacks: WannaCry 2.0, NotPetya, Operation Cloud Hopper and the attempted cyberattack against the Organisation for the Prohibition of Chemical Weapons (OPCW). The sanctions targeted the following (Official Journal of the European Union, 2020):

- Four members of Unit 74455 of Russia's military intelligence agency (GRU) for the NotPetya and the hacking of the Wi-Fi system for OPCW in Hague in April 2018. The Council also enlisted the GRU for attacking the Ukrainian Electricity grid in 2015.
- Two Chinese citizens who are known as of "Advanced Persistent Threat 10" (APT10) and the technological development company Huaying Haitai for their involvement in an attack on information systems of companies in the six continents and in the EU and service provider located in the EU such as Swedish Ericson, which was named Operation Cloud Hopper.
- The Lazarus group, which consists of the North Korean company Chosun Expo for the Wanna Cry 2.0 ransomware attack, the collapse of the British NHS servers and millions of losses for the affected private sector. The WannaCry 2.0 disrupted information systems around the world by targeting information systems with

ransomware attacks and blocking access to data. It affected the information systems of companies inside the EU.

The attribution of cyberattacks to Chinese, Russian and North Korean entities and individuals is considered to be a bold move for the EU. It demonstrates clearly that the EU and its member-states have embraced the need to be more active than passive, when it comes to cybersecurity. After the announcement of the cyber sanctions regime by the Council of the European Union, the US, the UK, Australia and Canada publicly supported this policy initiative. On the contrary, Russia and China criticized the EU for following a restrictive position instead of using a diplomatic tool like the dialogue.

On 11 September 2020 the Horizontal Working Party on Cyber Issues started the discussions for a second cyber sanctions package by the EU (Council of the European Union, 8 September, 2020). The Bundestag hack on 2015 triggered the above package. This cyberattack resulted in the exfiltration of 16GB of data of the German Parliament's information technology network. In October 2020 the European Council announced the second package of cyber sanctions against the head of GRU, Igor Kostyukov and the GRU officer, Dmitriy Badin and the GRU Unit 26165 (also known as APT28). The European Council had already announced sanctions for Kostyukov which included a travel ban and asset freeze in January 2019 for the Salisbury chemical attack on Sergei Skripal and his daughter. Moreover, the German authorities issued an arrest warrant for Badin in May 2020 for the Bundestag hack. This cyber sanctions package referred to more EU travel restrictions on Badin, since they could not arrest him because he was not on EU territory (Council of the European Union, 22 October, 2020). Only six out of twenty-seven EU member-states publicly endorsed the second cyber sanctions package. The Netherland's Ministry of Foreign Affairs published a written statement and the other member-states, Austria, Belgium, Denmark, Estonia and Latvia only published a supportive post in Twitter.

In March 2021, the Finnish Central Criminal Police and the Finnish Security Intelligence Service attributed the breach of the Finnish Parliament's information system in 2020 to the Chinese hacker group Advanced Persistent Threat 31 (APT31) (SUPO, 2021). In April 2021, The Computer Emergency Response Team of the EU Institutions, Bodies and Agencies (CERT-EU) stated that six EU institutions, bodies and agencies were affected by the cyberattack of Solar Winds (European Parliament, 2021). In July 2021, the EU High Representative Josep Borrell published the declaration that malicious cyber activities which affected EU's economy, security, democracy and society, have been conducted from the Chinese territory. The APT31 is responsible for the exploitation of the Microsoft Exchange servers which undermined the security and integrity of thousands of information systems in the EU. He also stated that they have detected cyber malicious activities from one more Chinese hacker group the Advanced Persistent Threat 40 (APT40) (Council of the European Union, 19 July 2021). Few days later, the CERT-FR of the French cybersecurity agency ANSSI, stated that they have detected malicious cyber activities from APT31 (CERTFR, 2021). On 24 September 2021 Borrell declared that the GRU Ghostwriter, a Russian hacker, was trying to conduct malicious cyber activities against the public sector. These activities aimed to undermine the democratic values and processes of the EU and thus Brussels would consider taking further steps (Council of the European Union).

The EU has already adopted two cyber sanctions regimes and they are discussing the adoption of a third one. During the presidency of Portugal, it was decided to prolong the framework for sanctions for one more year till 18 May 2022 (Council of the European Union, 17 May, 2021). The lack of collective attribution in the EU and its member-states is an obstacle. Taking into consideration that many EU member-states, especially the smaller ones, do not have the efficient capabilities and intelligence networks to effectively attribute such malicious activities (European Commission, 13 June, 2018).

5 US sanctions in cyberspace

The US security policy in the past decade used sanctions and especially economic and trade sanctions to counter security threats. The last three presidencies of the US imposed sanctions to thousands entities and individuals. President Obama imposed sanctions on an average of 500 entities per year for human rights violations, nuclear proliferation, violation of territorial sovereignty and hacking incidents. Sanctions were also enacted by Trump's presidency. President Joe Biden imposed sanctions to Myanmar's military leaders who executed the coup, on the government of Nicaraguan for the unfair elections and Russia for the hacking incidents. The US include the sanctions regime in their cybersecurity strategy of 2012 when Obama's government publicly attributed Iranian Ministry of Intelligence and Security (MOIS) for its support to terrorist groups (Hezbollah) and their hacking activities. They imposed a total of 311 cyber sanctions, Russia (141), Iran (112) and North Korea (18) (US Department of the Treasury, 2012). The US Treasury Department has imposed cyber sanctions to 13 individuals and 19 entities during 2021 (US Department of the Treasury, 21 September 2021).

The US cybersecurity strategy is based on defence, deterrence and response. Defence is hard to achieve due to the rapid evolution of ICT's techniques, so the intrusion is an easy task for the perpetrator. The US stated that the procedure of deterrence will be by denial or efforts that aim to persuade adversaries that the US can prevent malicious cyber activities, but also deterrence by cost imposition or measures that are designed to both threaten and carry out actions to impose costs against actors who release cyberattacks or other malicious cyber activities against the US (US Department of the Treasury, 2012). In the context of deterrence, the US government and intelligence services do not provide evidence in public regarding the hacking efforts on the US critical infrastructure.

The US adopts a more offensive than defensive attitude as a response to the increasing cyber violent behaviour by other actors. General Paul Nakasone stated that "We have learned that defending our military networks requires operations outside of our military networks…proactively hunt for adversary malware on our own networks rather than simply waiting for an intrusion to be identified" (Tucker, 2020). In other words, the US counter cyber threats by actively interfering with offensive operations, like undermining and limiting the abilities of perpetrators, blocking its competitor's campaigns and by hacking-back. This active approach protected the US elections in 2018 and 2020 and prevented a number of malicious cyber activities. However, defence, deterrence and response failed to prevent the malicious cyber activities in the Microsoft Exchange servers in 2017 and 2021 and the Solar Winds in 2020. As the Cyberspace Solarium Commission stated about the effectiveness of deterrence, "Today most cyber actors feel undeterred if not emboldened, to target our personal data and public infrastructure…through our inability or unwillingness to identify and punish our cyber adversaries, we are signalling that interfering in American elections or stealing billions in US intellectual property is acceptable" (Cyberspace Solarium Commission, 2020).

US sanctions are categorized to primary and secondary ones. Primary sanctions are imposed on a US actor for security issues which are taking place within the US. The secondary sanctions are imposed by the Office of Foreign Assets Control (OFAC) or the State Department, on a non-US person (Comply Advantage). The OFAC is under the US Department of the Treasury, and imposes economic and trade sanctions against malicious state and non-state behaviour. The OFAC sanctions can be a program that blocks a government and contains broad geographically trade restrictions, or can be more limited, such as a program that sanctions specific individuals (OFAC, 2017).

Following, the cyberattack to Sony Pictures Entertainment by the North Korean hacking group, Lazarus in 2014, the US administration announced cyber sanctions regime in 2015. The Executive Order (E.O.) "Blocking the

Property of Certain Persons Engaging in Significant Malicious Cyber-Enabled Activities", allowed the imposition of sanctions to individuals and entities for their participation in or contribution to malicious cyber activities (The White House, April 2015).

After the 2016 US presidential elections interference, Obama amended the E.O. of 2015 regarding the sanctions regime and referred to two Russian intelligence services (GRU and Federal Security Service (FSB)), to four individual officers of the GRU and to three companies that provided support for that incident (The White House, 2016). This E.O. referred to the sanctioning of malicious Russian cyber activity and focused on cyber-enabled malicious activities regarding the critical infrastructure, the network of computers and the misappropriation of economic resources. These persons who were responsible for the elections hacking, called as "personae non gratae", forcing them to leave the US within 72 hours. The sanctions regime included diplomatic and economic measures. This proves how much the government was reluctant to adopt a more offensive stance and meaningful punishments against Russia in order to prevent future interference. This case illustrates the problem of attributing cyberattacks to specific individuals or entities, because the perpetrator's location is in either hostile foreign jurisdictions with non-existent law enforcement (Russia and China) or with non-existent legal framework (Southeast Asia).

For the period of Obama's presidency, the cyber deterrence was a catchphrase, due to its willingness to build a strong and resilient defence in its information network systems, to recover rapidly from malicious cyber activities and to conduct cyberattacks as a punishment to adversaries for these disruptions (White House Report on Cyber Deterrence Policy, 2015). The US face the following challenge, how to respond to a cyberattack and avoid retaliation such as the large-scale Iranian DDoS attacks, Operation Ababil between 2011 and 2013 that followed the Stuxnet (FBI, 2016). The same concerns about unintended costs and retaliation were expressed during the US government's decision-making process on its response to the 2016 Russian election interference. It is reported that Obama had approved offensive cyber operations against the Russian critical infrastructure. But these operations were not implemented, because Washington considered that they could lead to a political escalation, especially during the pre-election period (Miller, Nakashima & Entous, 2017).

The Trump administration expanded cyber sanctions regime through the Presidential Documents and publicly attributed five entities and 19 individuals for malicious cyber activities for interference in the US elections of 2016 and NotPetya, but also as a response to the Russian efforts to

25

destabilize the US (Federal Register, 2018). Two entities and six individuals had already been sanctioned for the 2016 US elections and Yahoo! of 2014. The NotPetya attack on 2017 targeted primarily Ukrainian companies and institutions, but it also affected organizations, companies and critical infrastructure outside the Ukrainian territory, resulting to economic loss of 10 billion dollars. The US attributed this major destructive cyberattack to Russia (White House, 2018; US Department of The Treasury, 15 March 2018). The sanctions regime did not clearly punish the perpetrators of NotPetya cyberattack, but was considered as a response to the hostile attitude of Russia against the US.

The WannaCry 2.0 and NotPetya cyber incidents confirm how complicated and sophisticated the process of attribution is, since no sensitive information and methods of perpetrator's were published, but also the time that it took to publicly attribute these attacks. The WannaCry 2.0 was conducted in May 2017 and attributed in December of the same year. Likewise, the NotPetya was conducted in June 2017, whereas the attribution was announced in February 2018 (White House, 2018). Based on the above, it is obvious that large-scale cyberattacks cannot be timely attributed, because there are few perpetrators that possess such capabilities.

According to the 2018 Department of Defense Cyber Strategy, the US will work with likeminded states to deter cyber-threats through the sharing of information and best practices, enhancing the attribution process and promoting joint actions. The US military can carry out activities in and out of cyberspace in order to collect information, disrupt malicious cyber activities and respond to these activities, below the level of armed conflict (US Department of Defense, 2018).

In September 2019, the US government imposed sanctions to hacking group Lazarus Group and its two sub-groups, Bluenoroff and Andariel, which had connections to North Korea's government and its intelligence bureau, the Reconnaissance General Bureau (RGB). These groups targeted government, military, financial, manufacturing, media, entertainment and international shipping companies, and critical infrastructure. Lazarus Group was involved in the WannaCry 2.0 ransomware attack in 2017, which had large-scales effects and was publicly attributed by many countries, and for the Sony Pictures Entertainment attack in 2014. The Bluenoroff conducted cyberattacks worldwide against financial institutions in 2018 and had attempted to steal 1.1 billion dollars. The Andariel was reported in 2015 for cyberattacks against South Korea's government. The sanctions included the prohibition of property and interests of North Korean entities, and of any entities that are owned directly or indirectly by North Korean entities, that are in the US or in the possession or control of US citizens (US Department of The Treasury, 2019).

During the COVID-19 pandemic, the online payments and activities have increased and some cyber actors released malicious cyber activities that affected the financial institutions, cyber insurance firms and digital forensics companies. The OFAC published an advisory report on the potential sanctions risks for facilitating ransomware payments and it referred to large-scale cyberattacks with huge economic loss. The large-scale cyberattacks are the following: 1) the Cryptolocker infected more than 234,000 computers from 2013 to 2016, 2) the SamSam ransomware by Iranians cyber actors gained access to information from government institutions and companies from 2015 to 2018, 3) the WannaCry 2.0 in 2017 infected more than 300,000 computers from 150 countries 4) the Lazarus Group, Bluenoroff and Andariel, North Korean's hacking groups which conducted cyberattacks from 2014 to 2018 and 5) the Evil Corp, a Russian cybercriminal group that used the Dridex malware to infect ICTs programs in over 40 countries and cause 100 million in theft. It also referred, that the OFAC imposed sanctions to these actors for conducting the above mentioned cyber malicious activities, and other actors for supporting them (US Department of the Treasury, 2020). On 19 October 2020, the U.S Department of Justice publicly attributed six Russian officers of GRU Unit 74455, also known as Sandworm, for conducting malicious cyber activities against the 2017 French Elections, the 2018 PyeongChang Winter Olympic Games (Olympic Destroyer), the Ukrainian Government in 2016 and Georgian Government in 2019, but they do not impose any further sanctions (Department of Justice, 2020).

The US government published in 2021 an E.O for the harmful foreign activities of Russia and imposed economic sanctions. They also publicly attributed to the Russian government, the Russian intelligence services and Russian technology companies the Solar Winds hack of 2020, the US elections interference of 2020 and the poisoning of Kremlin politician Alexei Navalny in 2018 (The White House, April 15, 2021; US Department of The Treasury, 2021).

6   Concluding remarks

Countering the security challenges that cyberspace poses is not an easy task. The US and the EU are the only two actors that have used sanctions as a policy option to counter the complex threats that derive from this domain. As in any case were sanctions are used, the imposition of restrictive measures raises once more the question of whether sanctions are truly effective or whether their utility is restricted in their symbolic nature. In the case of cyber sanctions thought, this question is even more difficult to answer due to the unique and complex nature of cyberspace, where reliable attribution remains not only a technological challenge, but also or rather more, a political one.

As regards the EU, the imposition of cyber sanctions serves as a hard test on whether the Union is willing to become a reliable cybersecurity provider. Brussels have to choose between attributing cyberattacks and thereby jeopardising its relations with other countries, and not responding to cyber threats with cyber sanctions and thus choosing a more preferable policy option. So far the record is mixed. The EU imposed cyber sanctions, but lacked public support, since only six out of the twenty-seven member-states publicly endorsed the second cyber sanctions package (Soesanto, 2020). Till now, the imposition of cyber sanctions are against individuals, although threats and attacks are designed and ordered by states. As a result, the perpetrators could unleash cyberattacks against the same targets or new targets in the near future.

Considering the US, Washington has taken specific decisions, but always under the veil of uncertainty due to the complexity of cyberspace and the non-existence of proper management of this realm. The management of cyber threats involves political, technical and economic challenges along with the adoption of precautionary measures. These precautionary measures will lead to the enhancement of resilience and effective deterrence. The interaction between cyberspace and international politics creates several dilemmas regarding the appropriate response and how, misconceptions, collateral damage and further escalation can be avoided. These dilemmas existed and were obvious in the Obama's and Trump's administrations but also now in the Biden's one.

Cyber sanctions is a policy option that has been utilised by both the US and the EU and will most probably be also used by other great powers like China and Russia. This is a vicious circle. Cyber sanctions are an ineffective tool of response, due to technical reasons such as the existence of unclear evidence, false links and untraceable perpetrators. Nevertheless, the political value of the cyber sanctions regime lays in its symbolism. By imposing cyber sanctions, the EU demonstrates its willingness to respond and preserve its core values and its sovereignty. It is safe to conclude that the cyber sanctions regime is one more option in the EU's toolbox. The US is under no illusion that sanctions alone will be enough to change the behaviour of malicious actors in cyberspace, but the imposition of restrictive measures remains an attractive policy option for both diplomatic and symbolic reasons. Whether cyber sanctions will prove to be a hammer or not, remains to be seen.

References

Abazi, V. and Eckes, C. (2018), *'Closed evidence in EU courts: Security, secrets and access to justice'*, Common Market Law Review, 55(3) https://kluwerlawonline.com/journalarticle/Common+Market+Law+Review/55.3/COLA2018069

Baldwin A. David, (1985) *Economic Statecraft*, Princeton University Press, New Jersey.

CERT-FR, (21 July 2021), *'Campagne d'attaque du mode opératoire APT31 ciblant la France'*, https://www.cert.ssi.gouv.fr/ioc/CERTFR-2021-IOC-003/

Charter of the United Nations, *Article 39, 40 & 41*, https://legal.un.org/repertory/art1.shtml

Comply Advantage, *'Primary & Secondary Sanctions'* https://complyadvantage.com/insights/primary-secondary-sanctions/

Council of the European Union, (16 April 2018), *'Council conclusions on malicious cyber activities – approval'*, Brussels https://data.consilium.europa.eu/doc/document/ST-7925-2018-INIT/en/pdf

Council of the European Union, (17 May 2021), *'Cyberattacks: Council prolongs framework for sanctions for another year'*, https://www.consilium.europa.eu/en/press/press-releases/2021/05/17/cyberattacks-council-prolongs-framework-for-sanctions-for-another-year/

Council of the European Union, (18 October 2018), *'European Council meeting–Conclusions'*, Brussels https://www.consilium.europa.eu/en/press/press-releases/2018/10/18/20181018-european-council-conslusions/

Council of the European Union, (19 July 2021), 'China: Declaration by the High Representative on behalf of the European Union urging Chinese authorities to take action against malicious cyber activities undertaken from its territory', https://www.consilium.europa.eu/en/press/press-releases/2021/07/19/declaration-by-the-high-representative-on-behalf-of-the-eu-urging-china-to-take-action-against-malicious-cyber-activities-undertaken-from-its-territory/

Council of the European Union, (22 October 2020), *'Malicious cyberattacks: EU sanctions two individuals and one body over 2015 Bundestag hack'*, Press office - General Secretariat of the Council, Brussels https://www.consilium.europa.eu/en/press/press-releases/2020/10/22/malicious-cyberattacks-eu-sanctions-two-individuals-and-one-body-over-2015-bundestag-hack/pdf

Council of the European Union, (24 September 2021), *'Declaration by the High Representative on behalf of the European Union on respect for the EU's democratic processes'* https://www.consilium.europa.eu/en/press/press-releases/2021/09/24/declaration-by-the-high-representative-on-behalf-of-the-european-union-on-respect-for-the-eu-s-democratic-processes/

Council of the European Union, (28 June 2018), *'European Council conclusions'*, Brussels https://www.consilium.europa.eu/en/press/press-releases/2018/06/29/20180628-euco-conclusions-final/

Council of the European Union, (30 July 2020), 'Declaration by the High Representative Josep Borrell on behalf of the EU: European Union response to promote international security and stability in cyberspace', Brussels https://www.consilium.europa.eu/en/press/press-releases/2020/07/30/declaration-by-the-high-representative-josep-borrell-on-behalf-of-the-eu-european-union-response-to-promote-international-security-and-stability-in-cyberspace/

Council of the European Union, (7 June 2017), Draft *Council Conclusions on a Framework for a Joint EU Diplomatic Response to Malicious Cyber Activities ("Cyber Diplomacy Toolbox")*, Brussels https://data.consilium.europa.eu/doc/document/ST-9916-2017-INIT/en/pdf

Council of the European Union, (8 September, 2020), '*Horizontal Working Party on cyber issues*', Brussels https://data.consilium.europa.eu/doc/document/CM-3442-2020-INIT/en/pdf

Cyberspace Solarium Commission, (11 March 2020), '*Cyberspace Solarium Commission Report*', *https://www.fdd.org/analysis/2020/03/11/cyberspace-solarium-commission-report/*

Department of Justice, (19 October 2020), 'Six Russian GRU Officers Charged in Connection with Worldwide Deployment of Destructive Malware and Other Disruptive Actions in Cyberspace', *https://www.justice.gov/opa/pr/six-russian-gru-officers-charged-connection-worldwide-deployment-destructive-malware-and*

European Commission, (2021), 'Restrictive measures', https://ec.europa.eu/info/business-economy-euro/banking-and-finance/international-relations/restrictive-measures-sanctions_en

European Parliament, (13 April 2021), 'EN P-001112/2021 Answer given by Mr Hahn on behalf of the European Commission', https://www.europarl.europa.eu/doceo/document/P-9-2021-001112-ASW_EN.pdf

European Union External Action Service, (3 August 2016), 'European Union sanctions' https://eeas.europa.eu/headquarters/headquarters-homepage/423/european-union-sanctions_en

FBI, (2016), '*Iranians charged with hacking US financial sector*', FBI, https://www.fbi.gov/news/stories/iranians-charged-with-hacking-us-financial-sector

Federal Register, (21 September 2018), 'Presidential Documents, Executive Order 13849, Authorizing the Implementation of Certain Sanctions Set Forth in the Countering America's Adversaries Through Sanctions Act', https://home.treasury.gov/system/files/126/caatsa_eo.pdf *https://eur-lex.europa.eu/legal-content/EN/TXT/PDF/?uri=CELEX:32019D0797&from=GA*

Ivan Paul, (18 March, 2019), '*Responding to cyberattacks: prospects for the EU Cyber Diplomacy Toolbox*', European Policy Centre https://www.epc.eu/en/Publications/Responding-to-cyberattacks-EU-Cyber-Diplomacy-Toolbox~218414

Kapsokoli Eleni, (2020), 'EU Cybersecurity Governance: A Work in Progress', in "Views on the Progress of CSDP", ESDC 1st Summer University Book, edited by Fotini Bellou and Daniel Fiott, European Security and Defence College, Doctoral School on CSDP, Publications Office of the European Union, Luxembourg
https://www.researchgate.net/publication/346274333_Eleni_Kapsokoli_EU_Cyb
ersecurity_Governance_A_Work_in_Progress_in_Views_on_the_Progress_of_
CSDP_ESDC_1st_Summer_University_Book_edited_by_Fotini_Bellou_and_D
aniel_Fiott_European_Security_and_Defence_C

Liaropoulos Andrew, (July 2018), *'The Uses and Limits of Cyber Coercion'*, Proceedings of the 17th European Conference on Cyber Warfare and Security, University of Oslo, 28-29 June 2018
https://www.researchgate.net/publication/326265321_The_Uses_and_Limits_of
_Cyber_Coercion_Proceedings_of_the_17th_European_Conference_on_Cyber_
Warfare_and_Security_University_of_Oslo_28-29_June_2018

Libicki Martin, (1 March 2017), *'It takes more than offensive capability to have an effective cyberdeterrence posture'*, Testimony before the House Armed Services Committee
https://www.rand.org/content/dam/rand/pubs/testimonies/CT400/CT465/RAND
_CT465.pdf

Miller G., Nakashima E. and Entous A., (23 June, 2017), *'Obama's secret struggle to punish Russia for Putin's election assault'*, Washington Post,
https://www.washingtonpost.com/graphics/2017/world/national-security/obama-
putin-election-hacking/?utm_term=.858072115a9a

Moret Erica and Pawlak Patryk, (July 2017), *'The EU Cyber Diplomacy Toolbox: towards a cyber-sanctions regime?'*, European Union Institute for Security Studies
https://www.iss.europa.eu/sites/default/files/EUISSFiles/Brief%2024%20Cyber
%20sanctions.pdf

Official Journal of the European Union, (17 May 2019a), 'COUNCIL DECISION (CFSP) 2019/797 of 17 May 2019 concerning restrictive measures against cyber-attacks threatening the Union or its Member States', Brussels

Official Journal of the European Union, (17 May 2019b), 'COUNCIL REGULATION (EU) 2019/796 of 17 May 2019 concerning restrictive measures against cyberattacks threatening the Union or its Member States', Brussels
https://eur-lex.europa.eu/legal-content/GA/TXT/?uri=CELEX%3A32019R0796

Official Journal of the European Union, (30 July 2020), 'COUNCIL DECISION (CFSP) 2020/1127 amending Decision (CFSP) 2019/797 concerning restrictive measures against cyberattacks threatening the Union or its Member States', Brussels https://eur-lex.europa.eu/legal-
content/EN/TXT/?uri=CELEX:32020D1127

Pawlak Patryk and Biersteker Thomas, (October, 2019) *'Guardian of the Galaxy: EU cyber sanctions and the norms in cyberspace'*, Chaillot Paper/155
https://www.iss.europa.eu/content/guardian-galaxy-eu-cyber-sanctions-and-
norms-cyberspace

Soesanto Stefan, (20 November, 2020), *'Europe has no strategy on cyber sanctions'*, Lawfare Institute in Cooperation with Brookings https://www.lawfareblog.com/europe-has-no-strategy-cyber-sanctions

SUPO Finnish Security Intelligence Service, (18 March 2021), *'Supo identified the cyber espionage operation against the parliament as APT31'* https://supo.fi/en/-/supo-identified-the-cyber-espionage-operation-against-the-parliament-as-apt31

Taylor Brendan, (2010), *'Sanctions as Grand Strategy'*, 1st Edition, Routledge.

The White House, (1 April 2015) Office of the Press Secretary, *'Executive Order: Blocking the Property of Certain Persons Engaging in Significant Malicious Cyber-Enabled Activities'*, *https://obamawhitehouse.archives.gov/the-press-office/2015/04/01/executive-order-blocking-property-certain-persons-engaging-significant-m*

The White House, (2015), *'Report on cyber deterrence policy'*, *https://obamawhitehouse.archives.gov/the-press-office/2015/01/13/securing-cyberspace-president-obama-announces-new-cybersecurity-legislat*

The White House, (2018), 'Statement from the Press Secretary', *https://trumpwhitehouse.archives.gov/briefings-statements/statement-press-secretary-25/*

The White House, (April 15, 2021) *'FACT SHEET: Imposing Costs for Harmful Foreign Activities by the Russian Government'*, https://www.whitehouse.gov/briefing-room/statements-releases/2021/04/15/fact-sheet-imposing-costs-for-harmful-foreign-activities-by-the-russian-government/

The White House, 'Office of the Press Secretary, (29 December 2016), *FACT SHEET: Actions in Response to Russian Malicious Cyber Activity and Harassment'*, https://obamawhitehouse.archives.gov/the-press-office/2016/12/29/fact-sheet-actions-response-russian-malicious-cyber-activity-and

Tucker Eric, (25 August, 2020), *'Military's top cyber official defends more aggressive stance'*, The Associated Press, https://www.defensenews.com/news/your-military/2020/08/25/militarys-top-cyber-official-defends-more-aggressive-stance/?contentFeatureId=f0fMztk16BnMbkh&contentQuery=%7B%22section%22%3A%22%2Fhome%22%2C%22from%22%3A15%2C%22size%22%3A10%2C%22exclude%22%3A%22%2Fnews%2Fyour-military%22%7D

US Department of Defense, (2018), *'Summary 2018 Department of Defense Cyber Strategy'*, USA https://media.defense.gov/2018/Sep/18/2002041658/-1/-1/1/CYBER_STRATEGY_SUMMARY_FINAL.PDF

US Department of The Treasury, (13 September 2019) *'Treasury Sanctions North Korean State-Sponsored Malicious Cyber Groups'*, https://home.treasury.gov/news/press-releases/sm774

US Department of The Treasury, (15 April, 2021), *'Treasury Sanctions Russia with Sweeping New Sanctions Authority'*, https://home.treasury.gov/news/press-releases/jy0127

US Department of The Treasury, (15 March 2018) *'Treasury Sanctions Russian Cyber Actors for Interference with the 2016 U.S. Elections and Malicious Cyberattacks'*, https://home.treasury.gov/news/press-releases/sm0312

US Department of the Treasury, (16 February 2012), '*Treasury Designates Iranian Ministry of Intelligence and Security for Human Rights Abuses and Support for Terrorism*', https://www.treasury.gov/press-center/press-releases/Pages/tg1424.aspx

US Department of the Treasury, (21 September 2021), '*Publication of Updated Ransomware Advisory; Cyber-related Designation*' https://home.treasury.gov/policy-issues/financial-sanctions/recent-actions/20210921

US Department of the Treasury, (October 1, 2020) *Advisory on Potential Sanctions Risks for Facilitating Ransomware Payments*, https://home.treasury.gov/system/files/126/ofac_ransomware_advisory_10012020_1.pdf

US Department of the Treasury, Office of Foreign Assets Control (OFAC), (3 July 2017), 'Cyber-related sanctions program'

Van den Herik Larissa, (2014), 'Peripheral Hegemony in the Quest to Ensure Security Council Accountability For its Individualized UN Sanctions Regimes' *https://papers.ssrn.com/sol3/papers.cfm?abstract_id=2448176*

Author biography

Eleni Kapsokoli is a Ph.D. candidate at the University of Piraeus, Department of International and European Studies, Greece and Ph.D. Fellow of the European Doctoral School. She holds a bachelor's degree in Political Science and Public Administration and a master's degree in International Relations and Strategic Studies. Her main research interests are international security, terrorism, cybersecurity and cyberterrorism.

Chapter Two

The EU in the Era of Digital Geopolitics and the Challenge of Digital Sovereignty

Andrew N. Liaropoulos

University of Piraeus, School of Economics, Business and International Studies, Greece

aliarop@unipi.gr

Abstract: Over the past two decades digital technologies have become the main driver of globalization. They have influenced the way societies interact, how companies deliver services and how people are governed. The coronavirus pandemic highlighted the increased digitalization in all aspects of society, but also the risks, dependencies and vulnerabilities that accompany this technological transformation. The digital domain is no stranger to the great power competition. There is a race for technological leadership, for controlling digital technologies and for regulating them. Policymakers around the world have realized the importance of the digital domain on their countries' security and autonomy and have issued sovereignty claims on cyberspace. The European Union - an actor that aims to ensure that governments, the private sector, civil society organisations and end users around the world promote an open, free, and secure cyberspace - has recently added the concept of digital sovereignty in its political vocabulary. European digital sovereignty relates not only to the well-established ability of the EU to regulate digital technologies and set global standards in the digital domain, but also to its strategic autonomy, to its ability to compete in the arena of digital geopolitics and to reduce its dependencies. The EU needs to secure its digital economy, society and democracy, but also acknowledge its inherent constrains and the risks associated with protectionism and digital decoupling.

Keywords: EU, sovereignty, strategic autonomy, digital sovereignty, digital geopolitics

1   Introduction

Over the past years the EU has faced several security challenges in the digital sphere (Carrapico & Barrinha 2017; Christou 2019) and gradually developed policies and institutions (Kapsokoli 2020) that aim to safeguard its citizens in this new domain. Adding to that, the coronavirus pandemic revealed the extent to which data, networks and digital technologies constitute the backbone of modern societies. As a result, the calls within the EU to increase the level of autonomy in its industrial and technological base have increased (Aktoudianakis 2020). It is in this context that digital sovereignty (Timmers 2019; Christakis 2020; Floridi 2020; Hobbs 2020) became the latest buzzword in the corridors of Brussels. Bearing in mind that sovereignty is regarded as a foundational concept of international politics, even though an essentially contested one (Biersteker & Weber 1996; Krasner 1999), it is challenging to examine how it is applied in the digital realm. Cyber sovereignty, digital sovereignty, information sovereignty, technological sovereignty and data sovereignty are only some of the terms that have entered the relevant literature over the last two decades (Liaropoulos 2017; Pohle & Thiel 2020; Mueller 2020) and enriched the debate on the nature of sovereignty and governance.

It is even more thought-provoking to consider how digital sovereignty is understood in the context of the EU, since the term sovereignty does not even appear in the EU constitutive treaties (Christakis 2020, 9). In addition, sovereignty relates to national security, which under the EU treaties is reserved for the member-states. In view of the fact, that the very idea of 'European sovereignty' (Leonard & Shapiro 2019) - let alone a digital one - is a rather vague concept, it is necessary to develop an understanding of this hard to define term. Trapped between Chinese techno-nationalism and the US model of surveillance capitalism, the EU needs to define a strategy on how to shape its digital future.

Taking for granted that a widely accepted and comprehensive approach on the topic of digital sovereignty is lacking, this chapter analyses the European discourse on digital sovereignty. It reviews the concept of sovereignty and explores the way it is applied in the European digital domain. The goal is to highlight the dilemmas and constrains that the EU is facing in relation to regulating the digital domain, avoiding technological protectionism, promoting cyber-resilience, and playing the game of digital geopolitics. To do that, the chapter first analyses the concept of sovereignty, which embodies an internal and an external/international dimension. The first refers to the idea of a supreme decision-making and enforcement authority over a given territory and population. The latter refers to the absence of a supreme international authority and therefore the independence of sovereign states. This typology is also applied in the case of digital sovereignty (Christakis 2020). Next, the chapter reviews EU's capacity in regulating its digital domain, but also in acting autonomously in the arena of digital geopolitics. Considering that digital technologies are profoundly affecting every aspect of our societies, from cybersecurity and techno-nationalism to data localization and internet governance, it is important to study how Europe aspires to tackle these issues.

2 From sovereignty to digital sovereignty

There is no doubt, that sovereignty is the primary organizing principle of international politics, but also one of the most controversial terms. Despite its rich intellectual history, there is still disagreement regarding the role and significance of sovereignty in contemporary politics. From the early works of Jean Bodin, Thomas Hobbes, and Immanuel Kant to contemporary scholars like Carl Schmitt and Stephen Krasner, state sovereignty has been related to the people's right to establish an identity and protect self-determination against external interference, but also to domestic atrocities and genocide (Slomp 2008, 33). Sovereignty is closely linked to concepts like governance, security, independence, and democracy.

A popular perception of sovereignty is the one that discerns between the internal and the external/international sovereignty. The former is understood as the supreme power that the state has over its citizens within its borders and therefore the supreme decision-making and enforcement authority over a specific territory and towards a population. The latter is understood as the absence of a superior power to states. International sovereignty represents the principle of self-determination in the absence of a supreme international authority (Slomp 2008, 40-42). In the international context, sovereignty meets independence. States, regardless of their power status, are considered sovereign and independent and enjoy equal rights under international law (Christakis 2020, 5). This is also reflected in the UN Charter, in the principles of sovereign equality, Article 2(1), territorial integrity Article 2(4) and non-intervention Article 2(7) (Aalberts 2016, 186). Therefore, sovereignty does not only mean authority within a distinct territorial entity, but it also implies equal membership of the modern states system.

Sovereignty - a concept that continues to trigger conceptual battles - becomes even more complex when applied in a domain with no clear physical borders. To begin with, is cyberspace beyond the reach of state sovereignty? How do states perceive and exercise their sovereignty in relation to information and communication technologies (ICTs)? Is it possible for states to apply territorial jurisdiction in a borderless space? Can cyberspace be governed and regulated, or should we perceive it as a case of global commons? (Wu 1997; Mueller 2010; DeNardis 2014). Discussing the idea of sovereignty in relation to cyberspace has a short, but nevertheless, rich history. After all, it relates to issues of cybersecurity, to the development of norms of responsible state behaviour and potentially to the construction of an international cyber-order (Liaropoulos 2014; Mueller 2020, 784).

In the early days of the Internet development, the notions of territory and governance seemed rather irrelevant in this human-made and spaceless domain. Indicative of this are the views of John Perry Barlow, the founder of the Electronic Frontier Foundation (EFF). In 1996, in his manifesto titled *A Declaration of the Independence of Cyberspace* he states the following: "Governments of the Industrial World, you weary giants of flesh and steel, I come from Cyberspace, the new home of Mind. On behalf of the future, I ask you of the past to leave us alone. You are not welcome among us. You have no sovereignty where we gather. We have no elected government, nor are we likely to have one...Cyberspace does not lie within your borders." (1996). For utopians, cyberspace is a separate entity with little or ideally no top-down regulation since it can be self-regulated. Again, in the words of Barlow "Where there are real conflicts, where there are wrongs, we will identify them and address them by our means. We are forming our own Social Contract. This governance will arise according to the conditions of our world, not yours. Our world is different." (1996). From a different theoretical angle, Mueller argues against sovereignty in cyberspace. His thesis is that we cannot impose jurisdictional borders on cyberspace, simply because borders in cyberspace do not align with the territorial jurisdictions of states. According to Mueller, cyberspace due to its unique technical structure, should be approached as global commons and regulated as such (2020).

The issue of exercising sovereignty in relation to cyberspace comes down to whether the latter is indeed a non-territorial and borderless domain. To approach this issue, it is critical to distinguish between the physical and non-physical elements of cyberspace. Stephen Gourley differentiates between the domain (the medium) and the space. He refers to the physical aspects as the cyber domain - anything that enables users to transmit, store, and modify digital data - and to the non-physical aspects as cyber space (written as two words). Cyber activities take place through the cyber domain in cyber space (2013, 278). The cyber domain is an artificial and human-made construct with geographical ties over a specific territory. This infrastructure is terrestrially based and, therefore, not immune from state sovereignty. Thereby, states can exercise their sovereignty through the cyber domain. According to Gourley the territoriality principle allows states to control cyber activities occurring within and across their borders, and the effects principle gives them jurisdiction over external activities that cause effects internally. Applying the same analogy for the non-physical aspects of cyberspace is tricky. The reason is that there is no universal approach regarding the sovereignty of data/information (2013, 279-280).

The exercise of state sovereignty in cyberspace raises two issues (Cornish 2015, 157). First, it conflicts with the idea of cyberspace as a global common; and second, it could result in the fragmentation of cyberspace. Regarding the idea of cyberspace as a global common, in sharp contrast to sea and air that are limited by geographical boundaries, cyberspace is a human-made domain that is not constrained by physical space. In relation to size, cyberspace is unbounded. In sharp contrast to the domains of land, sea and air that are limited, cyberspace itself is growing and evolving as information technology expands and develops. Contrary to popular belief, cyberspace does not meet the legal criteria of global commons and is not free as are the atmosphere and ocean (Betz & Stevens 2011, 107). Paradoxically, although cyberspace seems borderless, it is bounded by the physical infrastructures that facilitate the transfer of data and information. Such infrastructures are mostly owned by the private sector and are located within the sovereign territory of states. Therefore, it would be more precise to argue that cyberspace comprises a global common infrastructure, but is not a global common (Cornish 2015, 158).

In 2015, the United Nations Governmental Group of Experts confirmed that sovereignty, international norms, and principles that derive from state sovereignty apply to state conduct of ICTs activities and to their jurisdiction over ICTs infrastructure within their territory (United Nations General Assembly 2015). Thus, the principle of sovereignty in relation to cyberspace is essentially uncontested. What is contested though, are the norms that relate to sovereignty, since states do not share the same understanding on the free flow of information, privacy, anonymity and national (cyber)security. Over the past years, many states, mainly authoritarian ones, have used the sovereignty card - information, data, technological and digital sovereignty - to restrain internet freedoms and exercise digital surveillance (Kamasa 2020).

The hard reality of international relations is that cyberspace itself is not an independent sovereign entity and that states have explored ways to exercise their sovereign power. The global digital ecosystem relies on physical apparatuses, tangible properties that states physically control and nothing can prevent states from regulating the digital activities of their citizens. Indicative of this point are the cases of the General Data Protection Regulation (GDPR) and the US Cloud Act. GDPR applies to data controllers, which are not established in the EU, as long as they process data that is related to offer of goods or services to data services in the EU or monitor the behaviour of individuals located in the EU. Likewise, the US Cloud Act enables law enforcement authorities to request data that is in the possession, custody and control of a US company, even if such information may be stored in a server that is placed outside the US (Celeste 2021).

The digital realm reflects the current international system, where national interests, geopolitical ambitions and ideologies inevitably clash. The digital domain is a battlespace for great power competition. Great powers like China and the US are locked in a technological war competing over leadership in the fields of 5G, cloud storage, computer chip development and artificial intelligence (AI). In August 2020, President Donald Trump published executive orders targeting the viral video application TikTok and messaging application WeChat. The orders declared that these two applications would be blocked from processing transactions for US citizens and from being downloaded in US application stores, due to security concerns. According to the Trump administration, these measures were taken to protect US citizens from the collection of their data by the Chinese government. Another example of this digital war is the ban of Huawei as a supplier of American telecom infrastructure. Furthermore, Huawei is prohibited from purchasing computer chips that are produced outside the US with American technology (Moerel & Timmers 2021, 5). China on the other hand, is building its own internet based on different values and is exporting its vision of techno-authoritarianism to other countries (Freedom House 2021, 7). The Chinese social media platform WeChat, the Alibaba online marketplace and the Baidu search engine have created a digital ecosystem distinct from the one dominated by US technological giants such as Facebook, Amazon and Google.

To conclude, digital sovereignty is about controlling, possessing, and regulating the digital realm. Thus, it is about data and AI, standardization processes and hardware, as well as about services like social media or e-commerce and infrastructures like satellites and internet's undersea cables. Having conceptualized an understanding of what sovereignty entails in relation to the digital ecosystem, we turn our analysis to the concept of European digital sovereignty.

3 The EU as a digital colony

The EU is a unique actor. It is not a state, but the Union is much more than just an intergovernmental organization. Putting aside for a moment the theories of European integration, the democratic deficit and the legal nature of this sui generis organization, any discussion about European sovereignty, and especially a digital one, raises eyebrows. After all, the idea of removing sovereignty from national capitals to recreate it in Brussels is a complex issue, in both conceptual and political terms. Whether European sovereignty implies the weakening of national sovereignties, the creation of a shared sovereignty or the construction of collective sovereignty is a strong theoretical exercise that meets the political reality of European power politics.

A quick review of the policy papers that the EU has published and the statements that key officials have made over the last three years, highlights the anxiety that the EU will not be able to effectively regulate its digital universe, protect its citizens' data and compete successfully with China and the US in the arena of digital geopolitics (European Commission 2019; Christakis 2020; Hobbs 2020). References made by EU policymakers to digital or technological sovereignty and digital autonomy imply that if the EU is a weak actor in the digital domain, this will affect its ability to regulate its digital services and protect both its infrastructure and values. Furthermore, a powerless EU will be unable to shape the development of global norms regarding cyberspace governance.

The quest for digital sovereignty is rooted in a perception that the EU has been digitally colonized. It is a fact, that non-EU companies, especially US and Asian ones, have dominated the European digital market. EU dependencies are evident in the cases of cloud and data infrastructures, 5G connectivity and AI. In the 2019 Forbes Top 20 digital companies list (Forbes 2019), only one EU company - Deutsche Telekom - made it to the list, while US companies claimed 12 spots; China and Japan two each; and Hong Kong, South Korea, and Taiwan one each. Likewise, in AI the EU is lagging both the US and China, in terms of private investment and adoption of AI technologies by the private sector and by the public sector (European Commission 2018; Castro, McLaughlin & Chivot 2019). With respect to communication infrastructure Europe still has two dominant players, Nokia and Ericsson, although their position is challenged by US and mainly Chinese competitors, such as Huawei. The global landscape of telecommunication operators is quite diverse, but the European market is fragmented with many national players and few giants like Deutsche Telecom, Telefonica, Vodafone and Orange (EIT Digital 2020, 9).

The global cloud storage service market is largely dominated by US and Chinese companies. In particular, Amazon accounts for 45% of the market share, Microsoft 17.9%, Alibaba 9.1%, Google 5.3% and Tencent 2.8% (Aktoudianakis 2020, 4). The inefficient control over data that is produced in the EU, but is stored abroad is a major concern for both governments and businesses. Most of the data that is generated in the EU is stored with US cloud providers because there are hardly any European alternatives. As a result, citizens, businesses and public authorities in the EU are at risk since their data is stored under potentially conflicting jurisdictions. This is problematic and has raised concerns within the EU, because US intelligence and law enforcement agencies can access this data under the US Cloud Act. In 2020 in a landmark decision, the EU Court of Justice (CJEU) struck down the EU-US Privacy Shield agreement, one of the most widely used mechanisms allowing US companies to transfer and store EU personal data in the US. The CJEU overturned in July 2020 the Privacy Shield agreement, which allowed data transfers between European and US companies, but without providing the legal protection in the US that users enjoy in Europe. Because this data could be tapped by US authorities without EU citizens being able to take effective action against it, the Court declared it invalid. The invalidation of the Privacy Shield agreement demonstrated the problems related to conflicting regulations and EU's overreliance on foreign cloud and data storage solutions (Aktoudianakis 2020, 5; Christakis 2020, 20).

Furthermore, by storing data abroad, the EU cannot take full advantage from the available meta-data, to identify consumer habits, minimise costs and modernise supply chains. As a result, Europe's digital economy becomes less competitive (Aktoudianakis 2020, 4). Technological giants like Google, Apple, Facebook, Amazon and Microsoft, the so-called GAFAM, are collecting massive amounts of personal data and their economic model - data capitalism - is largely based on the collection and exploitation of online users' data to generate profit (Zuboff 2019; Madiega 2020, 3-4). By gaining access to crucial data about online behaviour and consumer habits, these companies have a major competitive advantage in relation to other players. This allows them to act as gatekeepers to the European digital market. Furthermore, GAFAM's harvesting of data can be used for manipulation of online public discourse (Aktoudianakis 2020, 4).

Since 2019, the EU expressed its concern about the potential reliance of its member-states on Chinese 5G infrastructure (NIS Cooperation Group 2019). The European Parliament has expressed concern about the growing role of Chinese tech companies, calling for action to reduce such dependencies (Aktoudianakis 2020, 6). Even though, Huawei was not banned, despite the pressure exercised by the US, certain member-states restrained Huawei's role in their networks (Morris 2020). The choice of 5G operators, infrastructures and their suppliers are directly linked to national security and sovereignty. Any decision about 5G cannot be made solely on terms of quality and price (Duchâtel & Godement 2019). Even though, Chinese companies offer high quality at a low price, there is a concern that the Chinese government could influence companies like Huawei to monitor or even shut down critical infrastructure whenever it wants (Grüll 2020). The US sanctioned the company and demanded Europe to follow. Brussels left the decision to the states. For example, Spain hired Huawei, whereas the Czech Republic decided not to. Germany took the middle way, welcoming all companies as long as they adhere to a catalogue of safety criteria. For example, suppliers must give a declaration of confidence that no information will reach foreign authorities and that they can refuse to disclose confidential information from or about their customers to third parties (Grüll 2020).

As stated above, the global cloud market is dominated by US and Chinese technological giants and therefore the EU is concerned about the lack of control over data produced in its territory (Madiega 2020, 4). As a result, the European Commission highlighted the need to deploy European designed cloud solutions (Nextcloud 2019) and began discussions with the German and French governments, which have already launched the GAIA-X cloud project. Such initiatives aim to build a resilient digital infrastructure. This development is regarded, as a step towards digital sovereignty because the EU had stood up for its values and the rights of its citizens (Grüll 2020). A European alternative to the US providers is on the way. GAIA-X, is a platform where customers can find providers that meet certain criteria, such as compliance with the GDPR. By building cloud services, the EU seeks to keep in Europe data generated on the continent and to protect that information from foreign governments (Burwell & Propp 2020, 9). US companies are also welcomed to participate if they comply with these standards (Grüll 2020). This is an example of how Europe can extend its digital sovereignty, through clear sets of criteria, which companies must meet to be allowed to enter the internal market. Some EU member-states, including Belgium, Bulgaria, France, Germany, Greece, Luxembourg, the Netherlands, Poland, Romania, and Sweden have taken a further step, by enacting data localization measures that exclude certain categories of data from being relocated outside their territory (Burwell & Propp 2020).

Last, but not least, the EU must seriously consider its chip shortage. The COVID-19 pandemic and the technological war between the US and China, vividly illustrated how dependent the EU is on imports of raw materials like the semiconductors. Bearing in mind, that the latter are at the core of the global technological race, it is no surprise, that the European Commission announced its willingness to proceed with the Chips Act in the first half of 2022, in order to secure Europe's supply of microchips, encourage innovation and strengthen industrial capacity (Kamasa 2021).

4   Regulate to dominate: The EU as a regulatory power in the digital domain

EU's dependencies and weaknesses draw only one part of the picture. Over the last years, the EU has responded to the growing economic and political importance of the digital economy, as well as to the security concerns of its citizens, by launching a series of regulatory initiatives (Hobbs 2020, 47). To begin with, the EU launched the Digital Single Market in 2015 to reduce barriers to digital activity between the member-states and improve access to online services and products for citizens and businesses. After the 2013 revelations by Edward Snowden, of significant US government surveillance of European citizens' communications, including German Chancellor Angela Merkel's mobile phone, trust in the US took a significant blow and raised serious concerns regarding the cohesion of the transatlantic partnership. Snowden's global surveillance revelations triggered the debate about data protection within the EU (Rossi 2018). As a result, the EU passed the GDPR.

This privacy legislation imposed strict conditions on the handling of EU citizens' personal information, even if that data or citizen was physically outside the EU. When it came into effect in May 2018, companies around the world found themselves having to comply with GDPR. As a result, the EU is regarded as a standard setter in privacy and data protection, since many countries have incorporated GDPR provisions in their national legislation (Madiega 2020, 3). Although creating EU digital sovereignty was rarely mentioned at the time, both the Digital Single Market plan and GDPR were clearly intended to enhance EU digital capabilities and provide citizens with a form of control, over their own personal data (Hobbs 2020, 47). Since then, the idea of greater European sovereignty over the digital realm has gained more ground. Indicative of the above is the reference made by Ursula von der Leyen in her statement over her policy priorities, where she called for the EU to "achieve technological sovereignty in some critical technology areas" (Von der Leyen 2019). Likewise, the European Commission stressed the importance of technological sovereignty and the need to ensure that the EU has a secure, high-quality digital infrastructure and the ability to develop and sustain key cutting-edge technologies (Hobbs 2020, 48).

In defence of Brussel's ability to exercise its influence as a global regulatory power in the digital domain, we must stress that the EU is perceived to be a global leader in establishing standards related to online activities that are intended to safeguard its citizens and ensure an ethical approach to the dilemmas posed by the digital world (Blancato 2019; Christakis 2020, 17-20; Hobbs 2020, 49). The "right to be forgotten" and restrictions regarding hate speech are two examples of this trend. Based on the European Commission's voluntary Code of Conduct on Countering Illegal Hate Speech, many digital companies, including Facebook, Twitter, YouTube and Microsoft, adopted measures to control the content that appears on their platforms (Bradford 2020a; 132). Likewise, on February 2020, the European Commission issued three documents, a declaration about shaping Europe's digital future, a white paper on AI and the European strategy for data.

These documents include rules, which ensure that data collected and controlled within the EU, is managed according to ethical standards that place privacy in the epicentre. The EU's approach towards AI is a human centric one, meaning that the EU requires compliance with fundamental rights, regardless of whether these are explicitly protected by EU treaties, such as the Treaty on European Union or by the Charter of Fundamental Rights of the European Union. Thus, the AI Act will prohibit most facial recognition systems and force the AI systems to inform citizens if they are exposed to an algorithm that might affect their behaviour (Czarnocki 2021, 4). Likewise, the Digital Services Act, proposes rules intended to reinforce European norms on content, consumer protection, and platform liability. By obliging service providers to comply with transparent terms of service, the Act aims to limit the power of major players, like GAFAM, to censor content (Czarnocki 2021, 4). In parallel, the European data strategy that was adopted in February 2020, aims to create European data spaces that will be used for economic and societal reasons (European Commission 2020). In these data spaces, EU companies and citizens will be able to control their data. By emphasizing on infrastructure, key industries, creation of data spaces and by promoting a set of norms for responsible state behaviour in the digital world, the EU aspires to gain more control over how digital activities are conducted within Europe and therefore how its citizens are treated in the digital realm.

It should be noted, that EU regulations often have a global impact. Bearing in mind that the EU is one of the world's largest consumer markets, most multinational corporations accept its terms of business as the price of admission. To escape the cost of complying with multiple regulatory regimes around the world, many companies often extend EU rules to their operations globally. That is why so many large non-EU companies follow the EU's GDPR in their operations (Bradford 2020b). Since the introduction of the GDPR there is growing pressure in the US for a federal standardization on data privacy and cybersecurity (EIT Digital 2020, 6). Thus, it is fair to argue that the so-called "Brussels Effect" is in play in the digital domain.

Apart from exercising its regulatory power in standard-setting international organizations, like the United Nations and the International

Telecommunication Union, the EU and some of its-member states have also invested on building technological alliances and approaching like-minded states in terms of constructing a preferable international technological order (Cohen & Fontaine 2020). Grouping of like-minded states – meaning techno-democracies, in the form of Democracy 10 (D10) or Techno-Democracies 12 (T-12) are welcome developments in terms of building digital cooperation but should not be treated as a panacea. The agenda of such multilateral initiatives would include common norms and standards for advanced technologies and more resilient supply chains, but also defending the democratic-liberal order against techno-autocracies like China and Russia (Jain et al 2021). Such a group of like-minded states - loosely including the G7, meaning US, UK, France, Germany, Italy, Canada, Japan, plus Australia, South Korea and the EU - is a strong democratic club, but many regions like Southeast Asia, Africa and Latin America, are under-represented. This elite club of techno-democracies will not be able to reach to the rest of the world and especially to the so-called swing states like India, Indonesia, Kenya, Brazil and South Africa. Such groupings are not only restrictive, since they exclude potential 5G network providers like Finland and Sweden and major manufacturers of semiconductors like the Netherlands and Taiwan, but they also lack a clear strategy. It is uncertain whether they aim to shape norms and strengthen partnership or counter digital authoritarianism and China's technological rise (Pannier 2021, 5-7). Even if this initiative is limited to the transatlantic community, it is not certain that this alliance will speak necessarily with a common voice. There is not only a great digital divide between the democratic and the authoritarian world, but also one, even though smaller, between the two sides of the Atlantic. After all, the EU and the US need to resolve several issues, like personal data protection, responsibility for content, competition protection and regulation of AI systems (Czarnocki 2021, 6).

5 Digital geopolitics and the EU

In sharp contrast to the popular belief that Europe is a rather weak player in the digital domain, the above section has illustrated the ability of the EU to exercise its power and regulate its digital sphere. Technology regulation is very important, and the GDPR data privacy regulation proved that the EU can be a champion in this field. Nevertheless, this is only one aspect of digital sovereignty. Another aspect and an equally important one, is that of digital geopolitics. The latter involves not only the politics of digital platforms that privileges certain technological giants, and the competition over the control of data, but also the division between liberal powers - US and the EU - and authoritarian ones - China and Russia - in relation to Internet freedoms and cyberspace governance. Trapped between the US Cloud Act and Chinese 5G providers, Brussels needs to balance between data localization and techno-nationalism on the one hand, and the lack of a dominant industrial and technological base on the other hand (European Commission 2019).

To begin with, the EU must alter its approach on technology. Technology is not neutral. Throughout history, technology has been a game changer, it enabled major power shifts and created economic and military advantages. As such, the EU cannot shape its digital strategy merely on regulations, norms and ethics. The EU simply cannot afford to ignore the geopolitics of digital technology. It seems that despite the strong rhetoric about a geopolitical union, the EU still feels uncomfortable when it comes to traditional power politics. After all the EU's spirit is market-driven and dominated by technocrats. We should bear in mind, that from the very beginning, the European project left high politics in the hands of the states. The EU bureaucracy does not perceive the world in terms of hard power, coercion and relative gains, but mainly in terms of market regulation.

Illustrative of this, is the way the EU treats data. The EU is a large, yet fragmented market that prioritises the regulation of data, whereas both China and the US are focusing on gathering an enormous amount of data to fuel their algorithms and produce consumer profiles and patterns of predictions. The EU has a human-centric approach that focuses on ethics, privacy and digital rights. Its competitors on the other hand, simply dominate the digital market. Europe is dependent on cloud services and digital platforms offered by Google, Amazon, Apple and Microsoft and their Chinese competitors, Alibaba, Baidu and Tencent (EIT Digital 2020, 9). It is no secret that China aspires to control all digital infrastructure that reaches into the EU through the Belt and Road Initiative. The Digital Silk Road is far more than an infrastructure project. It is part of a strategy to construct a more Sino-centric digital order. Apart from building a global data infrastructure, China is also exporting surveillance technologies to dictators and authoritarian regimes throughout the developing world (Insikt Group 2021; Liaropoulos 2021). So far, the EU has no answer to China's Digital Silk Road, or to its campaign to establish a digital currency.

Adding to that, the recent technological war between the US and China revealed the risk of potential disruptions to critical supply chains, like in the case of semiconductors (European Commission 2019, 8). The EU risks becoming exposed to global technological wars if it does not invest in home grown technological solutions. Nevertheless, efforts to enhance digital autonomy should not lead to policies of protectionism. Despite short term benefits, protectionism can hinder global trade and cost prosperity and jobs in the EU. The latter needs to address its vulnerabilities productively, by exploring its competitive advantages and investing in innovation (Aktoudianakis 2020; Christakis 2020).

6 Conclusion

Digital technologies are nowadays an essential part of the everyday life of citizens, companies and institutions in the EU, but the digital market is dominated by American and Chinese technological giants. Considering its inability to fully control the data and digital infrastructure that is associated with its citizens and institutions, the EU is competing to exercise sovereignty on its digital ecosystem and thereby preserve its core values (Celester 2021). In common with the early days of the Cold War, Europe is experiencing a superpower squeeze. This digital superpower squeeze places the EU between the emergent China and the US, which is struggling to retain its technological advantage. A global race for digital supremacy that includes AI, semiconductors and quantum computing and influences national security, global trade, and civil society, is already underway, and the EU despite its many assets, is lagging behind. It is in this environment that the debate on Europe's digital sovereignty is much needed (Christakis 2020; Hobbs 2020). The digital sovereignty narrative aims to build a consensus regarding the need to safeguard European leadership in certain technological areas. By becoming resilient and autonomous, the EU will be able to avoid geopolitical coercion in critical technological sectors.

The purpose of the analysis in this chapter was not to identify a course of action for Brussels, but rather to highlight the political dilemmas that the EU is facing (European Commission 2019). The EU has launched many policies and instruments over the years, but a wide arsenal of policy tools remains at its disposal. Building a strong industrial and technological base in the digital sector, bolstering its digital diplomacy, and improving its cyber-resilience are top priorities. Cases such as the Huawei 5G highlight the need to develop policies that will strengthen Europe's technological competitiveness (Duchâtel & Godement 2019). Above all, the EU needs to crystallize a strategic vision, about its future. To do that, the EU must first acknowledge its vulnerabilities and value the risks and controversies of becoming a digital fortress. Choosing between data localization and anti-trust policies and risking a technological / data war with either the US or China, is not an easy decision to make. Geopolitical antagonisms will only escalate as the digital domain becomes critical to an increasing number of actors and thus Europe must make a meaningful and concrete decision. Simply put, the EU cannot ignore digital geopolitics.

References

Aalberts, T. (2016) "Sovereignty", in Berenskoetter, F. (ed) *Concepts in World Politics,* Sage, London.

Aktoudianakis, A. (2020) "Fostering Europe's Strategic Autonomy. Digital Sovereignty for growth, rules and cooperation" European Policy Centre, Brussels, December, [online], https://www.epc.eu/en/publications/Fostering-Europes-Strategic-Autonomy--Digital-sovereignty-for-growth~3a8090

Barlow, J.P. (1996) "Declaration of the Independence of Cyberspace", [online], https://www.eff.org/cyberspaceindependence.

Betz, D.J. & Stevens, T. (2011) Cyberspase and the State: Towards a Strategy for Cyber Power, Routledge, Oxford.

Biersteker, T.J. & Weber C. eds. (1996) *State Sovereignty as a Social Construct,* Cambridge University Press, Cambridge.

Blancato, F. (2019) "Regulate to Dominate: The Geopolitics of Standard-Setting in Digital Technologies and its Strategic Implications for the EU", UNU Institute on Comparative Regional Integration Studies, Policy Brief no.8, Bruges, [online], https://cris.unu.edu/regulate-dominate-geopolitics-standard-setting-digital-technologies-and-its-strategic-implications

Bradford, A. (2020a) The Brussels Effect. How the European Union rules the World, Oxford University Press, New York.

Bradford, A. (2020b) "Hey, US Tech: Here Comes the Brussels Effect", Ghazen Global Insights, December 17, [online], https://www8.gsb.columbia.edu/articles/chazen-global-insights/hey-us-tech-here-comes-brussels-effect

Burwell, F. & Propp, K. (2020) "The European Union and the Search for Digital Sovereignty: Building Fortress Europe or preparing for the New World?", Atlantic Council, *Future Europe Initiative, Issue Brief,* June, [online], https://www.atlanticcouncil.org/in-depth-research-reports/issue-brief/the-european-union-and-the-search-for-digital-sovereignty/

Carrapico, H. & Barrinha, A. (2017) "The EU as a Coherent (Cyber)Security Actor?", *Journal of Common Market Studies,* Vol. 55, No. 6, pp. 1254-1272.

Castro, D., McLaughlin, M. & Chivot, E. (2019) "Who is winning the AI Race: China, the EU of the United States?", *Center for Data Innovation,* [online], https://euagenda.eu/publications/who-is-winning-the-ai-race-china-the-eu-or-the-united-states

Celeste, E. (2021) "Digital Sovereignty in the EU: Challenges and Future Perspectives" in Fabbrini, F. Celeste E. & Quinn, J. (eds), *Data Protection Beyond Borders. Transatlantic Perspectives on Extraterritoriality and Sovereignty,* Hart Publishing, Oxford.

Christakis, T. (2020) "'European Digital Sovereignty': Successfully Navigating Between the 'Brussels Effect' and Europe's Quest for Strategic Autonomy", Multidisciplinary Institute on Artificial Intelligence/Grenoble Alpes Data Institute, [online], https://ssrn.com/abstract=3748098.

Christou, G. (2019) "The collective securitization of cyberspace in the European Union", *West European Politics,* Vol. 42, No. 2, pp.278-301.

Cohen, J. & Fontaine, R. (2020) "Uniting the Techno-Democracies. How to Build Digital Cooperation", *Foreign Affairs*, Vol. 99, No. 6, pp. 112-122.

Cornish, P. (2015) "Governing cyberspace through constructive ambiguity", *Survival*, Vol. 57, No. 3, pp. 153-76.

Czarnocki, J. (2021) "Saving EU digital constitutionalism through the proportionality principle and a transatlantic digital accord", *European View*, [online], https://journals.sagepub.com/doi/full/10.1177/17816858211055522

DeNardis, L. (2014) *The Global War for Internet Governance*, Yale University Press, New Haven.

Duchâtel, M. & Godement, F. (2019) "Europe and 5G: the Huawei Case", Policy Paper, Institut Montaigne, Paris, June, [online], https://www.institutmontaigne.org/en/publications/europe-and-5g-huawei-case-part-2

EIT Digital, (2020) "European Digital Infrastructure and Data Sovereignty. A policy perspective", [online], https://www.eitdigital.eu/fileadmin/files/2020/publications/data-sovereignty/EIT-Digital-Data-Sovereignty-Summary-Report.pdf

European Commission, (2018) "USA-China-EU plans for AI: where do we stand?", *Digital Transformation Monitor*, [online], https://ec.europa.eu/growth/tools-databases/dem/monitor/sites/default/files/DTM_AI%20USA-China-EU%20plans%20for%20AI%20v5.pdf.

European Commission, (2019) "Rethinking Strategic Autonomy in the Digital Age", *EPSC Strategic Note*, Issue 30, [online], https://op.europa.eu/en/publication-detail/-/publication/889dd7b7-0cde-11ea-8c1f-01aa75ed71a1/language-en.

European Commission, (2020) "A European strategy for data", available at https://ec.europa.eu/info/sites/info/files/communication-european-strategy-data-19feb2020_en.pdf.

Floridi, L (2020) "The Fight for Digital Sovereignty: What it is, and why it matters, especially for the EU" *Philosophy & Technology*, Vol. 33, pp. 369-378.

Forbes, (2019) "Top Digital Companies – 2019 Ranking", [online], https://www.forbes.com/top-digital-companies/list/.

Freedom House, (2021) "Freedom on the Net 2021. The Global Drive to control Big Tech", [online], https://freedomhouse.org/

Gourley, S.K. (2013) "Cyber sovereignty", in Yannakogeorgos, P. & Lowther, A. (eds), *Conflict and cooperation in cyberspace*, Taylor & Francis, New York.

Grüll, P. (2020) "Geopolitical Europe aims to extend its sovereignty from China", EUACTIV.DE, 11 September, [online], https://www.euractiv.com/section/digital/news/geopolitical-europe-aims-to-extend-its-digital-sovereignty-versus-china/.

Hobbs, C. (2020) "Europe's Digital Sovereignty: From Rulemaker to Superpower in the Age of US-China Rivalry", *European Council on Foreign Relations*, [online], https://ecfr.eu/publication/europe_digital_sovereignty_rulemaker_superpower_age_us_china_rivalry/

Insikt Group, (2021) "China's Digital Colonialism: Espionage and Repression along the Digital Silk Road", *Cyber Threat Analysis – China*, [online], https://www.recordedfuture.com/china-digital-colonialism-espionage-silk-road/

Jain, A. et al (2021). "From the G7 to a D-10: Strengthening Democratic Cooperation for today's challenges", Atlantic Council, [online], https://www.atlanticcouncil.org/wp-content/uploads/2021/06/From-the-G7-to-a-D10-Strengthening-Democratic-Cooperation-for-Todays-Challenges.pdf

Kamasa, J. (2020) "Internet Freedom in Retreat", *CSS Analyses in Security Policy*, No.273, ETH, Zurich.

Kamasa, J. (2021) "Microchips: Small and Demanded", *CSS Analyses in Security Policy*, No.295, ETH, Zurich.

Kapsokoli, E. (2020) "EU cybersecurity governance: A work in progress", in Bellou, F. & Fiott, D. (eds) *Views on the progress of CSDP*, ESDC 1st Summer University Book, Luxembourg.

Krasner, S.D. (1999) *Sovereignty: Organized hypocrisy*, Princeton University Press, Princeton.

Leonard, M. & Shapiro, J. eds. (2019) "Strategic Sovereignty: How Europe can regain the capacity to act", [online], https://ecfr.eu/archive/page/-/ecfr_strategic_sovereignty.pdf

Liaropoulos, A. (2014) "Cyberspace, Sovereignty and International Order", ISN ETH Zurich [online], https://www.files.ethz.ch/isn/188212/ISN_176144_en.pdf

Liaropoulos, A. (2017) "Cyberspace governance and state sovereignty", in Bitros, G.C & Kyriazis, N.C. (eds) *Democracy and an Open-Economy World Order*, Springer, Heidelberg.

Liaropoulos, A. (2021) "Exporting Chinese Digital Authoritarianism", RIEAS [online], https://www.rieas.gr/researchareas/editorial/4673-exporting-chinese-digital-authoritarianism

Madiega, T. (2020) "Digital Sovereignty for Europe', *EPRS - European Parliamentary Research Service*", [online], https://www.europarl.europa.eu/RegData/etudes/BRIE/2020/651992/EPRS_BRI(2020)651992_EN.pdf

Moerel, L. & Timmers, P. (2021) "Reflections on Digital Sovereignty", *Research in Focus, EU Cyber Direct*, [online] https://eucyberdirect.eu/research/reflections-on-digital-sovereignty

Morris, I. (2020) "Europe is showing Huawei the exit", *Light Reading*, 9 September, [online] https://www.lightreading.com/5g/europe-is-showing-huawei-exit/d/d-id/763814

Mueller, M.L. (2010) Networks and States: The Global Politics of Internet Governance, MIT Press, Cambridge.

Mueller, M.L. (2020) "Against Sovereignty in Cyberspace", *International Studies Review*, Vol. 22, No. 4, pp.779-801.

Nextcloud, (2019) "EU governments chose independence from US cloud providers with Nextcloud", 27 August, [online], https://nextcloud.com/blog/eu-governments-choose-independence-from-us-cloud-providers-with-nextcloud/

NIS Cooperation Group, (2019) "EU coordinated risk assessment of the cybersecurity of the 5G networks", Report, 9 October [online], https://ec.europa.eu/commission/presscorner/detail/en/IP_19_6049

Pannier, A. (2021) "Europe in the Geopolitics of Technology. Connecting the Internal and External Dimensions", IFRI - French Institute of International Relations, 9 April, [online], https://www.ifri.org/en/publications/briefings-de-lifri/europe-geopolitics-technology-connecting-internal-and-external

Pohle, J. & Thiel, T. (2020) "Digital Sovereignty", *Internet Policy Review*, Vol.9, Issue 4, pp.1-19.

Rossi, A. (2018) "How the Snowden Revelations Saved the EU General Data Protection Regulation", *The International Spectator*, Vol. 53, No. 4, pp. 95-111.

Slomp, G. (2008) "On Sovereignty", in Salmon, T.C. & Imber, M.F. (eds) *Issues in International Relations,* Routledge, New York.

Timmers, P. (2019) "Strategic Autonomy and Cybersecurity", EU Cyber Direct, Supporting EU Cyber Diplomacy, [online], https://eucyberdirect.eu/content_research/strategic-autonomy-and-cybersecurity/

United Nations General Assembly, (2015) "Report of the Group of Governmental Experts on Developments in the Field of Information and Telecommunications in the Context of International Security", [online], https://dig.watch/sites/default/files/UN%20GGE%20Report%202015%20%28A-70-174%29.pdf

Von der Leyen, U. (2019) "A Union that strives for more'', Political Guidelines for the next European Commission 2019 - 2024, October 9, [online], https://op.europa.eu/en/publication-detail/-/publication/43a17056-ebf1-11e9-9c4e-01aa75ed71a1

Wu, T.S. (1997) "Cyberspace Sovereignty? - The Internet and the International System", *Harvard Journal of Law and Technology,* Vol. 10, No. 3, pp. 647-666.

Zuboff, S. (2019) *The Age of Surveillance Capitalism*, Profile Books Ltd, London

Author biography

Dr Andrew N. Liaropoulos is Assistant Professor in University of Piraeus, Department of International and European Studies, Greece. He is also a senior analyst in the Research Institute for European and American Studies (RIEAS) and a member of the editorial board of the Journal of European and American Intelligence Studies (JEAIS).

Chapter Three

Towards an International Framework for Cyber Cooperation based on Global Commons

Brett van Niekerk [1,2]**, Shadi Alshdaifat**[3] **and Trishana Ramluckan**[1,4]

[1] University of KwaZulu-Natal, South Africa
[2] Durban University of Technology, South Africa
[3] University of Sharjah, UAE
[4] Educor Holdings, South Africa
brettv@dut.ac.za; vanniekerkb@ukzn.ac.za
salshdaift@sharjah.ac.ae
ramluckant@ukzn.ac.za

Abstract: Global Commons are areas covered by international treaty frameworks and are often open for all states. Usually they are designated as protected areas for environmental preservation and scientific research, with limitations on military operations in order to preserve peace. The concept of Global Commons have been considered as a model for cyberspace. However, facilities related to global commons have been affected by cyber-incidents, raising the questions of both suitability as well as how proposed international law on cyberspace will impact on areas considered as Global Commons. The chapter will investigate the relevance of the various Global Commons treaty frameworks to cybersecurity taking into account previous cyber-security incidents to assess the sufficiency of international law for these protected areas regarding cyber-incidents. Based on these considerations, a framework for international cooperation in cyberspace is proposed.

Keywords: Area protection, Cyber-attack, Cyber-security, International Cooperation, International Security

1 Introduction

Cyberspace is becoming increasingly prevalent in international security, resulting in a growing focus on the applicability of international humanitarian law (IHL) to cyberspace. Militaries are also considering cyberspace as a fifth domain of operations, alongside air, sea, land and space (US Department of

Defense, 2010). In 2019 and 2020, countries began releasing their national perspectives on the application of IHL cyber-operations and cyberspace (Finnish Ministry for Foreign Affairs, 2020; Ministére des Armées, 2019; Netherlands Parliament, 2019).

In addition, international non-governmental organisations and multi-stakeholder groups have proposed norms for cyberspace, such as the United Nations Group of Governmental Experts on developments in the field of information and telecommunications in the context of international security (UN General Assembly, 2015), *The Paris Call for Trust and Security in Cyberspace* (2018), and the Global Commission for the Stability of Cyberspace (GCSC, 2019).

The concept of Global Commons has been suggested by some authors as a model or basis for laws and treaties for cyberspace; however, some raise concerns and highlight possible challenges with this proposal (DiploFoundation, 2015; Guarino & Iasiello, 2017; Marauhn, 2013; Stadnik, 2017; Ziolkowski, 2013a). In addition, cyber-attacks have been seen to affect systems in areas considered global commons, providing a unique perspective to discuss the applicability and limitations of international laws for cyberspace from the perspective of cyberspace as a global commons. This chapter aims to discuss the suitability of three global commons areas, namely space, Antarctica and the high seas, as models for cyberspace by contrasting potential challenges that might arise from cyber-attacks against systems in these areas. According to Alshdaifat, van Niekerk and Ramluckan (2021), aspects of different Global Commons treaties should be incorporated into a treaty for cyberspace; based on these, the chapter proposes a groundwork for a cooperation in cyberspace.

Section 2 presents a background to global commons in terms of the relevant international legal frameworks as well as the relevant physical characteristics. Cyber-attacks related to global commons are described in Section 3, and their implications for international law are discussed in Section 4. A discussion on the applicability of global commons to international cyber cooperation is conducted in Section 5, followed by a proposed framework for cooperation in cyberspace in Section 6. Section 7 contains further discussion, and Section 8 contains the conclusion.

2 Background to Global Commons

This section provides an overview of various the physical environments and legal frameworks related to global commons. Governance of the international commons is not customary; it is laid out in treaties including the 1967 Outer

Space Treaty (NASA, 2006), the 1982 United Nations Convention on the Law of the Sea (UNCLOS), and to a lesser extent in the 1959 Antarctica Treaty System (Kriwoken & Keage, 1989).

2.1 United Nations Convention on the Law of the Sea

The 1982 United Nations Convention on the Law of the Sea (UNCLOS) sets out a number of aspects related to the sea, such as territorial waters, conservation, rights of passage for commercial and non-commercial government vessels, submarine vessels, undersea cables, broadcasts from international waters, piracy and other criminal transportation of goods, and dispute resolution. The UNCLOS is particularly detailed, and considers a number of variations, such as specific clauses for archipelagos, and for migratory fish versus those that are predominately found in territorial waters (UN, 1982).

The UNCLOS specifies territorial waters (i.e. sovereign space) as 12 nautical miles from the low tide mark, extending to the sea floor and into airspace. Coastal states may still provide control for a further 12 nautical miles in what is known as the contiguous zone in order to prevent any infringement of the laws or regulations related to its territorial waters, immigration, or customs. Beyond the territorial waters, or in the high seas, all nations have freedom of navigation and overflight. It is also indicated that the high seas shall be used for peaceful purposes and no state may claim sovereignty over a portion of the high seas (UNCLOS, 1982).

As we are dealing with the cyber security scenario, the consideration on undersea cables and broadcasting from the high seas are pertinent. Unauthorised broadcasts are considered as sound radio or television broadcasts from a vessel or structure in the high seas, that is meant for reception by the general public and contrary to international regulations (distress calls are exempt). In terms of undersea cables, all states have the right to lay cables on the continental shelf and on the sea bed beyond the continental shelf. The Convention indicates that states who have jurisdiction over persons or a vessel which sails under their flag are liable for the damage to undersea cables, unless reasonable measures taken to avoid damage can be proved (UNCLOS, 1982).

The average depth of the Oceans is 3688m (Eakins and Sharman, 2010), and the deepest point is approximately 11,000m in the Mariana Trench (Daily Telegraph Reporter, 2011). The oceans cover approximately 71% of the Earth's surface (Eakins and Sharman, 2010).

2.2   Outer Space

The Outer Space Treaty of 1967 indicates that outer space, which includes the moon and celestial bodies, is open to all states for exploration and scientific investigation, which should be conducted to benefit all countries. International cooperation is encouraged in this regard. Nations may not claim sovereignty or attempt to appropriate any area of outer space, and all activities should be conducted in a manner that maintains international peace and security in accordance with relevant international laws (NASA, 2006).

Following the focus on maintaining international peace and security, weapons of mass destruction in orbit or stationed in outer space are prohibited, and no weapons testing or military manoeuvres may be conducted, nor can any military installations be established in outer space; however, military personnel and any facility may be used for peaceful exploration of space (NASA, 2006).

Any object (or personnel) launched into outer space, or constructed or installed in outer space, shall remain under the jurisdiction, control, and ownership of the state when in outer space. In addition, any state that is a signatory of the treaty is liable if an object is damaged that is launched (or attempted to be launched) from its territory or if the state contracted the launch from another state's infrastructure. To facilitate cooperation and the global benefit, any state signatory of the treaty may have access to another state's equipment and installations on a reciprocal basis (NASA, 2006).

In addition to the Outer Space Treaty, a legal framework was established for the purposes of developing and operating the International Space Station. The basis of the framework is the International Space Station Intergovernmental Agreement, signed in 1998 (US Department of State, 1998). This is supported by four memoranda of understanding, and a number of bilateral implementing arrangements (European Space Agency, 2021). In general, the agreement is aligned to the Outer Space Treaty in that it promotes cooperation for peaceful purposes, and the components of the International Space Station remain the jurisdiction of the states that contributed it. In contrast, the agreement prohibits claims against other partners for damage caused by International Space Station operations (European Space Agency, 2021). Of particular note is a specific clause on criminal jurisdiction, where a nation affected by criminal actions by a person of another nationality in orbit my request criminal jurisdiction (US Department of State, 1998).

Outer space is considered to begin at approximately 100km from the planet, where the number of oxygen molecules decreases to a point that the 'sky' loses the blue colour and appears black (Howell, 2017). Most man-made orbiting objects are outside of this point. Geostationary satellites, mainly used for communication satellites, orbit at an altitude of approximately 36,000km. Low Earth Orbit is between 160km and 1000km and is commonly used for satellites for imaging (European Space Agency, 2020); the International Space Station orbits in this zone at approximately 400km (Mathewson, 2016). Medium Earth Orbit is between low Earth orbit and the geosynchronous orbits, and is commonly used for navigation satellites (European Space Agency, 2020).

The temperatures in space are harsh; the 'shady side' of the International Space Station can be as low as -150 °C and this increases to 121 °C on the 'sunny side'. These temperatures necessitate a number of thermal controls in order to keep the temperature constant without forming condensation (Frost, 2018). Any manned space craft or station will require many life support systems to regulate not only temperature, but air quality and pressure, as well as waste and water management.

2.3   The Antarctic Treaty System

The Antarctic Treaty System (ATS) is the combination of the Antarctic Treaty (1959) and other agreements stemming from this. The Antarctic Treaty is interpreted as giving the continent the status of territory open for use in an unobstructed situation by any of the states, including those not among the parties to this treaty. This status permits the treatment of Antarctica as international territory, the legal status of which is similar to that of the high seas, air, or space; in particular, the governing treaties of Antarctica share many similarities with UNCLOS as a protected international commons. However, this is the main difference between the legal system of the Arctic and Antarctica in so far as the treaty enshrined the right of states to exercise personal and territorial jurisdiction over potential territorial claims.

There is limited communication infrastructure in Antarctica serving the research stations and vessels. Most communication is based mainly on satellite connections, but limited private mobile phone connections are available near some facilities. In 2015, 90% of the total data capacity to the continent was through the primary relay which supported 50Mbit/s (CIA, 2020; Roberts, 2015). Despite this, Antarctica has the Internet domain .AQ and most of those residing in the zone are considered Internet users (CIA, 2020; Roberts, 2015). During the summer months the population within the zone is approximately 5000, mostly researchers at research stations on the continent or surrounding islands, and vessels supporting these (CIA, 2020; Roberts, 2015).

Any territory or ocean south of 60°S Latitude is encompassed by The Antarctic Treaty Zone (The Antarctic Treaty, 1959). Antarctica has been described as "the coldest, windiest and driest continent on Earth" (Australian Antarctic Program, 2019), and is considered as one of the harshest environments on the planet. Wind gusts have been known to reach 200km/h, and sustained winds of 100km/h can last for days (Australian Antarctic Program, 2019). The average inland temperature is -60 °C, and can range from a low of -80 °C in winter to -30 °C in summer. The coastal areas are milder with an average temperature of -10 °C, with lows of -40 °C in winter and ranging up to 10 °C in summer (Australian Antarctic Program, 2019; Roberts, 2015). With such hostile conditions, a cyber-attack affecting a vessel or research facility could be potentially catastrophic if critical systems are disrupted.

As the Antarctica Treaty Zone is considered a Common Heritage of Mankind (i.e. international land), Antarctica should be treated as a peaceful land without the deployment of troop units, it cannot serve as a place for military operations, and ensure environmental safety. However, there are increasing tensions within the ATS due to some newcomers not following existing processes, raising concerns that disputes over contested territorial claims may intensify (Espach and Samaranayake, 2020).

3 Cyber security incidents related to Global Commons

3.1 Cyber-attacks against maritime systems

A number of incidents have affected the maritime sector; many of these can be considered cyber-crimes and did not necessarily affect operations on the high seas, but research is showing vulnerabilities on many vessel systems, and there have been occasions where sea-going vessels have been affected by cyber incidents (van Niekerk, 2016). Examples of these include:

- It was reported that three oil rigs had their safety systems remotely disabled in 2009 (Kravets, 2009);
- In 2009 Royal Navy warships had systems infected by malware (Page, 2009);
- An oil rig drifted off its drill site after malware disrupted the navigation systems in 2013 (Knox, 2015; Swanbeck, 2015);
- A malware infection rendered an oil rig unseaworthy for over two weeks (Wagstaff, 2014); and,

- In 2021 leaked documents reportedly from Iranian cyber units illustrated their research into hacking the ballast systems of commercial vessels (Haynes, 2021).

A number of systems that ships rely on have been shown to be vulnerable to interference (Wagstaff, 2014; van Niekerk, 2016). In 2013 researchers successfully demonstrated spoofing of Global Positioning System (GPS) signals to divert a yacht off course (Vaas, 2013); it was reported in 2015 that a European port's operations were disrupted for 12 hours due to a disgruntled employee jamming the GPS signals (Knox, 2015). In 2013 researchers also illustrated the possibility of spoofing and interfering with the automatic identification system (AIS) installed on commercial vessels (Balduzzi, Wihoit & Pasta, 2013). In 2021 it was reported that fake positions of warships are appearing on AIS; often these fake positions were located inside the territorial waters of a foreign nation (Harris, 2021).

3.2 Cyber-attacks and space systems

Cyber-security of satellite systems is of growing concern (Garner, 2020; Holmes, n.d.), and the US Space Development Agency director is reported as stating that cyber-attacks against satellite systems is more concerning than kinetic attacks from anti-satellite missiles (Erwin, 2021). Accordingly, the mission of the US Space Force includes cyber-security and cyber-warfare, as is evident from their recruiting (Airforce.com, 2021), and the US Air Force is considering "space-centered cyber training" (Vincent, 2022). Both Schubert (2021) and Holmes (n.d.) indicate that tools that can be used to target satellites are becoming more easily accessible; however, Schubert also raises the possibility of related attacks such as electromagnetic pulses. In addition, space electronic warfare can use radio frequency signals to jam or interfere with communications to and from satellites (Rajagopalan, 2019). In 2012 concerns over vulnerabilities in GPS systems were raised (Emspak, 2012), and the GPS spoofing and jamming examples described in Section 3.1 illustrate these concerns. Hudaib (2016) provides an overview of electronic attack and network security considerations for satellite systems, as well as common security mechanisms employed.

A reported cyber-incident that affected space systems was when the US National Oceanic and Atmospheric Administration implemented incident response measures in 2014 after a state-sponsored cyber-attack, which ultimately affected satellites, including weather satellites (Flaherty, Samenow & Rein, 2014). In 2020, a "hack-a-sat" competition was held at the Defcon conference, where participants would attempt to hack a satellite and the associated ground control (Scoles, 2020). This competition illustrates the growing significance of cyber threats to space systems. Hudaib (2016) provides an overview of a number cases where satellite broadcasts were 'hijacked', illustrating that a combination of electronic warfare and cyber-attacks could be used to interfere with satellites, their users, and their controllers. A satellite was reportedly damaged after hackers managed to rotate the satellite so the camera pointed towards the sun, and a hacking group claimed to have stolen software that would allow it to control military satellites (Hudaib, 2016). In 2022, reports surfaced of broadband satellite services from Vaisat being disrupted in Europe due to a suspected "cyber incident" (Greig, 2022).

The interference of safety systems on oil rigs described in Section 3.1 has some hypothetical relevance to space systems. Should a populated space system (e.g. space station or capsule) be affected by a cyber-incident, the results could be catastrophic as this could result in loss of temperature control, air pressure, or other life support systems. Malicious code that affects the reporting of sensors during docking between a space station and capsule could result in physical damage should the capsule arrive too fast or at the wrong angle; likewise, re-entry with impacted sensors could be disastrous.

3.3 Cyber-attacks and Antarctica

Despite Antarctica having limited infrastructure, connectivity and population, cyber-incidents have occurred on the continent, including:

- A hacker compromising of the backup and data acquisition servers of the National Science Foundation's Degree Angular Scale Interferometer radio telescope in 2003 (Poulsen, 2004);
- An extortion attempt by Romanian hackers stole data from the Amundsen-Scott South Pole Station in 2003. There were some incorrect reports that this affected the life support systems and put the researcher's lives were in danger (Poulsen, 2004).
- Three research stations in the Antarctic were compromised in 2015 and used as staging points for cyber-criminals to target US and European government agencies (Roberts, 2015).

In addition, the incidents affecting sea going vessel systems (Section 3.1) and GPS or satellite systems (Section 3.2) are relevant to the Antarctic environment. An incident affecting an Antarctic program research ship's systems may hinder resupply of the bases or delay the departure of those at the bases. Interfering with navigation, such as spoofed GPS signals, can result in vessels deviating from known safe zones into more hazardous waters. The disablement of the oil rig's safety systems supports the concern about life support systems mentioned above. In the harsh environment of Antarctica, any degradation of life support system functions could have dire consequences. Disruption of communications or weather information may result in unpreparedness or the inability to make distress calls.

The importance of cyber-security for Antarctic programmes has been recognised. The contract for the US Antarctic Program's cybersecurity was won by security firm Kratos in 2021 (InfoSecurity Magazine, 2012). The US Antarctic Program also has a dedicated information security webpage that lists all the relevant information, including policies and awareness training initiatives (USAP, c. 2020).

The incidents mentioned above illustrate that research facilities in Antarctica have been affected by cyber-attacks, and therefore the potential for further incidents exists. Whilst the known incidents were perpetrated by cyber-criminals, this does raise the possibility for nation-state cyber-operations to target the research facilities and research vessels directly or indirectly through the disruption of satellites used for navigation, communications, and weather information. Due to the limited connectivity and redundancy of the connections, Antarctica's Internet access and communications in general can be considered to be susceptible to distributed-denial-of-service (DDoS) attacks. Research data is a prime target as is illustrated in the above examples, especially since state-backed cyber-espionage operations have been increasing, such as those targeting vaccine development during the COVID-19 pandemic (Cimpanu, 2020). A cyber-capable nation may find obtaining research relevant to its national interests easier to obtain through cyber-espionage that conducting the research itself on the continent.

4 An international humanitarian law perspective on cyber-attacks on Global Commons

International Humanitarian Law (IHL) provisions are generally dated and do not explicitly consider cyber-operations. As the increasing prevalence of information technologies as a tool for conflict is relatively young in comparison to IHL and was considered to constitute a "revolution of military affairs" (Cordesman, 2014; Dombrowski and Ross, 2008), it has been posited that IHL is ill-equipped for cyberspace and cannot be adequately applied in cyber-warfare (Dunlap, 2011). An opposing view is that the absence of explicit references to cyber-operations in IHL does not exclude cyber-operations from IHL (Ferraro, 2015); in fact, the UN GGE report declares that international law does apply to activities in cyberspace and this view was supported by the UN Open Ended Working Group (UNGA, 2021) and the

Association for Progressive Communications' proposed Internet Rights Charter (APC, 2006). International law has explicit provisions to prohibit or limit the use of certain weapons, such as anti-personnel mines or biological and chemical weapons; however, the general rules apply to the use of any weapon system. Specifically, Article 36 of Protocol I Additional to the Geneva Conventions (1979: 21) states that "[i]n the study, development, acquisition or adoption of a new weapon, means or method of warfare, a High Contracting Party is under an obligation to determine whether its employment would, in some or all circumstances, be prohibited by this Protocol or by any other rule of international law applicable to the High Contracting Party". This indicates that international law is sufficiently broad to include the use of cyber-weapons.

Despite the above-mentioned differing views, a number of key considerations should to be taken into account (Schmitt, 2017):

- Did the cyber-incident breach national sovereignty?
- Did the cyber-incident affect critical national processes (e.g. elections)?
- Did the cyber-incident result in equivalent damage or impact to that of a physical armed attack?

It is considered difficult to determine the answers to some of these questions; often the difficulty is related to the fact that accurately attributing the origin of the incident to another nation remains (Schmitt, 2017). It is through this lens that this section considers the relevance of cyber-attacks and areas designated as Global Commons.

Sovereign claims in Global Commons are often restricted by the relevant legal frameworks. Both the ATS and outer space treaties indicate that there can be no sovereign claims in those areas, and the UNCLOS specifies zones of national waters. Similarly, Ayers (2016) considers that cyberspace has no boundaries and therefore nations can have no sovereign claims. A cyber-attack that is conducted against a facility in the ATS zone or outer space cannot be considered to have breached a nation's sovereignty if there can be no sovereign claims in the area. However, can a state cyber-operation be considered a breach of sovereignty if it targets a facility (or part thereof) or a vessel under the jurisdiction of another nation if it is in an international zone? As facilities or sea-going vessels are unlikely to contain or affect critical national processes, claims of interference will not be relevant for cyber-operations against them. Assessing the application of IHL to cyber-operations and deciding on the appropriate responses will be further complicated in cases where sovereignty cannot be claimed.

In the event that a cyber-attack results in significant physical damage to a facility in a Global Commons, or loss of life as a result of disruption of critical life-support systems (e.g. in space or Antarctica), can this incident be considered as either an act of war or an armed attack? Some national perspectives on cyber-operations allow for the possibility of a cyber-attack to be classed as a use of force or an armed attack in cases where the consequences of the cyber-attack are equivalent or similar to that of a physical use of force or armed attack (Ministère des Armées, 2019; Netherlands Parliament, 2019). Following on from these interpretations, a cyber-operation against a facility in a Global Commons area resulting in death or injury of its occupants or significant physical disruption of the facility's operation can constitute the use of force or an armed attack, taking into account the severity of the incident. In addition to the afore-mentioned conditions being met, attribution indicating the responsible nation-state will also be required to make such a case. However, in remote locations with hostile environments (e.g. outer space or Antarctica) it is unlikely the necessary on-site skill sets will be available to provide adequate incident response and the necessary digital forensic investigations, In addition, it is unlikely that persons with such skills will be transported to the locations timeously, particularly in Antarctica or outer space. As most of the systems are operational, there will be no option but to continue using them during an investigation, which will complicate the extraction of digital evidence.

Military cyber-operations conducted in or against certain areas where treaties prohibit military action can be considered as a breach of those treaties (Schmitt, 2017). The specific example provided by Schmitt (2017) was the Antarctic Treaty System, but the breach also applies to similar scenarios, such as the Outer Space Treaty. For a breach to occur, two criteria need to be met: firstly, the aggressor nation needs to be a signatory of the treaty in order for them to have breached it; and secondly, there will need to be adequate attribution not just to the aggressor state, but specifically to its military organisations. An additional challenge is that of 'digital collateral damage', where a military cyber-operation affects a facility or vessel in space, Antarctica or in the high seas, even through the affected facility or vessel was not the intended target. When a military cyber-operation causes collateral damage in a protected area, it may need to be determined if the operation originated within the protected territory or externally. Should the operation have originated externally and was not intended to target entities within a protected territory, then it is possible to argue that a treaty prohibiting military action in such an area was not breached. As cyberspace is not identical to the physical world, determining where a cyber-operation took place is more challenging. Is it deemed to have occurred at the originating point of the cyber-operation, at the targeted systems, where other remote systems were utilised, or at all points through which network traffic related to the cyber-operations traversed? This specific definition becomes important when considering if a cyber-operation has breached clauses of a treaty limiting military operations.

Jurisdictional challenges may also arise when considering cyber-incidents, such as those described in Section 3 where systems of ocean-going vessels and Antarctic facilities were affected. The very nature of a Global Commons is that nations do not have sovereign claims. However, some treaties may prescribe jurisdictional claims, for example the jurisdiction of flagged vessels under the UNCLOS or specific modules of the International Space Station. Within a cyberspace context, nations can exercise jurisdiction over systems within their territorial boundaries (Schmitt, 2017). However, jurisdiction of what is called the 'public core of the Internet' by the GCSC (2019) remains unresolved. A dedicated multinational cyber-policing force or forum may need to be established for jurisdiction over the 'public core', similar to the cyber- peacekeeping force that was proposed by Dorn and Webb (2019).

An additional challenge is that of monitoring compliance in cyberspace, whether it is adherence to a specific treaty, voluntary norms or international humanitarian law. For example, small removeable storage devices can be used to transport malicious code undetected into a protected area, leaving no network trace of the security incident until the device is connected to a network. In addition, in the cyber realm the knowledge of how to conduct a cyber-attack is often just as important. By comparison, military equipment and weapons of mass destruction have a much larger physical size in addition to other signatures that can be detected. This makes the concept of inspections as is often used for compliance inefficient when considering cyberspace. The UN GGE report (UNGA, 2015) raised a number of areas that are required in addition to the norms, including confidence building measures which can aid in indicating compliance to treaties. The Organisation for Security and Cooperation in Europe (OSCE, 2016) proposes 16 confidence building measures for cyberspace, which can be used or adapted to aid in verifying compliance of treaties or agreements related to cyberspace.

5 Applicability of Global Commons to international cyber cooperation

A number of authors propose that cyberspace should be given the status as an area of Global Commons similar to the existing three described above (DiploFoundation, 2015; Guarino & Iasiello, 2017; Marauhn, 2013; Stadnik,

Brett van Niekerk, Shadi Alshdaifat and Trishana Ramluckan

2017; Ziolkowski, 2013a), particularly from the perspectives of jurisdictional analysis and that it is perceived that cyberspace has no borders and does not fall into a single nation's sovereignty (Ayers, 2016; Menthe, 1998). However, Kaushik (2021) indicates that characteristics of cyberspace are different from the traditional concept of a Global Commons in that it is mostly managed by private organisations, it is not physical, it focuses on the transfer of information rather than goods, and it is manmade. Areas considered as Global Commons are usually defined by treaties in order to facilitate the governance of the area and the international cooperation associated with the area (Guarino & Iasiello, 2017; Marauhn, 2013). However, there is no specific treaty in place regarding cyberspace (Marauhn, 2013), and the majority of international cooperation revolves around proposed voluntary norms, such as those proposed in the UN GGE 2015 (UNGA, 2015) report and the GCSC (2019) report. The foundations of nation-level international cooperation in cyberspace are still being negotiated through processes such as the UN GGE UN OEWG (Digital Watch, 2021).

In considering sovereignty, both the ATS and Outer Space Treaty do not allow for sovereign claims, although the UNCLOS does indicate that there are territorial waters beyond which is considered as the High Seas. In terms of cyberspace, the servers, infrastructure, and governance of that infrastructure is subject to the laws of the nation in which they reside and nations do have sovereignty over cyber infrastructure in their territory (Schmitt, 2017). An approach to encoding sovereignty for cyberspace is that infrastructure internal to a nation is then subject to that nation's sovereignty, but the interconnections among nations that essentially make the global Internet work, (what the GCSC report (2019) terms the "public core" of the Internet) form the area of Global Commons. However, Kaushik (2021) indicates this is an imperfect solution, and does not fully consider the complexities of cyberspace.

For jurisdiction, both the UNCLOS and the International Space Station treaty do consider national jurisdiction, which is applied to a vessel sailing under the nation's flag, or the module of the International Space Station. In a similar manner, Schmitt (2017) indicates nations can have jurisdiction over cyber infrastructure within their territory, and extraterritorial jurisdiction is possible for situations where severe adverse effects are experienced due to IT services outside of the territory being disrupted. Therefore, jurisdiction can be dealt with in a similar manner to sovereignty, where the Global Commons of cyberspace refer to the public core, and nations have jurisdiction within their territories, with mechanisms in place to request and/or provide extraterritorial jurisdiction in certain circumstances.

65

A challenge with treaties for cyberspace is the ability to verify compliance, particularly due to difficulties in attributing cyber-operations, and the ease of hiding the operations. This complexity of enforcing treaties in cyberspace is noted by Shackelford (2017). Therefore, inspections will not be an effective mechanism for verifying compliance in cyberspace, which contrasts with clauses in treaties for areas of Global Commons such as Article VIII(3) of the *The Antarctic Treaty of 1959* which includes inspections as the key mechanism for verifying compliance and the Outer Space Treaty allowing for inspections of space vehicles or related facilities. Alternative mechanisms are required in cyberspace, which are found in part in the concept of confidence building measures, which is included in the UN GGE 2015 report (UNGA, 2015) and 16 measures are proposed by the OSCE (2016). Borghard and Lonergan (2018) discuss the confidence building measures for cyberspace and conclude that they are necessary to prevent cyber conflict. In a similar manner, the measures can be adapted for managing accusations of non-compliance.

Both the ATS and Outer Space Treaties prohibit the militarisation of the respective environments. By contrast, the high seas have previously experienced sea battles and warships do transit through the open ocean. There is recognition that there is existing military use of cyberspace, and military cyber-operations are likely to continue, in addition to the presence of other malicious actors (GCSC, 2017; Kaushik, 2021). This raises the challenge of a virtual equivalent of arms control. Shackelford (2017) considers it infeasible to ban code or software that could be used for cyber-attacks as this could hinder defensive preparedness. Tools and techniques that are used to conduct cyber-attacks are often derived from tools specifically meant to test an organisations' cyber-security, and the techniques that a military cyber-operation may use can be similar to that of cyber-crime. Ziolkowski (2013a:167) proposes that nations adopt "precautionary measures concerning potential cyber threats posing a significant risk of damage of a transboundary nature". This is supported by the above-mentioned norms (GCSC, 2017; UNGA, 2015), and the concept can be considered to be similar to the *Protocol on Environmental Protection to the Antarctic Treaty of 1991*. In addition, confidence building measures are traditionally used in arms control (Ziolkowski, 2013c), and equivalents for cyberspace have been proposed as discussed above.

While there is potential for governing cyberspace with current international law, it is continually evolving, as are the technologies and situations in Antarctica and outer space. Therefore, in the future it may be necessary to introduce provisions in international law to cater for the changes and differences in cyberspace as malicious or aggressive operations become more prevalent. For example, nations not following processes under the ATS can be seen as analogous to situations where non-signatories in a treaty for cyberspace breach clauses, hiding behind the difficulty in attribution. However, the issue of cyberspace governance remains controversial and unresolved, particularly cyberspace becoming a Common Heritage of Mankind (Alshdaifat, 2018; Baslar, 1998). A phase in achieving this goal is to agree upon and introduce an international regulatory system. In addition, an independent authority may be required to assist with the governance of the treaty, similar to the Secretariat of the Antarctic Treaty (2021). The next section proposes a basis for cooperation in cyberspace based on aspects of the three global commons.

6   Proposed cyber cooperation framework

As indicated by Alshdaifat, van Niekerk and Ramluckan (2021), a single framework or treaty from a Global Commons area will be insufficient for a treaty for cyberspace, but aspects from all three may be combined to provide the basis. This section proposes the basis for a legal framework for cooperation in cyberspace based on mappings from the three Global Commons. Figure 1 proposes the possible relevant frameworks or treaties from which specific clauses or principles for cooperation in cyberspace and be taken.

The proposed basis for a treaty or framework for cyberspace cooperation includes the following elements:

- **Sovereignty**: Similar to UNCLOS, a nation's sovereignty over cyberspace extends to its territorial boundaries. The precise definition of what constitutes the boundaries may need to be clarified. For example, undersea cables could be considered as the landing point or where they cross into territorial waters. The "public core" of the Internet needs to be defined, and should be excluded from any sovereignty claims.
- **Jurisdiction**: Similar to the UNCLOS and ISS agreement, cyber infrastructure based within a nation's territory will be subject to their jurisdiction. Due to the prevalence of cross-border information flow and cyber-crime, some agreement on the processes for requesting extra-territorial jurisdiction should be included. As with sovereignty the "public core" of the Internet needs to be defined, and a possible independent governance body with multi-national representation should be instituted with jurisdiction over the "public core".

Alternatively, an existing Internet governance organisation could take this role.

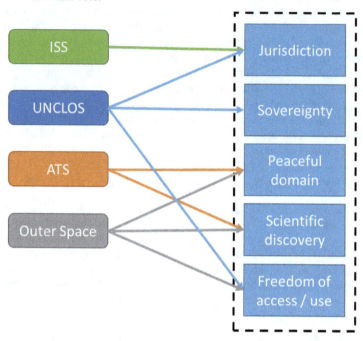

Figure 1: Mapping of Global Commons legal framework to a proposed treaty for cooperation in cyberspace

- **Peaceful domain:** the "public core" of the Internet and related cyber infrastructure should not be targeted or used to conduct military cyber-operations. In considering cyberspace as a peaceful domain, the norms of responsible state behaviour in cyberspace can be adopted or adapted from the existing proposed norms.
- **Scientific discovery**: cyberspace should be used to support scientific discovery. This may imply the need to implement measures to mitigate disinformation, which often counters scientific information (this discussion falls outside the scope of this chapter).
- **Freedom of access and use:** The "public core" of the Internet and related cyber infrastructure should be accessible by all. Limitations need to be placed on this clause, including protecting privacy as well as critical systems and data.

As mentioned in the points above, an international organisation may be needed to govern the public aspects of the Internet and cyberspace.

7 Discussion

Global commons are naturally occurring protected spaces, usually with a focus on scientific discovery. As described above, proposals have been made that cyberspace should be adopted as a fourth Global Commons. However, cyberspace differs in that it is man-made and therefore subject to significant changes in the way it operates or is structured. Cyberspace has evolved rapidly, with malicious activity as well as online military and intelligence operations already occurring. In addition, as Shackelford (2017) indicates, banning tools or software that can be employed offensively prevents development of security technologies and these tools are already prevalently used by cyber-criminals. This implies that the use of cyberspace for purely peaceful purposes and scientific discovery may be idealistic and beyond reach. Therefore, it is more practical to consider the public core of the Internet as protected, where the GCSC (2017) proposes a definition for the public core. Cyber-operations are then permissible, although the public core cannot be interfered with. To further support the peaceful use of cyberspace, current proposals of norms and confidence building measures can be included.

Given the nature of cyberspace, there may be additional challenges when considering sovereignty, jurisdiction, and breaches thereof or non-compliance with a treaty or agreement. Unlike other global commons, cyberspace lacks a natural physical boundary that can easily be defined. Cyberspace is a connection of networks, computers, and related communications infrastructure. Therefore, some of these components are found in almost all countries. It is therefore not possible to prohibit sovereign claims or jurisdiction in cyberspace when the connected infrastructure resides within a nation's territory. Therefore, sovereignty and jurisdiction should apply to cyber infrastructure with a nation's borders, and the public core is considered neutral and outside of national claims. When there are claims of a breach of sovereignty or a treaty, there needs to be some attribution to support the claims indicating the malicious or contravening activity was conducted by a state or was state sponsored.

A limitation to any treaty or agreement is that those who have not signed are not bound by the treaty. Within cyberspace, this means that nations that are not signatories can still conduct cyber-operations without repercussions prescribed by the treaty. In addition, due to the difficulty of attribution, signatories may still attempt cyber-operations in contravention of the treaty in the hope that they will not be identified. This again supports Shackleford's

(2017) position that banning all cyber weapons or tools with offensive uses is not feasible as injured states may not be able to adequately respond to cyber-attacks. Traditional measures for verifying compliance such as inspections are not realisable in cyberspace, therefore additional measures not considered in the existing global commons frameworks are required: that of confidence building measures and norms of responsible behaviour. These may also mitigate the uncertainties when enforcing treaties or applying international law in cyberspace. An independent organisation can be used to support the facilitation of the treaty and act as an intermediary for confidence building measures and governance matters.

Based on the perspectives discussed in this chapter, cooperation in cyberspace on Global Commons does have merit, although there are still limitations and complexities. No one treaty system will be suitable on its own, but by combining aspects from the various treaties for common spaces as well as additional existing proposed mechanisms for cyberspace, an adequate framework for cooperation in cyberspace similar to a common space can evolve. The framework proposed above provides a basis for cooperation, although not all challenges have been resolved and further discussion and diplomacy will be required.

8   Conclusion

The areas of Global Commons have been proposed as a potential model upon which a treaty for cyberspace could be developed. Whilst the existing treaties show promise, challenges may arise when considering their clauses in a cyberspace context. Due to the nature of the Global Commons areas, which are usually remote and only accessible by limited persons (in particular Antarctica and outer space), providing the necessary support to investigate cyber-incidents to provide attribution will be difficult. These areas also may be reliant on limited dedicated communication systems, which make them susceptible to cyber-attacks. Due to restrictions on sovereignty and jurisdiction, concepts of an armed attack or use of force become more complicated. Cyberspace differs in that it is manmade as opposed to being a naturally occurring physical space, and there is a wider ability to access cyberspace as compared to the global commons areas. Therefore, a single treaty for a global commons area is unlikely to be adequate for cooperation in cyberspace. Despit this, some aspects of each of the treaties could be used to form a basis for cooperation in cyberspace, with other proposed measures to mitigate possible shortcomings. This chapter proposed such a basis, with a focus on sovereignty, jurisdiction, freedom of access, peaceful use, and scientific discovery. In addition, voluntary norms of responsible state behaviour in cyberspace and confidence building measures were included to support aspects of the proposed framework. We emphasize that further discussion is required regarding multi-stakeholder engagement and governance of cyberspace.

References

Airforce.com (2021) Learn More About U.S. Space Force Careers, [online], accessed 7 September 2021, https://www.airforce.com/spaceforce.

Alshdaifat, S.A. (2018) "Who Owns What in Outer Space? Dilemmas regarding the Common Heritage of Mankind", Pécs Journal of International and European Law (vol II), 21-43.

Alshdaifat, S.A., van Niekerk, B., and Ramluckan, T., (2021) "Antarctica and Cyber-security: Useful Analogy or Exposing Limitations?" Proceeding of the 20th European Conference on Cyber Warfare and Security, pp. 18-24.

Association for Progressive Communications, (2006) APC Internet Rights Charter, November, [online], accessed 25 February 2022, https://www.apc.org/sites/default/files/APC_charter_EN_1.pdf

Australian Antarctic Program. (2019) Antarctic Weather, 18 February, [online], accessed 28 December 2020, https://www.antarctica.gov.au/about-antarctica/weather-and-climate/weather/

Ayers, C.E. (2016) Rethinking Sovereignty in the Context of Cyberspace, Carlisle Barracks, Pennsylvania: U.S. Army War College. Available at: https://www.hsdl.org/?view&did=802916

Balduzzi, M., Wihoit, K., & Pasta, A. (2013). Hey Captain, where's your ship? Attacking vessel tracking systems for fun and profit, 11th Annual Hack in the Box (HITB) Security Conference in Asia, [online], accessed 10 September 2021, https://conference.hitb.org/hitbsecconf2013kul/materials/D1T1%20-%20Marco%20Balduzzi,%20Kyle%20Wilhoit%20Alessandro%20Pasta%20-%20Attacking%20Vessel%20Tracking%20Systems%20for%20Fun%20and%20Profit.pdf

Baslar, K., (1998) The Concept of the Common Heritage of Mankind in International Law, The Hague: Martinus Nijhoff Publishers.

Borghard, E.D., and Lonergan, S.W., (2018) Confidence Building Measures for the Cyber Domain, *Strategic Studies Quarterly* 12(3), 10-49.

Cordesman, A.H., (2014) The Real Revolution in Military Affairs, Center for Strategic and International Studies, 5 August, [online], accessed 25 February 2022, https://www.csis.org/analysis/real-revolution-military-affairs

CIA. (2020) Antarctica, The World Factbook, [online], accessed 4 January 2021, https://www.cia.gov/the-world-factbook/countries/antarctica/

Cimpanu, C., (2020) "US formally accuses China of hacking US entities working on COVID-19 research", *Zero Day*, 13 May, [online], accessed 18 May 2020, https://www.zdnet.com/article/us-formally-accuses-china-of-hacking-us-entities-working-on-covid-19-research/

Daily Telegraph Reporter. (2011) "Scientists map Mariana Trench, deepest known section of ocean in the world", The Telegraph, 8 December, [online], accessed 7

September 2021,
https://web.archive.org/web/20111208045125/http://www.telegraph.co.uk/earth/
environment/8940571/Scientists-map-Mariana-Trench-deepest-known-section-
of-ocean-in-the-world.html

Digital Watch (2021) UN GGE and OEWG, Geneva Internet Platform, [online],
https://dig.watch/processes/un-gge

DiploFoundation, (2015) The Internet as Common Heritage of Mankind, 22
December, [online], accessed 27 February, https://diplomacy.edu/blog/internet-
common-heritage-mankind/

Dombrowski, P., and Ross, A.L., (2008) "The Revolution in Military Affairs,
Transformation and the Defence Industry", *Security Challenges* 4(4), 13-38.

Dorn, A.W., and Webb, S., (2019) "Cyberpeacekeeping: New Ways to Prevent and
Manage Cyberattacks", International Journal of Cyber Warfare and Terrorism
9(1), 19-30.

Dunlap, C.J., (2011) "Perspectives for Cyber Strategists on Law for Cyberwar",
Strategic Studies Quarterly 5(1), 81-99.

Eakins, B.W. and Sharman, G.F., (2010) Volumes of the World's Oceans from
ETOPO1, NOAA National Geophysical Data Center, Boulder, CO, [online],
accessed 7 September 2021,
https://web.archive.org/web/20150311032757/http://ngdc.noaa.gov/mgg/global/
etopo1_ocean_volumes.html.

Emspak, J. (2012) GPS vulnerable to dangerous hacks and spamming, NBC News, 7
May, [online], accessed 10 September 2012,
https://www.nbcnews.com/id/wbna47324401

Erwin, S. (2012) DoD space agency: Cyber attacks, not missiles, are the most
worrisome threat to satellites, Space News, 14 April, [online], accessed 10
September 2021, https://spacenews.com/dod-space-agency-cyber-attacks-not-
missiles-are-the-most-worrisome-threat-to-satellites/

Espach, R., and Samaranayake, N., (2020), "Antarctica is the New Arctic: Security
and Strategy in the Southern Ocean", CNA, 17 March, [online], accessed 12
March 2021, https://www.cna.org/news/InDepth/article?ID=40

European Space Agency. (2020) Types of orbits, 30 March, [online], accessed 10
September 2021,
https://www.esa.int/Enabling_Support/Space_Transportation/Types_of_orbits

European Space Agency. (2021) International Space Station legal framework,
[online],
https://www.esa.int/Science_Exploration/Human_and_Robotic_Exploration/Inte
rnational_Space_Station/International_Space_Station_legal_framework.

Ferraro, T., (2015) "The ICRC's legal position on the notion of armed conflict
involving foreign intervention and on determining the IHL applicable to this
type of conflict", International Review of the Red Cross 97(900), 1227-1252.
Available at https://international-review.icrc.org/articles/icrcs-legal-position-
notion-armed-conflict-involving-foreign-intervention-and-determining

Frost, R. (2018) How Difficult Is It To Keep The Space Station Warm?, Quora, 24
October, [online] accessed 10 September 2021,

https://www.forbes.com/sites/quora/2018/10/24/how-difficult-is-it-to-keep-the-space-station-warm/?sh=1d699dea4af7

Garner, T. (2020) Why Satellite Cybersecurity Must Be Prioritized in the New Frontier, NextGov, 1 May, [online], accessed 10 September 2021, https://www.nextgov.com/ideas/2020/05/why-satellite-cybersecurity-must-be-prioritized-new-frontier/164977/

Global Commission on the Stability of Cyberspace. (2019) Advancing Cyberstability, Final Report, November, [online], accessed 7 January 2021, https://cyberstability.org/wp-content/uploads/2020/02/GCSC-Advancing-Cyberstability.pdf

Greig, J. (2022) Viasat says 'cyber event' is causing broadband outages across Europe, ZDNet, 28 February, [online], accessed 2 March 2022, https://www.zdnet.com/article/viasat-confirms-cyberattack-causing-outages-across-europe/

Guarino, A., and Iasiello, E., (2017) "Imposing and Evading Cyber Borders: The Sovereignty Dilemma", Cyber, Intelligence and Security 1(2), 1-20.

Harris, M. (2021) Phantom Warships Are Courting Chaos in Conflict Zones, Wired, 29 July, [online], accessed 10 September 2021, https://www.wired.com/story/fake-warships-ais-signals-russia-crimea/

Haynes, D. (2021) Iran's Secret Cyber Files, Sky News, [online], accessed 10 September 2021, https://news.sky.com/story/irans-secret-cyber-files-on-how-cargo-ships-and-petrol-stations-could-be-attacked-12364871

Holmes, M. (n.d.) The Growing Risk of a Major Satellite Cyber Attack, Via Satellite, [online], accessed 10 September 2021, http://interactive.satellitetoday.com/the-growing-risk-of-a-major-satellite-cyber-attack/

Howell, E. (2017) What is space?, Sapce.com, 8 June, [online], accessed 10 September 2021, https://www.space.com/24870-what-is-space.html

Hudaib, A.A.Z. (2016) Satellite Network Hacking & Security Analysis, International Journal of Computer Science and Security 10(1), 8-55.

InfoSecurity Magazine., (2012) Kratos gets $16 million cybersecurity contract for US Antarctic Program, 29 May, [online], accessed 22 November 2020, https://www.infosecurity-magazine.com/news/kratos-gets-16-million-cybersecurity-contract-for/

Kaushik, D., (2021) Cyberspace as A Global Commons, South Asia Journal, 3 February, [online], http://southasiajournal.net/cyberspace-as-a-global-commons/

Knox, J. (2015) Coast Guard Commandant on Cyber in the maritime domain, Coast Guard Maritime Commons, 15 June, [online], accessed 10 September 2021, http://mariners.coastguard.dodlive.mil/2015/06/15/6152015-coast-guard-commandant-on-cyber-in-the-maritimedomain/

Kravets, D., (2009) "Feds: hacker disabled offshore oil platforms' leak-detection system", Wired, 18 March, [online], accessed 28 December 2020, http://www.wired.com/2009/03/feds-hacker-dis/

Kriwoken, L.K., and Keage, P.L., (1989) "Introduction: the Antarctic Treaty System", In: J. Handmer (ed.), Antarctica: Policies and Policy Development,

Centre for Resource and Environmental Studies, Canberra: Australian National University, 1-6.

Marauhn, T., (2013) "Customary Rules of International Environmental Law - Can they Provide Guidance for Developing a Peacetime Regime for Cyberspace?" in: Ziolkowski, K. (ed.), Peacetime Regime for State Activities in Cyberspace, NATO CCDCOE: Tallinn, Estonia, pp. 465-484.

Mathewson, S. (2016) How to Spot the International Space Station Location with New NASA Tool, Space.com, 9 November, [online], accessed 10 September 2021, https://www.space.com/34650-track-astronauts-space-new-interactive-map.html

Menthe, D.C., (1998) "Jurisdiction in Cyberspace: A Theory of International Spaces", Michigan Telecommunications and Technology Law Review 4(1), 69-103. Available at: http://repository.law.umich.edu/mttlr/vol4/iss1/3

Ministére des Armées, (2019) International Law Applied to Operations in Cyberspace, [online], accessed 18 January, https://www.defense.gouv.fr/content/download/567648/9770527/file/internation al+law+applied+to+operations+in+cyberspace.pdf

Ministry for Foreign Affairs, (2020) Finland published its positions on public international law in cyberspace, Government of Finland, 15 October, [online], accessed 2 November 2020, https://valtioneuvosto.fi/en/-/finland-published-its-positions-on-public-international-law-in-cyberspace

National Aeronautics and Space Administration (NASA). (2006) The Outer Space Treaty of 1967, [online], accessed 25 January 2021, https://history.nasa.gov/1967treaty.html

Netherlands Parliament, (2019) Appendix: International law in cyberspace, 26 September, [online], accessed 8 January 2020, https://www.government.nl/binaries/government/documents/parliamentary-documents/2019/09/26/letter-to-the-parliament-on-the-international-legal-order-in-cyberspace/International+Law+in+the+Cyberdomain+-+Netherlands.pdf

Organization for Security and Co-operation in Europe, (2016) OSCE Confidence-Building Measures to Reduce the Risks of Conflict Stemming from the Use of Information and Communication Technologies, Decision No. 1202, 10 March, [online], accessed 22 February 2022, https://www.osce.org/files/f/documents/d/a/227281.pdf

Page, L. (2009) MoD networks still malware-plagued after two weeks, The Register, 20 January, [online], accessed 10 September 2021, https://www.theregister.com/2009/01/20/mod_malware_still_going_strong/

Paris Call for Trust and Security in Cyberspace (2018), 12 November, [online], accessed 18 January 2019, https://www.diplomatie.gouv.fr/IMG/pdf/paris_call_cyber_cle443433.pdf

Poulsen, K., (2003) "South Pole 'cyberterrorist' hack wasn't the first", *The Register*, 19 August, [online], accessed 22 November 2020, https://www.theregister.com/2004/08/19/south_pole_hack/

Protocol Additional to the Geneva Conventions of 12 August 1949, and relating to the Protection of Victims of International Armed Conflicts, (1977), United

Nations Treaty Series 3, 8 June, [online], accessed 9 January 2021, https://www.refworld.org/docid/3ae6b36b4.html.

Protocol on Environmental Protection to the Antarctic Treaty (1991). Secretariat of the Antarctic Treaty: Buenos Aires, Argentina. Available at: https://www.ats.aq/e/antarctictreaty.html

Rajagopalan, R.P. (2019) Electronic and Cyber Warfare in Outer Space, The United Nations Institute for Disarmament Research, [online], accessed 10 September 2021, https://www.unidir.org/files/publications/pdfs/electronic-and-cyber-warfare-in-outer-space-en-784.pdf

Roberts, P., (2015) "Petulant Penguin Attacks Use Antarctica As Base", *Security Ledger*, 1 April, [online], accessed 22 November 2020, https://securityledger.com/2015/04/petulant-penguin-attacks-use-antarctica-as-base/

Schmitt, M.N. (2017) Tallinn Manual 2.0: On The International Law Applicable to Cyber Operations, Cambridge: Cambridge University Press.

Schubert, F. (2021) Protecting everyday life – How Airbus protects satellite systems against attacks, Airbus, [online], accessed 10 September 2021, https://airbus-cyber-security.com/news/protecting-everyday-life-how-airbus-protects-satellites-against-attacks/

Scoles, S., (2020) "The Feds Want These Teams to Hack a Satellite—From Home", Wired, 6 August, [online], accessed 28 December 2020, https://www.wired.com/story/the-feds-want-these-teams-to-hack-a-satellite-from-home/

Secretariat of the Antarctic Treaty (2021) The Secretariat of the Antarctic Treaty, [online], accessed 10 September 2021, https://www.ats.aq/e/secretariat.html

Shackelford, S.J., (2017) "The Law of Cyber Peace", Chicago Journal of International Law 18(1), 1-47. Available at: http://chicagounbound.uchicago.edu/cjil/vol18/iss1/1

Stadnik, I., (2017) "What is an International Cybersecurity Regime and how we can Achieve it?" Masaryk University Journal of Law and Technology 11(1), 129-154.

Swanbeck, S. (2015) Coast Guard Commandant Addresses Cybersecurity Vulnerabilities on Offshore Oil Rigs, Centre for Strategic and International Studies, 22 June, [online], accessed 10 September 2021, https://www.csis.org/blogs/strategic-technologies-blog/coast-guard-commandant-addresses-cybersecurity-vulnerabilities

The Antarctic Treaty (1959), 1 December, Conference on Antarctica: Washington D.C. Available at: https://www.ats.aq/e/antarctictreaty.html

United Nations Convention on the Law of the Sea (1982). 10 December, United Nations. Available at: https://www.un.org/Depts/los/convention_agreements/texts/unclos/unclos_e.pdf

United Nations General Assembly (2015), Developments in the field of information and telecommunications in the context of international security, A/AC.290/2021/CRP.2, 10 March.

United Nations General Assembly (2021), Open-ended working group on developments in the field of information and telecommunications in the context of international security, A/RES/70/237, 23 December.

US Antarctic Program (c. 2020), USAP Information Security Program, [online] accessed 12 March 2021, https://www.usap.gov/technology/sctninfosec.cfm

US Department of Defense, (2010) The Quadrennial Defense Review, February, [online], accessed 9 January 2021, https://archive.defense.gov/qdr/QDR%20as%20of%2029JAN10%201600.pdf.

US Department of State, (1998) Space Station, Treaties and Other International Acts Series 12927, [online], accessed 26 February 2022, https://www.state.gov/wp-content/uploads/2019/02/12927-Multilateral-Space-Space-Station-1.29.1998.pdf

Vincent, B. (2022) Air Force Eyes Space-Centered Cyber Training, NextGov, 18 February, [online], accessed 22 February 2022, https://www.nextgov.com/cybersecurity/2022/02/air-force-eyes-space-centered-cyber-training/362189/

Vaas, L. (2013) $80 million yacht hijacked by students spoofing GPS signals, Naked Security, 31 July, [online], accessed 10 September 2021, https://nakedsecurity.sophos.com/2013/07/31/80-million-yacht-hijacked-by-students-spoofing-gps-signals/

van Niekerk, B., (2016) "Analysis of Cyber-Attacks against the Transportation Sector", in: Korstanje, M.E. (ed.), *Threat Mitigation and Detection of Cyber Warfare and Terrorism Activities*, IGI Global: Hershey, PA, pp. 68-91.

Wagstaff, J. (2014) All at sea: global shipping fleet exposed to hacking threat, Reuters, 24 April, [online], accessed 10 September 2021, https://www.reuters.com/article/us-cybersecurity-shipping-idUSBREA3M20820140424

Ziolkowski, K., (2013a) "General Principles of International Law as Applicable in Cyberspace", in: Ziolkowski, K. (ed.), Peacetime Regime for State Activities in Cyberspace, NATO CCDCOE: Tallinn, Estonia, pp. 135-188.

Ziolkowski, K., (2013b) "Peacetime Cyber Espionage – New Tendencies in Public International Law", in: Ziolkowski, K. (ed.), Peacetime Regime for State Activities in Cyberspace, NATO CCDCOE: Tallinn, Estonia, pp. 425-464.

Ziolkowski, K., (2013c) Confidence Building Measures for Cyberspace – Legal Implications, NATO CCDCOE: Tallinn, Estonia

Author biographies

Dr Brett van Niekerk is a senior lecturer in IT at the Durban University of Technology. He serves as chair for the International Federation of Information Processing Working Group on ICT in Peace and War, and the co-Editor-in-Chief of the International Journal of Cyber Warfare and Terrorism. He has numerous years of information/cyber-security experience in both academia

and industry, and has contributed to the ISO/IEC information security standards. In 2012 he graduated with his PhD focusing on information operations and critical infrastructure protection. He is also holds a MSC in electronic engineering and is CISM certified.

Dr Shadi A. Alshdaifat earned a Bachelor's degree in law (LLB) from Mu'tah University, Jordan (2001). He also holds a master's degree in International and Comparative Law (LLM) from Dedman School of Law at Southern Methodist University, Dallas, Texas (2009). He also holds Science Juridical Doctorate from Golden Gate University School of Law San Francisco, California (2012). Currently he is an Associate Professor of Public International Law in the University of Sharjah.

Dr Trishana Ramluckan is the Research Manager at Educor Holdings and an Honorary Research Fellow at the University of KwaZulu-Natal's School of Law. Prior to this she was a Postdoctoral Researcher in the School of Law and an Adjunct Lecturer in the Graduate School of Business at the University of KwaZulu-Natal. She is a member of the IFIP working group on ICT Uses in Peace and War and is an Academic Advocate for ISACA. She is also the Editor-in- Chief of the Educor Multidisciplinary Journal (EMJ). In 2017 she graduated with a Doctor of Administration specialising in IT and Public Governance and in 2020 she was listed in the Top 50 Women in Cybersecurity in Africa. Her current research areas include Cyber Law and Information Technology Governance.

Chapter Four

Cyber Power Diffusion: Global, Regional and Local Implications

Eduardo Izycki

King's College, London, United Kingdom
Universidade de Brasília, Brasília, Brazil
eduardo.izycki@kcl.ac.uk; eduardo.izycki@aluno.unb.br

Abstract: One of the most striking features of the 21st century is the widespread adoption of information technology in every aspect of the modern life of individuals, society, or nation-states. Interconnectivity will increase exponentially in the years to come with the adoption of 5G networks, the internet of things (IoT), large volumes of information (Big Data), and the use of machine learning (artificial intelligence). As a result, economic activity and ordinary life will be even more exposed to the threat of cyber offensive actions. While many studies focus on the worst-case scenario where cyber offensive actions will provoke a cyber-armageddon, they fail to provide empirical evidence to support it. This chapter provides empirical data regarding the current state of cyber conflict. For that purpose, an algorithm to collect and process the empirical data was built and used to examine hypotheses. As a result, this research gathered evidence of 29 different countries engaging in cyber offensive actions and 86 nations acquiring cyber offensive technologies from private vendors. The numbers challenge the average perception of concentration of cyber capabilities in a few "traditional" actors. This entails that cyberspace, as an operational theatre, favours the diffusion of power among nation-states. The majority of cyber offensive actions are a variation of traditional instruments of statecraft such as surveillance, espionage, and disinformation, potentialized by cyberspace's peculiar characteristics. In this sense, cyber offensive capabilities are providing alternatives for the bargaining and interactions to nation-states below the threshold of the use of force. Actors are able to achieve strategic outcomes and influence the balance of power without having to resort to an armed attack and minimize the risk of a military or nuclear response from their targets.

Keywords: cybersecurity, cyber warfare, cyber conflict, state-sponsored cyber-operations, cyber-power, cyberspace.

1 Introduction

The debate regarding cyber-operations is often fuelled by worst-case scenarios. Threat inflation is part of the cybersecurity vendors routine and also governments want to take advantage of discourse to enhance their prerogatives and powers in cyberspace.

However, following the steps of Valeriano and Maness (2018), this chapter analyses empirical data about cyber offensive actions performed – or sponsored – by nation-states, instead of focusing on hypothetical cyber-attacks scenarios.

In order to clarify the scope of cyber-operations considered in this chapter, this research considered four types of offensive cyber capabilities in place:

- **Surveillance:** the ability to surreptitiously access the digital communication, location of users (online or offline), data usage, and metadata produced (United Nations 2019).
- **Disinformation:** the adoption of the information disorder theoretical framework, which includes false information (inadvertently or deliberately) or genuine information or opinion to cause harm (Wardle and Derakhshan 2017).
- **Espionage:** unauthorized access to a system to collect information for immediate use or to manipulate the decision-making process in the long-term (Valeriano, Jensen and Maness 2018).
- **Sabotage/Degradation:** attempts to physically compromise the target's ability to operate properly (Valeriano, Jensen and Maness 2018).

By creating an empirical base of over two thousand documents, this chapter provides a picture that defies the average perception of concentration of cyber capabilities in a few "traditional" actors. The number of stakeholders and their behaviour description is an innovative contribution that will affect future policy decisions based on accurate observations of cyberspace.

The chapter is divided into 4 sections. After the introduction, a methodology section describes the dataset gathering and the information processing. The third section is a discussion on offensive cyber capabilities based on the empirical evidence presented. A proposed taxonomy of state-actors based on their behaviour is also offered. The final section is concluding remarks and the prospects for cyber conflicts based on the evidence gathered so far.

2   Methodology

A few previous works engaged in cyber-attack historical analysis such as Healey and Grindal (2013), the UNIDIR Cyber Index (2013), a study published by the Wall Street Journal (Valentino-DeVries, Thuy Vo and Yadron, 2015), the Council of Foreign Relations (2020), several open-source projects available at code sharing platforms (Bandla 2020), the Mitre Corporation (MITRE 2019), and the Malware Information Sharing Platform – MISP (2019).

The Digital Watch initiative, from the Geneva Internet Platform, is another source to be contrasted with the methodology used here. The Digital Watch focuses on strategic documents "national strategies, military doctrines, official statements, and credible media reports" that provide "offensive cyber capabilities" indicators (Digital Watch, 2021). Conversely, this chapter presents technical reports that describe actual cyber actions attributed to state-sponsored activity.

All these sources are relevant because they involve data collection regarding cyber-attacks. However, not all initiatives delved into the motivations, the goals, and the intended targets of the campaigns.

Despite numerous references to cyber-attacks in traditional media outlets, rarely do they include technical remarks or concrete evidence supporting their stories. They are often the product of human sources that disclose details about a cyber-attack, such as the attribution of authorship, techniques employed, and the target's compromise level. However, without backing this up with data and concrete evidence, a story can be told to serve a political purpose, whether to be detrimental to the victim or the alleged perpetrator of the cyber-attack.

Therefore, to evaluate the current condition of cyber conflicts, this research sought objective data concerning cyber-attacks and Nation-State offensive capabilities. The goal is not to rely solely on conventional news, instead, the research identified sources of technical reports that could withstand a rigorous analysis. As a result, this research relied on four major sources:

- **technical reports** by cybersecurity private companies and national incident response teams (CSIRTs);
- **independent studies** by non-governmental organizations and universities;
- **information leakage** suffered from private vendors of spyware and governmental agencies;
- **reports** from export controls of European countries.

These four sources of information provide insight into distinct features of Nation-State offensive cyber capabilities.

The first two – technical reports and independent studies – are clustered together for collection and processing. They usually describe complex campaigns that are frequently referred to as Advanced Persistent Threats (APT). They display detailed information about sophisticated long-term campaigns conducted or sponsored by Nation-States. The data provided by these documents is strong evidence of both offensive cyber capability and intent, given that they analyse actual cyber-attacks.

This research gathered 1,885 technical reports describing cyber-attacks from 2008 to 2020. The research organized the documents into campaigns or groups based on who the attacks were attributed to, which resulted in 461 different threat-actors.

2.1   Technical reports and independent studies

The technical reports and independent studies collection process was made possible by creating and maintaining automated Python scripts, specially developed for this purpose.

The starting point was a sample-dataset provided at GitHub, the repository kbandla/APTnotes. This repository contained over 300 reports (from 2008 to 2016) from 20 different providers who described cyber-attacks considered APTs. Most of the reports were about offensive actions conducted by Nation-States and directed against other countries.

The tracking of technical reports and independent studies was a fundamental step towards the dataset for this research. Once those sources were identified, they were put into a daily monitoring routine. The Python scripts automatically "visited" the APT source's web pages to look for new reports or blog posts. Once the script found a new piece of information, they retrieved the content (e.g., web scraping). They sent an alert to notify a human supervisor in order to validate the collected item.

This process is operated incrementally. Thus, a new source can be included in the script, and the news reports are collected as they are published. The previous APT reports or blog posts are also collected retroactively to increase the dataset.

By December 2020 there were 234 different sources being monitored daily.

2.2   Data breaches

Data was also gathered from private vendors and state-sponsored APT threat actor's data breaches. The leaks have granted unprecedented access to the restricted private market and the development of offensive cyber capabilities.

There have been two major data breaches from offensive capabilities in private vendors: from Gamma Group in 2014 (WikiLeaks 2014), and from Hacking Team in 2015 (WikiLeaks 2015). The sheer volume of information disclosed is remarkable. The Gamma Group breach amounted to 40 GB and included customer information, manuals, training materials, and source code for the spyware sold. The Hacking Team leak included more than a million emails exchanged from the Italian branch, overseas offices, and government customers.

The CIA breach became known as Vault 7. The agency suffered a cyber-attack from a non-governmental group, and its cyber weapons were published online (WikiLeaks 2017). The leak was claimed by the Shadow Brokers, an alleged hacktivist group that wanted to sell the exploits and later publicize the tools used by the American intelligence agency. There is a suspicion that the Shadow Brokers were, in fact, a hacking group working for the Russian government, but no evidence supporting this was presented (Risk Based Security 2016).

An Iranian state-sponsored APT threat-actor also suffered a data breach. A group called Lab Dookhtegan (Cimpanu 2019), allegedly composed of dissidents from the Iranian Revolutionary Guard cyber branch, leaked information about Iranian hackers' personal identities, details about their attacks, and source code of offensive cyber capabilities. Lab Dookhtegan remains active to this day, publishing new information monthly.

In some cases, it was possible to infer that the entity responsible for the purchase was a military branch, law enforcement, or an intelligence agency based on the information released during the breaches.

2.3   Reports from exports controls

The fourth source for this research was reports collected from export controls publicized – the countries in which some private vendors have their headquarters. This data was available for only a few countries: the United Kingdom, Switzerland, Germany.

A third-party (McGrath, Novak and Gallagher 2016) gathered and indexed the open-source project called Transparency Toolkit. The data is available for download and online queries.

The reports did not identify the private vendor selling, nor the exact software being sold. However, they identified the country for whom the export license was issued. That helped as additional evidence of intent from the acquiring country.

2.4   Processing the data collected

The collected information comprises two datasets relevant for this chapter but with distinct characteristics. The technical reports provide information about actual offensive cyber capabilities. The second set was collected from the data breaches and granted information about countries' intent by developing or acquiring offensive cyber technology from private companies.

Both sets provide invaluable information about Nation-States offensive cyber capabilities. The first gives insights into 34 countries that have displayed offensive capabilities. The second set of information provides a detailed overview of the 86 countries that acquired offensive capabilities, although this dataset lacks evidence for their actual use.

The first dataset was analysed with Natural Language Processing. Spacy is a Python library that enables text processing and entity extraction without the loss of syntactical meaning. This processing step required more custom Python scripts for the adequate use of Spacy.

2.5   The classification and entity recognition

Python scripts for natural language processing were applied to the first dataset. This process included building custom dictionaries, removing stop-words from the text, word lemmatization, phrase matching, and text extraction.

The overarching goal of the scripts was looking for cyber-attack attribution (whether it was state-executed, state-sponsored, or a non-state actor), information on the victims (if it was a government and/or which industry it targeted), the countries affected by the attack, and the purpose of the cyber-attacks/campaigns (e.g., financial gain, espionage, sabotage). It was also possible to collect and classify MITRE Attack Techniques and CVEs employed during the offensive actions.

Every document processed was analysed following the aforementioned steps and when a match was found the information was added in a database. This allowed for multiple classifications of each document.

An additional classification was performed to cluster the reports into campaign/threat actors according to the myriad of names that private vendors use to refer to. Therefore, sources were classified as known APT groups based on the numerous names used by vendors. This was instrumental in performing analysis regarding the capabilities and intents of Nation-States.

The result was a dataset that classifies each document regarding authorship, if nation-affiliated, which group was attributed, the target's nature, and the duration of the cyber-attack/campaign.

2.6   Parsing structured data

The second dataset was built from structured data. The data breaches from Hacking Team, Gamma Group, Vault 7, and Lab Dookhtegan consisted of a huge volume of files. Wikileaks successfully indexed the files with a user-friendly interface. It allowed queries to search for countries that developed cyber weapons and those that acquired offensive cyber capabilities from private vendors. There was evidence to attribute the spyware purchased to a military force, law enforcement, or intelligence agency in some cases.

The evidence provided by both leaks is abundant. Besides commercial information about how the spyware operates; the e-mail communication, invoices from the purchases, and even spreadsheets detailing the buyers provided a full picture of this share of the cyber-weapons market.

On a few occasions, the second dataset's information was successfully correlated to the information collected in the first dataset (the intent was materialized in actual capabilities). This was the case for reports from The Citizen Lab and Amnesty International that corroborated the purchases of cyber offensive capabilities from Morocco, United Arab Emirates (UAE), Saudi Arabia, and Bahrain.

Based on the available information, this research considered a set of twelve private vendors as providers of offensive cyber capabilities: Amesys, Area SpA, Cyberbit, Dreamlab, Elbit, FinFisher, Hacking Team, Sandvine, NICE Systems, NSO Group, SS8, and Trovicor (Teach 2020).

Thus, the parsing of data searched for evidence of commercialization of cyber capabilities from those twelve providers to any Nation-State. Once the script identified a match to both conditions, it was added to the database for further analysis.

2.7 Threat actors and document clustering

A factor that improved attribution is the increase of evidence accumulated over the years. Threat actors have been monitored for long periods of time, and information is shared among multiple stakeholders in the cybersecurity community (Roth 2019). In most cases, only the correlation from different malware and campaigns over long periods of time allowed an attribution with a higher confidence level.

The clustering of documents within the same threat actor based on different methodologies is the minimal analytical unit for this research (MITRE 2019).

Despite significant improvements, attribution remains a challenge in cyberspace. Those mainly responsible for it are research institutions and private cybersecurity vendors, but even nation-states have attributed offensive cyber actions more often in the last few of years than during the early 2000's (Egloff and Wenger 2019).

The plausible deniability is also a concern because no state actor accepted or claimed responsibility for a particular offensive cyber action attributed to another country. It should be noted that the authorship of kinetic actions might remain unclear. Recent examples of those are the Malaysian Flight 17 (shot down over Ukraine, likely by militias armed with Russian equipment) and the Abqaiq–Khurais refinery attacks in Saudi Arabia (allegedly by Houthi rebels armed with Iranian drones). Neither of these attacks were clearly attributed.

Each document is processed individually and, if possible, is indexed to a threat actor (based on different methodologies provided by its original author). This set of documents allows the threat actors profiling: motivations, resources, targets, preferred sectors, and state-affiliation. It also allows for the cross-checking of references from multiple vendors, increasing confidence in the analytical process.

In order to avoid double-counting the same threat actor, the threat actors' synonyms are compliant with Roth (2018), MISP (2019), and MITRE Corporation (2019). This means that the most accurate landscape of threat actors available by the end of 2020 was taken. As new information is uncovered, groups with no established affiliation certainly will be tracked.

2.8 Merging the datasets

The main goal of this research is to portray a clear picture of the cyber offensive capabilities of Nation-States. To achieve that goal, it was necessary to combine the two datasets. Whenever available, the information collected was associated with a country (purchase, origin, or target), a date/period (acquisition or attack), and the victim's characteristics.

The compiled dataset is the basis for the Nation-State behaviour analysis accomplished in this research. It was possible to identify what demonstrated intent (acquired technology that enables cyber-attacks) and which states displayed actual offensive cyber capabilities (performing cyber actions).

The data concerning state-sponsored APT is a reliable indicator of intent and capability. The data gathered from offensive cyber capability acquisition is trustworthy evidence of nation states' intent.

3 Offensive cyber capabilities

Conventional wisdom suggests that there are only a handful of countries with meaningful offensive cyber capabilities. However, three variables observed in this chapter suggest the opposite, i.e., that there is diffusion of offensive cyber capabilities among countries:

- The existence of state-sponsored threat-actors in 29 different countries
- The similar complexity displayed in cyber attacks
- The acquisition of offensive cyber capabilities by an additional 66 countries

Cyber proxies are an additional source of offensive cyber capabilities. They encompass a broad range of actors such as cyber mercenaries and patriotic hackers (Maurer, 2018), and according to the United Nations Group on the use of mercenaries, they can perform actions such as "military and security services provided in cyberspace, including data collection and espionage"[1]. However, this research did not collect information specifically on these actors. It is an additional dimension that future research should explore.

The combination of the variables is used to profile nation-state offensive cyber behaviour into three distinct categories: Global, Regional, and Local.

---

[1] https://www.ohchr.org/EN/Issues/Mercenaries/WGMercenaries/Pages/Report-Cyber-Mercenaries-2021.aspx

3.1 State-sponsored activities

The data gathering process collected over 3,000 documents. After the analysis, 1,885 documents remained describing APTs campaigns/threat actors. The analysis performed a classification of each document concerning the support of state-actors.

The attribution process is a complex endeavor. Nevertheless, 1,034 documents (54.9%) establish some level of authorship. In most cases, the technical analysis identified the threat actor, its idiom, country, or origin region.

In some cases, there is the attribution of a threat-actor nationality, but there is no evidence that it had the support, sponsor, or acquiescence of the hosting country. In light of this, it became important to undertake this dichotomous classification within documents: state-sponsored attacks and independent threat actors from a particular country or region.

This research adopts Tim Maurer's notion of proxies acting on behalf of governments, i.e., when an intermediary conducts or contributes to an offensive cyber action that is enabled knowingly by a beneficiary (2018). Three forms of state-sponsored relationships are defined:

- Delegation: the principal grants authority to an agent to act on its behalf
- Orchestration: providing support (ideational or material) and directing them at particular targets
- Sanctioning: tolerates the actions of the threat-actor despite having the capabilities to stop it

From the documents with attribution, a total of 389 documents presented evidence of state-sponsored cyber offensive activities. The number represents 20,6% of the 1,885 documents. It is an impressive figure, especially in light of the common idea that attacks remain anonymous on the internet.

By grouping threat-actors into countries, there is evidence that 29 different nations have already performed offensive cyber actions, either directly or by sponsoring a threat actor (Figure 1). The list goes well beyond the traditional cyber powerhouses: China, Russia, Iran, Israel, North Korea, and the United States. It includes the likes of Bahrain, Egypt, Ethiopia, France, India, Iraq, Lebanon, Mexico, Morocco, Kazakhstan, Pakistan, Panama, South Korea, Syria, Saudi Arabia, Thailand, Togo, Turkey, the United Arab Emirates, the United Kingdom, Uzbekistan, Vietnam, and Yemen.

The number of countries capable of engaging in cyberspace is impressive. A comparison with different dimensions (such as land, air, sea, and space) would result in a smaller number of potential protagonists at the global level, rendering cyberspace a dimension with unprecedented nation-state competition with a relative reduction of power differentials (Nye 2010).

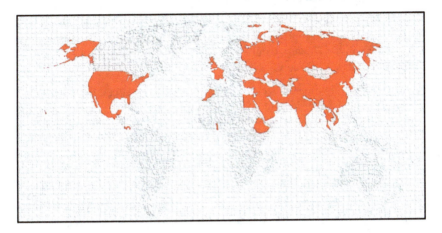

Figure 1: Countries with state-sponsored APT activity (2008-2020), Source: Izycki, Eduardo

3.2   Cyber-attack complexity

An interesting factor is the comparison of offensive cyber actions complexity. It is based on the CVE (Common Vulnerabilities and Exposures) and the Common Vulnerability Scoring System (CVSS).

By comparing the CVE's associated with the campaigns and the development of indigenous technology there is evidence to suggest that countries possess similar capabilities in terms of vulnerabilities exploited during state-sponsored APTs (Table 1).

The MITRE Attack is a knowledge base built as an open-source project to describe tactics and techniques observed in real-world attacks. The framework describes threat-actors behavior to prepare for a robust security process (MITRE Corporation 2017). This research uses the number of different tactics and techniques performed by threat-actors as an indicator of their ability to perform multiple actions. Thus, the bigger the number, the more versatile the threat actors are and more capable of offensive cyber actions.

The CVE is a database of publicly disclosed cybersecurity vulnerabilities. The vulnerabilities are classified according to a CVSS. The vulnerability ratings (Critical, High, Medium, and Low) are commonly used to prioritize vulnerability remediation activities.

The CVSS considers the attack vector, attack complexity, privileges required, user interaction, scope, and impact metrics (availability, integrity, and confidentiality). The less complex the attack and the more damage it causes, the higher its CVSS score.

After identifying the indicators in the original report sources, the threat actors were grouped according to their state-sponsored country. Countries with more identified threat-groups tend to have more CVE's explored over time. Thus, simply counting is not enough. An additional layer to the analysis is the proportion of the most severe CVE's being exploited. Threat-actors that exploit unique vulnerabilities are more versatile, and the ones that explore more severe vulnerabilities are considered more capable of offensive attacks.

The following table displays the proportion of CVE's according to their rating by CVSS standards. This evaluation is performed by NIST (National Institute of Standards and Technology).

Table 1: CVE's severity according to country (2008-2020)

Country	Critical	High	Medium	Low
Russia	70,1%	25,0%	4,9%	0,0%
China	64,1%	24,2%	9,4%	2,3%
North Korea	61,6%	38,4%	0,0%	0,0%
India	66,7%	33,3%	0,0%	0,0%
United States	63,6%	13,6%	22,7%	0,0%
Israel	62,5%	18,8%	18,8%	0,0%
Ethiopia	100,0%	0,0%	0,0%	0,0%
Turkey	61,5%	23,1%	15,4%	0,0%
United Kingdom	100,0%	0,0%	0,0%	0,0%
Kazakhstan	100,0%	0,0%	0,0%	0,0%

Country	Critical	High	Medium	Low
Mexico	100,0%	0,0%	0,0%	0,0%
Saudi Arabia	55,6%	44,4%	0,0%	0,0%
Morocco	62,5%	25,0%	12,5%	0,0%
South Korea	83,3%	16,7%	0,0%	0,0%
Panama	100,0%	0,0%	0,0%	0,0%
Egypt	100,0%	0,0%	0,0%	0,0%
UAE	62,5%	37,5%	0,0%	0,0%
Uzbekistan	100,0%	0,0%	0,0%	0,0%
Pakistan	100,0%	0,0%	0,0%	0,0%
France	18,8%	68,8%	6,3%	6,3%
Iran	100,0%	0,0%	0,0%	0,0%
Vietnam	0,0%	100,0%	0,0%	0,0%
Yemen	0,0%	50,0%	25,0%	25,0%

(Source: Izycki, Eduardo)

Moreover, the average difference between reported exploitation and the CVE registry year is also similar across countries. New CVE's tend to be explored by sophisticated actors, given that an exploit needs to be created for exploitation.

It is important to mention that there is a difference in terms of volume of actions and the number of targets that were attacked (Izycki, 2021).

Table 2: Total number of CVE's and average age (2008-2020)

Country	CVE's	Average Years
Russia	145	2,05
China	134	2,63
North Korea	74	2,61
India	31	2,10
United States	22	2,55
Iran	19	1,74

Country	CVE's	Average Years
Israel	16	1,94
Turkey	13	2,77
Pakistan	9	3,67
Ethiopia	8	2,75
UAE	8	1,63
Uzbekistan	8	1,63
United Kingdom	7	3,00
Kazakhstan	6	2,33
Egypt	6	3,00
Mexico	5	2,60
Saudi Arabia	5	2,60
Morocco	5	2,60
South Korea	5	2,60
Panama	5	2,60
Yemen	4	8,75
France	3	3,67
Vietnam	3	1,33

(Source: Izycki, Eduardo)

This suggests that offensive actions are performed by exploiting recent CVE's in a reproduced pattern among countries (except for Yemen).

All countries showed a tendency to explore Critical or High-level CVE's. This evidence suggests that despite differences in the number of threat-groups and volume of CVE's explored, the offensive cyber actions are similar regarding their severity.

3.3   Offensive cyber capabilities acquisition

The dataset also portrays a host of 86 countries that acquired offensive cyber capabilities from the private sector, although no concrete evidence of its use has been found so far. This staggering number suggests that offensive capabilities are widespread in cyberspace.

Based on the available data, this research considered a set of 12 private vendors as providers of offensive cyber capabilities: Amesys (France), Area SpA (Italy), Cyberbit (Israel), Dreamlab (Switzerland), Elbit (Israel), FinFisher (Germany and United Kingdom), Hacking Team (Italy), Sandvine (Canada), NICE Systems (Israel), NSO Group (Israel), SS8 (United States), and Trovicor (Germany).

Moreover, the purchasing of state-of-the-art offensive cyber capabilities was not a one-time deal; 45 countries (52,9%) acquired offensive solutions more than once (yellow countries in Figure 2). The remaining countries acquired a single cyber capability (green countries in Figure 2). The acquisition of more than one private solution for cyber offensive action is additional evidence of intent by countries to be assertive in cyberspace, as they display a clear desire to accumulate offensive cyber capabilities.

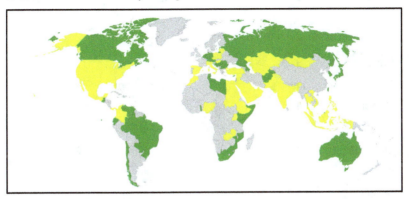

Figure 2: Cyber offensive acquisition from third party vendors (2008-2020), (Source: Izycki, Eduardo)

The 45 countries are listed below (Table 3) with the respective number of purchases observed.

Table 3: Countries with cyber offensive capabilities multiple acquisition (2008-2020)

Country	Purchases	Country	Purchases
Mexico	13	Saudi Arabia	6
UAE	8	United States	5
Egypt	7	Kazakhstan	5

Country	Purchases	Country	Purchases
Bahrain	5	India	2
Nigeria	5	Philippines	2
Oman	5	Zambia	2
Ethiopia	4	Yemen	2
Uzbekistan	4	Indonesia	2
Hungary	4	Mongolia	2
Pakistan	3	Bangladesh	2
Turkey	3	Switzerland	2
Syria	3	Kuwait	2
Morocco	3	Czechia	2
Thailand	3	Lithuania	2
Panama	3	Uganda	2
Qatar	3	Luxemburg	2
Singapore	3	Latvia	2
Spain	3	Turkmenistan	2
Malaysia	3	Honduras	2
Italy	3	Jordan	2
Sudan	3	Poland	2
Lebanon	2	Colombia	2
Vietnam	2		

(Source: Izycki, Eduardo)

The acquisition of multiple offensive cyber solutions suggests that the countries acquiring them intend to expand their repertoire since private vendors have different strategies to compromise targets and explore different vulnerabilities (Teach 2020).

Even advanced offensive cyber capabilities – for instance, exploring a zero-day vulnerability – might not be useful against the desired target if it is not vulnerable or does not have a particular hardware or software set-up. Hence, the willingness of countries to acquire offensive artifacts from more than one private vendor is considered as strong evidence of intent to perform offensive cyber actions.

Unlike conventional weaponry, where interoperability is a requirement, offensive cyber capabilities can and often do operate independently. Moreover, a threat-actor can use one artifact to compromise the target and another (from a different provider) to extract information (espionage) or send disruptive payloads (ransomware).

The cost of acquisition varies from the extension of services acquired. Still, the Remote-Control Service (also known as Galileo), provided by Hacking Team, cost less than 1 million dollars and yearly maintenance was lower than 200 thousand dollars (on average – reference to 2013/2014).

This indicates that the cost of acquisition for a state-of-the-art offensive cyber solution is negligible for a nation-state. Further, it is an explanation why countries display similar offensive cyber capabilities as shown in Section 3.2.

3.4 Profiling nation-state behaviour

The data gathered suggests that the overwhelming majority of cyber conflicts occur between long-standing rivals seeking to harm each other in the context of geopolitical disputes (Valeriano and Maness 2014). Although the dataset can provide no causal relationship, the regions targeted by a larger number of attacks were more inclined to acquire offensive cyber capabilities.

This research proposes a taxonomy of three categories: Global Players, Regional Contenders, and Local Actors.

3.4.1 Global players

The first cluster of countries is composed of China, Iran, Israel, Russia, the United Kingdom, and the United States. All six countries have indigenous offensive cyber capabilities. They have a high number of total and unique targets. They engage with high geographical dispersion (across at least five regions). Their objectives with cyber actions are mainly espionage and sabotage, and the preferred sectors are government and military.

Despite their similarities, Chinese and Iranian state-sponsored threat-actors also consistently engage in offensive cyber actions with surveillance purposes (respectively 5 and 2).

Table4: Global players main features

Country	Total Targets	Unique Targets	Espion age	Sabota ge	Preferred Targeted Sectors
China	316	61	23	0	Military (89), Government (62), Dissidents (52)
Russia	204	74	12	6	Military (98), Government (62), Diplomatic (51), Elections (46)
Iran	179	47	13	1	Military (32), Government (30), Energy (23)
United States	121	68	6	1	Military (8), Government (4), Industry (5), Nuclear (7),
Israel	31	21	1	2	Industry (9), Nuclear (8), Military (7)
United Kingdom	86	61	5	0	Military (4), Government (3), Nuclear (3)

(Source: Izycki, Eduardo)

Another difference relates to the cybercriminal actions performed by Chinese (10), Russian (9), and Iranian (3) state-sponsored threat-actors. This suggests that offensive capabilities are deployed by the same actors against a broad spectrum of targets and the state-sponsored actions are not a full-time commitment.

Moreover, these countries engage in multiple purpose campaigns simultaneously, suggesting they have a significant number of human resources, possibly recruiting from a thriving underground hacking community.

The United States and Israel engaged in an offensive cyber action against the Iranian nuclear program (Stuxnet). They unleashed threat-actors for the purposes of espionage, respectively the Equation Group (Falliere, Murchu and Chien 2011) and Duqu 2.0 (Kaspersky 2015).

Eduardo Izycki

The United States had another joint venture with the United Kingdom (and possibly with other Five Eyes countries). The Snowden leaks revealed that the GCHQ targeted attacks against the G20 Meeting as a state-conducted offensive cyber action (The Guardian 2013).

China used offensive cyber actions to conduct a long-term espionage campaign to speed up its technological development (FireEye 2013). Traditional espionage is also a frequent objective pursued by China through cyber means (Glyer, et al. 2020). Furthermore, there are a significant number of cases where the deployment of surveillance against its own citizens was observed (Amnesty International 2019).

Russia conducts multiple-layer pressure against its geopolitical goals, for instance, pressure on Estonia (Ashmore 2009), denial of service during the Georgian campaign (Georgia 2009), and destabilizing Ukraine (FireEye 2017). Its offensive cyber actions range from attacks against critical infrastructures, sophisticated disinformation campaigns, and multi-targeted espionage. The actions against the power supply in Ukraine are strong evidence of the versatility of Russian threat-actors, since the knowledge to target industrial protocols was necessary, and it is an unusual skill (Lipovsky 2016).

Iran conducts multiple campaigns against opposition figures, including nationals living abroad and in countries with geopolitical interests (Qatar, Bahrain, Syria, and Lebanon) (Gundert, Chohan and Lesnewich 2018). Simultaneously it engages against its regional rivals (Saudi Arabia - 11, Israel - 11, Turkey - 8, UAE - 7, Iraq - 6) to assert itself within the MENA region (Insikt Group 2019).

This tier demonstrates the ability to engage against different targets with different purposes, denoting versatility and resources to adapt to multiple targets. It is reasonable to assume that innovative actions are not a problem for this group. Thus, cybersecurity initiatives by their targets can be overcome by these threat-actors.

3.4.2 Regional contenders

The second group of countries is composed of France, India, Lebanon, North Korea, Pakistan, South Korea, Syria, Turkey, UAE, and Vietnam.

These ten countries display some level of self-made offensive cyber capabilities. They have multiple acquisitions of offensive cyber technologies from private vendors. Their actions are regionally oriented. Their objectives with cyber actions are mainly espionage, and the preferred sectors vary according to their own geopolitical imperatives.

Table 4: Regional contenders main features

Country	Espionage	Purchases	Targets in own region	Most Targeted Countries
France	3	0	33,3%	Iran (4), Algeria (3), Turkey (2), Germany (2)
North Korea	6	0	44,0%	South Korea (30), US (11), India (8), China (7), Russia (7)
Pakistan	4	3	60,7%	India (8), Pakistan (6), Others (1)
Lebanon	2	2	37,5%	Lebanon (4), US (3), Israel (3), Saudi Arabia (2), Jordan (2)
Turkey	3	3	56,5%	Syria (4), Turkey (3), Iraq (2), Albania (2)
Vietnam	1	2	85,0%	Vietnam (9), Cambodia (7) Philippines (6), China (5)
India	1	2	66,7%	Pakistan (6), China (4), Bangladesh (3), Sri Lanka (2)
Syria	0	3	87,5%	Syria (2), Lebanon (2), Saudi Arabia (2)
South Korea	1	1	70,6%	Russia (3), Japan (3) China (2), North Korea (2)
UAE	2	8	70,6%	UAE (3), Qatar (3), Bahrain (2), US (2)

(Source: Izycki, Eduardo)

Regarding the origins of their cyber offensive capabilities, all countries displayed some level of indigenous development. There were no acquisitions from France and North Korea, though the former has private companies selling technologies worldwide (Amesys/Bull and VUPEN).

France tends to act less regionally contained, targeting Algeria and Morocco probably due to their location and historical ties. The actions against Iran and Turkey are aligned with the negotiations for the Iranian Nuclear Deal that involved the three countries in 2015 (ESET 2015).

North Korea has a huge number of unique targets (64), but its offensive cyber actions are strongly skewed towards South Korea (18%) (Sherstobitoff, 2013). The actions against countries in other regions were mostly financially motivated against banks (SWIFT System) and cryptocurrency exchanges (Guerrero-Saade and Moriuchi 2017). North Korean threat-actors behave as organized cybercriminals, likely to circumvent the several embargoes imposed by the United States (Group-IB 2017).

South Korea also fits the profile of regionally oriented offensive cyber actions. However, the South Korean threat-actor remains shrouded in secrecy since most of the reports describe technical details without providing more details on its profile (Tencent 2019).

The case of India (Levene, Grunzweig and Barbehenn 2018) and Pakistan (Falcone et al. 2018) is a further demonstration of cyber actions' geopolitical orientation. Both countries have a nuclear balance, historically engaged in several skirmishes, and constantly face each other in cyberspace (Inskit Group 2016).

The MENA region is also prolific in examples of regional engagement. Lebanon (Lookout and EFF 2018), Syria (Hasbini, Pontiroli and Saad 2014), and Turkey (Arsene, et al. 2020) display preferential targets within the same region. The Syrian Civil War's intricate consequences are one of the main reasons for these three countries' cyber offensive actions.

The UAE case is unique because its national digital authority hired former employees from the National Security Agency (NSA) to conduct offensive cyber actions. Called Project Raven (Bing and Schectman 2019), the entire technical staff was outsourced, but they were physically in the UAE and constantly supervised by the Emiratis during campaigns against Bahrain, Qatar, and American targets (Bing and Schectman 2019).

Finally, the Vietnam case reaffirms the group's characteristics. Besides a clear targeting of Southeast Asian countries (Wright 2020), the main sector that Vietnamese threat-actors target is the maritime industry, perfectly aligned with the ongoing tensions in the South China Sea (Lassalle, Koessel and Adair 2017).

All countries in the group, except for Syria, performed offensive actions with the purpose of espionage. But financially motivated actions (North Korea,

Pakistan, Turkey, and India) and surveillance operations (Lebanon, Vietnam, and Syria) have also occurred.

The group's similarities reside in the nascent self-made offensive cyber capabilities, the acquisition from third parties, and the focus on targets within the region (actions are not as widespread as in the case of Global Players).

3.4.3   Local players

The third cluster of countries is composed of Bahrain, Egypt, Ethiopia, Iraq, Kazakhstan, Mexico, Morocco, Panama, Saudi Arabia, Thailand, Togo, Uzbekistan, and Yemen. These thirteen countries are dependent on private vendors to acquire or engage in offensive cyber actions. They have multiple providers. Their actions are focused on their own territory and citizens (occasionally targeting nationals abroad), and their objectives with cyber actions are mainly surveillance against dissidents and rival political organizations.

Table 5: Local players main features

Country	Purchases	Intelligence	Espionage	Surveillance	Political Targeting
Kazakhstan	5	3	1	1	3
Saudi Arabia	6	2	1	1	5
Ethiopia	4	1	1	1	4
Egypt	7	4	0	1	5
Uzbekistan	4	3	1	1	2
Morocco	3	1	0	1	4
Mexico	13	1	1	1	11
Bahrain	5	0	1	1	2
Yemen	2	0	0	2	2 (Tied)
Iraq	0	0	0	1	0
Thailand	3	0	0	1	2 (Tied)
Panama	3	2	0	1	1 (Tied)
Togo	1	0	0	1	1 (Tied)

(Source: Izycki, Eduardo)

Uzbekistan is the only country that displayed some level of indigenous development of cyber capabilities. The self-made capabilities – threat-actor named SandCat – were uncovered due to the developer's operational security flaw. The State Security Service (SSS) tested the offensive cyber tool in an uncontrolled environment where Kaspersky's anti-virus solution was installed, thus identifying the new malware (Zetter 2019).

All countries from this group show a preference for surveillance operations against citizens from their own countries. That is reinforced by the political targeting performed by all countries, except for Iraq (Senft, et al. 2014). The most frequent political targets were dissidents, expatriate communities, and rival political organizations or parties.

In Ethiopia (Marczak, et al. 2014), Kazakhstan (Galperin, et al. 2016), Saudi Arabia (Amnesty International 2018), Mexico (Scott-Railton, Marczak, et al. 2017), Morocco (Amnesty International 2019), and Panama (Marczak, Guarnieri, et al. 2014), the extraterritorial actions are targeted against the migrants or expatriate nationals living abroad. This means that offensive cyber actions are motivated by domestic reasons but the effects reach different parts of the world. That is empirical evidence of the strategic advantages introduced by operating in cyberspace.

Finally, despite local interests, this group exhibits intent to engage in cyberspace with multiple means. Twelve countries – excluding Iraq – acquired offensive cyber solutions. Except for Togo (Scott-Railton, Anstis, et al. 2020), all eleven countries acquired multiple solutions, and most of them (8) placed them in intelligence agencies.

4 Conclusions

The research in this chapter set out to provide a picture of power diffusion in cyberspace. As a result, it gathered evidence of 29 different countries engaging in offensive cyber actions (Section 3.1) and found that (at least) 86 nations acquired offensive cyber technologies from private vendors (Sections 3.3). The numbers are impressive, especially considering the widespread perception of concentration of cyber capabilities in a few "traditional" actors.

The number of actors and their similarities regarding exploited CVE's severity and age suggest diffusion of power, but there is hardly equality of cyber capabilities. Most countries depend on third-party technologies from the foreign private sector (Section 3.3). The roster of countries that have displayed self-made capabilities is small (20) – 16 countries with APT state-sponsored actors[2] and 4 countries with private providers[3] –, compared to the number of countries offensively capable (96).

In a belligerent scenario where there are trade embargos or hostilities, it is reasonable to conclude that the majority of countries would only be able to retain their offensive cyber capabilities if the original provider allowed it to continue. The dependence on private vendors can also be subject to a suspension order by a third-party host nation, in an analogous manoeuvre that suspends the sale of ammunition or equipment during a conflict.

The taxonomy proposed by this research suggests the presence of an evolving pattern regarding offensive cyber capabilities.

Countries begin acquiring offensive cyber capabilities from the private-sector and engaging in native targets as the first step in the offensive cyber capabilities ladder (Local Actors). As this leads to maturing offensive cyber capabilities and pressing geopolitical issues arise, countries use their repertoire to achieve geopolitical goals that would otherwise be unattainable by conventional measures (Regional Contenders). The final step would be the increase in indigenous offensive capabilities and the engagement in offensive campaigns beyond the country's vicinities (Global Players).

The conditions necessary for countries to scale up in the offensive cyber capabilities ladder are not fully clear. Given the fact that many Regional Contenders are not Information Technology and Communication leaders, offensive cyber capabilities can be developed a low cost.

This pattern is an opportunity that many states are resorting to. The low-cost ability to erode the advantages of geopolitical rivals and challenge the status-quo means that international dynamics is influenced by cyber capabilities, resulting in countries punching above their weight on the international stage (Barrinha and Renard 2020).

Cyber conflict is ambiguous and less oriented towards conventional military strategies, and international conflict studies lack the analytic tools to reframe strategies for it (Lewis 2021). The fact that cyber actions do not create an existential threat give states plenty of room to manoeuvre in cyberspace and to engage with competitors. This is seen by the cumulative effect that

---

[2] China, Russia, the United States, North Korea, the United Kingdom, Iran, Israel, France, Syria, Lebanon, India, Pakistan, Vietnam, Turkey, South Korea, and Uzbekistan
[3] Canada, Germany, Italy, and Switzerland

offensive cyber actions can achieve, i.e., a single action might not be relevant but repeated engagement can influence the relative balance of power.

Actors are able to achieve strategic outcomes and influence the balance of power without having to resort to an armed attack and minimize the risk of a military or nuclear response from their targets (Harknett and Smeets 2020).

The strategic board is being flooded by new stakeholders as more nations acquire and develop offensive cyber capabilities. It is important that policy-makers take into consideration the current state of affairs in cyberspace when preparing their strategies. The research described in this chapter is aimed to be a stepping stone for analysis based on evidence and not hyperbolical scenarios.

References

Amnesty International, 2018. *Amnesty International Among Targets of NSO-powered Campaign.* [Online]
Available at: https://www.amnesty.org/en/latest/research/2018/08/amnesty-international-among-targets-of-nso-powered-campaign/
[Accessed 2019].

Amnesty International, 2019. *Morocco: Human Rights Defenders Targeted with NSO Group's Spyware.* [Online]
Available at: https://www.amnesty.org/en/latest/research/2019/10/Morocco-Human-Rights-Defenders-Targeted-with-NSO-Groups-Spyware/
[Accessed 2020].

Amnesty International, 2019. *State-sponsored hackers target Amnesty International Hong Kong with sophisticated cyber-attack.* [Online]
Available at: https://www.amnesty.org/en/latest/news/2019/04/state-sponsored-cyber-attack-hong-kong/
[Accessed 2020].

Arsene, L., Tudorica, R., Vatamanu, C. & Maximciuc, A., 2020. *StrongPity APT – Revealing Trojanized Tools, Working Hours and Infrastructure.* [Online]
Available at: https://labs.bitdefender.com/2020/06/strongpity-apt-revealing-trojanized-tools-working-hours-and-infrastructure/
[Accessed 2020].

Ashmore, W. C., 2009. Impact of Alleged Russian Cyber Attacks. *Baltic Security & Defence Review.*

Australian Strategic Policy Institute, 2019. *Mapping China's Tech Giants.* [Online]
Available at: https://chinatechmap.aspi.org.au/#/map/f3-Surveillance
[Accessed 2020].

Bandla, K., 2020. *APTnotes data.* [Online]
Available at: https://github.com/aptnotes/data
[Accessed 12 2020].

Barrinha, A. & Renard, T., 2020. Power and diplomacy in the post-liberal cyberspace. *International Affairs 96(3).*

Bing, C. & Schectman, J., 2019. *American Hackers Helped UAESpy on Al Jazeera Chairman, BBC Host.* [Online]
Available at: https://www.reuters.com/investigates/special-report/usa-raven-media/
[Accessed 2020].

Bing, C. . & Schectman, J., 2019. *Project Raven.* [Online]
Available at: https://www.reuters.com/investigates/special-report/usa-spying-raven/
[Accessed 2019].

Cimpanu, C., 2019. *Source code of Iranian cyber-espionage tools leaked on Telegram.* [Online]
Available at: https://www.zdnet.com/article/source-code-of-iranian-cyber-espionage-tools-leaked-on-telegram/
[Accessed 2 2020].

Council on Foreign Relations, 2020. *Cyber Operations Tracker.* [Online]
Available at: https://www.cfr.org/cyber-operations/
[Accessed 12 2020].

Digital Watch, 2021. UN GGE and OEWG. [Online] Available at:
https://dig.watch/processes/un-gge/ [Accessed 28 Dec 2021].

Egloff, F. J. & Wenger, A., 2019. *Public Attribution of Cyber Incidents,* Zurich: Center for Security Studies (CSS), ETH Zurich.

Eichensehr, K., 2020. The Law & Politics of Cyberattack Attribution. *UCLA Law Review 67.*

ESET, 2015. *Dino – the latest spying malware from an allegedly French espionage group analyzed.* [Online]
Available at: https://www.welivesecurity.com/2015/06/30/dino-spying-malware-analyzed/
[Accessed 2018].

Falcone, R., Fuertes, D., Grunzweig, J. & Wilhoit, K., 2018. *The Gorgon Group: Slithering Between Nation State and Cybercrime.* [Online]
Available at: https://unit42.paloaltonetworks.com/unit42-gorgon-group-slithering-nation-state-cybercrime/
[Accessed 2019].

Falliere, N., Murchu, L. & Chien, E., 2011. *W32.Stuxnet Dossier,* s.l.: Symantec.

FireEye, 2013. *FireEye Uncovers Chinese Cyber Espionage Campaign Targeting European Ministries of Foreign Affairs.* [Online]
Available at: https://www.fireeye.com/company/press-releases/2013/fireeye-uncovers-chinese-cyber-espionage-campaign-targeting-european-ministries-of-foreign-affairs.html
[Accessed 2018].

FireEye, 2017. *At the Center of the Storm: Russia's APT28 Strategically Evolves its Cyber Operations.* [Online]
Available at: https://www2.fireeye.com/rs/848-DID-242/images/APT28-Center-of-Storm-2017.pdf
[Accessed 2018].

Freedom House, 2020. Freedom in the World 2020 A Leaderless Struggle for Democracy, s.l.: Freedom House.

Galperin, E., Quintin, C., Marquis-Boire, M. & Guarnieri, C., 2016. Operation Manul: I Got a Letter From the Government the Other Day...Unveiling a Campaign of Intimidation, Kidnapping, and Malware in Kazakhstan, s.l.: EFF.

Georgia, 2009. *Russian Cyberwar on Georgia.* [Online]
Available at: https://lawlordtobe.files.wordpress.com/2018/03/cyberwar-georgia.pdf
[Accessed 2018].

Glyer, C., Perez, D., Jones, S. & Miller, S., 2020. *This Is Not a Test: APT41 Initiates Global Intrusion Campaign Using Multiple Exploits.* [Online]
Available at: https://www.fireeye.com/blog/threat-research/2020/03/apt41-initiates-global-intrusion-campaign-using-multiple-exploits.html
[Accessed 2020].

Groll, E., 2019. *The Future Is Here, and It Features Hackers Getting Bombed.* [Online]
Available at: https://foreignpolicy.com/2019/05/06/the-future-is-here-and-it-features-hackers-getting-bombed/
[Accessed 2020].

Group-IB, 2017. *Lazarus Arisen: Architecture, Techniques and Attribution.* [Online]
Available at: https://www.group-ib.com/resources/threat-research/lazarus.html
[Accessed 2018].

Guerrero-Saade, J. A. & Moriuchi, P., 2017. *North Korea Targeted South Korean Cryptocurrency Users and Exchange in Late 2017 Campaign.* [Online]
Available at: https://go.recordedfuture.com/hubfs/reports/cta-2018-0116.pdf
[Accessed 2018].

Gundert, L., Chohan, S. & Lesnewich, G., 2018. *Iran's Hacker Hierarchy Exposed.* [Online]
Available at: https://go.recordedfuture.com/hubfs/reports/cta-2018-0509.pdf
[Accessed 2019].

Harknett, R. J. & Smeets, M., 2020. Cyber campaigns and strategic outcomes. *Journal of Strategic Studies.*

Hasbini, M. A., Pontiroli, S. & Saad, G., 2014. *The Syrian Malware House of Cards.* [Online]
Available at: https://securelist.com/the-syrian-malware-house-of-cards/66051/
[Accessed 2018].

Healey, J. & Grindal, K., 2013. *A Fierce Domain: Conflict in Cyberspace, 1986 to 2012.* s.l.:Cyber Conflict Studies Association.

Insikt Group, 2019. *Iranian Threat Actor Amasses Large Cyber Operations Infrastructure Network to Target Saudi Organizations.* [Online]
Available at: https://www.recordedfuture.com/iranian-cyber-operations-infrastructure/
[Accessed 2020].

Inskit Group, 2016. *Hacktivism: India vs. Pakistan.* [Online]
Available at: https://www.recordedfuture.com/india-pakistan-cyber-rivalry/
[Accessed 2018].

Izycki, E., 2021. Cyber Offensive Capabilities: a Glimpse Look into a Multipolar Dimension, Brasília, Brazil: Universidade de Brasília (UnB).

Izycki, E. & Vianna, E. W., 2021. *Critical Infrastructure: A Battlefield for Cyber Warfare?*. Tennessee Tech, USA, Academic Conferences International.

Kaspersky, 2015. *The Duqu 2.0 Technical Details*. [Online] Available at: https://media.kasperskycontenthub.com/wp-content/uploads/sites/43/2018/03/07205202/The_Mystery_of_Duqu_2_0_a_sophisticated_cyberespionage_actor_returns.pdf [Accessed 2018].

Kramer, F. D., 2009. *Cyberpower and National Security*. s.l.:University of Nebraska Press.

Lassalle, D., Koessel, S. & Adair, S., 2017. OceanLotus Blossoms: Mass Digital Surveillance and Attacks Targeting ASEAN, Asian Nations, the Media, Human Rights Groups, and Civil Society. [Online] Available at: https://www.volexity.com/blog/2017/11/06/oceanlotus-blossoms-mass-digital-surveillance-and-exploitation-of-asean-nations-the-media-human-rights-and-civil-society/ [Accessed 2019].

Levene, B., Grunzweig, J. & Barbehenn, B., 2018. *Patchwork Continues to Deliver BADNEWS to the Indian Subcontinent*. [Online] Available at: https://unit42.paloaltonetworks.com/unit42-patchwork-continues-deliver-badnews-indian-subcontinent/ [Accessed 2019].

Lewis, J., 2021. Toward a More Coercive Cyber Strategy. s.l., s.n.

Lipovsky, R., 2016. *New wave of cyberattacks against Ukrainian power industry*. [Online] Available at: https://www.welivesecurity.com/2016/01/20/new-wave-attacks-ukrainian-power-industry/ [Accessed 2019].

Lookout and EFF, 2018. *Dark Caracal: Cyber-espionage at a Global Scale*. [Online] Available at: https://info.lookout.com/rs/051-ESQ-475/images/Lookout_Dark-Caracal_srr_20180118_us_v.1.0.pdf [Accessed 2019].

Marczak, B. et al., 2018. BAD TRAFFIC - Sandvine's PacketLogic Devices Used to Deploy Government Spyware in Turkey and Redirect Egyptian Users to Affiliate Ads?. [Online] Available at: https://citizenlab.ca/2018/03/bad-traffic-sandvines-packetlogic-devices-deploy-government-spyware-turkey-syria/ [Accessed 2019].

Marczak, B., Guarnieri, C., Marquis-Boire, M. & Scott-Railton, J., 2014. *Hacking Team and the Targeting of Ethiopian Journalists*. [Online] Available at: https://citizenlab.org/2014/02/hacking-team-targeting-ethiopian-journalists/ [Accessed 2019].

Marczak, B., Guarnieri, C., Marquis-Boire, M. & Scott-Railton, J., 2014. *Mapping Hacking Team's "Untraceable" Spyware.* [Online]
Available at: https://citizenlab.ca/2014/02/mapping-hacking-teams-untraceable-spyware/
[Accessed 2019].

Marczak, B. et al., 2015. *Pay No Attention to the Server Behind the Proxy.* [Online]
Available at: https://citizenlab.ca/2015/10/mapping-finfishers-continuing-proliferation/
[Accessed 2019].

Marquis-Boire, M., Marczak, B., Guarnieri, C. & Scott-Railton, J., 2013. *You Only Click Twice.* [Online]
Available at: https://citizenlab.ca/2013/03/you-only-click-twice-finfishers-global-proliferation-2/
[Accessed 2019].

Martin , C., 2020. *Cyber weapons are called viruses for a reason: statecraft, security and safety in the digital age.* [Online]
Available at: https://thestrandgroup.kcl.ac.uk/event/ciaran-martin-cyber-weapons-are-called-viruses-for-a-reason-statecraft-security-and-safety-in-the-digital-age
[Accessed 2020].

Maurer, T., 2018. *Cyber Mercenaries: The State, Hackers, and Power.* Cambridge: Cambridge University Press.

McGrath, M., Novak, B. & Gallagher, K., 2016. *Surveillance Industry Index.* [Online]
Available at: https://sii.transparencytoolkit.org/
[Accessed 20 Nov. 2018].

MISP, 2019. *Malware Information Sharing Platform.* [Online]
Available at: https://www.misp-project.org/
[Accessed 10 05 2019].

MITRE, 2019. *Groups - MITRE ATT&CK.* [Online]
Available at: https://attack.mitre.org/groups/
[Accessed 2019].

Nye, J., 2010. *Cyber Power.* s.l.:Belfer Center for Science and International Affairs. Harvard Kennedy School,.

Nye, J., 2011. Nuclear Lessons for Cyber Security?. *Strategic Studies Quarterly 5(4),* pp. 18-38.

Nye, J., 2018. *Normative Restraints on Cyber Conflict,* s.l.: Belfer Center for Science and International Affairs.

Roth, F., 2018. *The Newcomer's Guide to Cyber Threat Actor Naming.* [Online]
Available at: https://cyb3rops.medium.com/the-newcomers-guide-to-cyber-threat-actor-naming-7428e18ee263
[Accessed 2019].

Roth, F., 2019. *APT Groups and Operations.* [Online]
Available at:
https://docs.google.com/spreadsheets/u/0/d/1H9_xaxQHpWaa4O_Son4Gx0YOIzlcBWMsdvePFX68EKU/pubhtml

Scott-Railton, J. et al., 2020. *Nothing Sacred - Religious and Secular Voices for Reform in Togo Targeted with NSO Spyware.* [Online]
Available at: https://citizenlab.ca/2020/08/nothing-sacred-nso-sypware-in-togo/
[Accessed 2020].

Scott-Railton, J. et al., 2017. *Reckless III - Investigation Into Mexican Mass Disappearance Targeted with NSO Spyware.* [Online]
Available at: https://citizenlab.ca/2017/07/mexico-disappearances-nso/
[Accessed 2019].

Senft, A., Dalek, J., Noman, H. & Crete-Nishihata, M., 2014. *Monitoring Information Controls in Iraq in Reaction to ISIS Insurgency.* [Online]
Available at: https://citizenlab.ca/2014/06/monitoring-information-controls-in-iraq/
[Accessed 2019].

Sherstobitoff, R., 2013. *Dissecting Operation Troy: Cyberespionage in South Korea.* [Online]
Available at: https://www.mcafee.com/enterprise/en-us/assets/white-papers/wp-dissecting-operation-troy.pdf
[Accessed 2018].

Teach, E., 2020. The Big Black Book of Electronic Surveillance. s.l.:Kindle Edition.

Tencent, 2019. *Be wary of blessings from the holidays - APT attack organization "Higaisa".* [Online]
Available at:
https://github.com/CyberMonitor/APT_CyberCriminal_Campagin_Collections/tree/master/2019/2019.11.04.Higaisa_APT
[Accessed 2020].

The Guardian, 2013. *GCHQ intercepted foreign politicians' communications at G20 summits.* [Online]
Available at: https://www.theguardian.com/uk/2013/jun/16/gchq-intercepted-communications-g20-summits
[Accessed 2018].

United Nations Institute for Disarmament Research (UNIDIR), 2013. *The Cyber Index: International Security Trends and Realities,* New York and Geneva: United Nations.

United Nations, 2019. Surveillance and Human Rights, Report of the Special Rapporteur on the Promotion and Protection of the Right to Freedom of Opinion and Expression, s.l.: United Nations.

Valentino-DeVries, J., Thuy Vo, L. & Yadron, D., 2015. *Cataloging the World's Cyberforces.* [Online]
Available at: https://graphics.wsj.com/world-catalogue-cyberwar-tools/
[Accessed 10 12 2020].

Valeriano, B., Jensen, B. & Maness, R., 2018. *Cyber Strategy: The Evolving Character of Power and Coercion.* Oxford: Oxford Scholarship Online.

Valeriano, B. & Maness, R. C., 2014. The dynamics of cyber conflict between rival antagonists, 2001–11. *Journal of Peace Research.*

Eduardo Izycki

Valeriano, B. & Maness, R. C., 2018. How We Stopped Worrying about Cyber Doom and Started Collecting Data. *Global Cybersecurity: New Directions in Theory and Methods,* pp. 49-60.

Voo, Julia; Irfan , Hemani; Jones, Simon; DeSombre, Winnona; Cassidy, Dan; Schwarzenbach, Anina, 2020. *National Cyber Power Index 2020,* s.l.: Harvard Kennedy School.

Wardle, C. & Derakhshan, H., 2017. Information disorder: Toward an interdisciplinary framework for research and policy making, s.l.: Council of Europe.

WikiLeaks, 2014. *SpyFiles 4.* [Online]
Available at: https://wikileaks.org/spyfiles4/customers.html
[Accessed 20 11 2018].

WikiLeaks, 2015. *Hacking Team.* [Online]
Available at: https://wikileaks.org/hackingteam/emails/
[Accessed 20 11 2018].

WikiLeaks, 2017. *Vault 7: CIA Hacking Tools Revealed.* [Online]
Available at: https://wikileaks.org/ciav7p1/
[Accessed 12 2020].

Wright, C., 2020. *New APT32 Malware Campaign Targets Cambodian Government.* [Online]
Available at: https://www.recordedfuture.com/apt32-malware-campaign/
[Accessed 2020].

Zetter, K., 2019. *Researchers Say They Uncovered Uzbekistan Hacking Operations Due to Spectacularly Bad OPSEC.* [Online]
Available at: https://www.vice.com/en/article/3kx5y3/uzbekistan-hacking-operations-uncovered-due-to-spectacularly-bad-opsec
[Accessed 2020].

Author biography

Eduardo Arthur Izycki is a Student of Masters in International Relations at the University of Brasília (UnB) and a public servant. Eduardo has worked on developing solutions for risk assessments in the cycle of major events in Brazil (2012-2016). He currently works in the Critical Infrastructure Protection Coordination of the Brazilian Institutional Security Office (GSI).

Chapter Five

Imaginable Cyberwar: Weaponization and Cyberespionage of e-Health Data

Samuel Wairimu

Karlstad University, Karlstad, Sweden

samuel.wairimu@kau.se

Abstract: The healthcare sector has become a preferred target by a number of cyber-attackers over the years. One of the major reasons for these attacks, apart from the less stringent cybersecurity measures, is the financial gain attached to personal health records and personally identifiable information on the dark web. However, with a change in the healthcare landscape as a result of the COVID-19 pandemic, the healthcare sector has not only seen intensified cyber-attacks from opportunistic attackers, but from state-sponsored attackers as well. While there are a broad range of cyber-attackers, the focus for this research is on state-sponsored attackers who demonstrate a high-level of sophistication, and whose motivations differ from other attackers. As such, the chapter sets out to discuss the nature of state-sponsored attackers and the impact they manifest when they weaponize e-Health data or gain access to intellectual property or sensitive/classified data in medical research in the context of cyberwar. To outline the impact, a comparison is made between non-state-sponsored cyber-attackers in relation to state-sponsored attackers through a qualitative approach supported by secondary research. The outcome indicates that targeting the healthcare sector in the context of cyberwar can result in active reconnaissance, data exfiltration, which can include ground breaking research data that can put a rival state at a competitive edge, and patient records, which can lead to the targeting of key and influential people within the government or state through personally identifiable information. To prevent these, the chapter further highlights a number of mitigations that can be implemented.

Keywords: State-Sponsored Attacker, e-Health, COVID-19, Cyber-Attacks

1 Introduction

The advantages of integrating information and communications technology (ICT) with the aim of supporting health are still being realised. From advancing clinical outcomes, to providing both quality and cost-effective healthcare services, the augmentation has created both vast and positive potential outcome in the delivery of healthcare services. As such, some governments across the globe are contributing towards the implementation of e-Health within their respective healthcare systems due to the aforementioned reasons. For instance, Sweden laid out a vision for e-Health, where the country aims to be the best in the globe by year 2025 in terms of taking advantage of e-Health to provide improved and equal healthcare services while promoting independence amongst healthcare consumers (Wickström, Regner and Micko, 2017).

Regardless of the current advances and the promises aligned with the use of e-Health, cyber-attacks against the healthcare sector have been prevalent over the years, and the threats continue to grow and adapt. In fact, it can be noted from the U.S. Department of Health and Human Services Breach Portal (HHS, 2021), that cyber-attacks against healthcare that have led to successful data breaches, thus affecting thousands to millions of individuals in terms of their privacy through maliciously accessed patient records, are on the rise. These attacks have been attributed to a number of cyber-attackers who differ in motivations and skills. Table 1 displays an overview of these attackers and their targets, while Table 2 shows their skills and contrasting motivations.

Table 1: Overview of attackers and their targets in the context of cyber-attacks in e-Health. These attacks can be directed toward a specific victim or could be random based on the attacker's motivations. Image adopted from (ISE, 2016).

Adversary	Patient Health Targeted (Specific Victims)	Untargeted (Indiscriminate)	Patient Records Targeted (Specific Victims)	Untargeted (Indiscriminate)
Individual/Small Group				Yes
Political Groups/ Hacktivists			Yes	
Organized Crime	Yes		Yes	Yes
Terrorism/Terrorist Organisations	Yes	Yes		
State-Sponsored Attackers (Nation States)	Yes	Yes	Yes	Yes

Table 2: Overview of attackers with their skills and motivations.

Adversary	Skills and Motivations
Individual/Small Group	Driven by financial gain, which is a key incentive when it comes to healthcare cyber-attacks (Martin *et al.*, 2017). This is because patient records contain PII such as Credit Card Information and Social Security Numbers (SSN), and PHI - which is deemed more valuable as it can be used for medical identify theft and insurance fraud (Coventry and Branley, 2018). Hence, these attackers are indiscriminate and mostly depend on unsophisticated means when launching an attack (ISE, 2016).
Political Groups/Hacktivists	In their paper, Coventry and Branley (2018) state that patient records contain information that can be leveraged in politics. Therefore, these groups can use such information to embarrass or coerce a well-known individual in the political arena for their own personal gain. In addition, they tend to less skilled and hence employ skilled people.
Organized Crime	Relies on highly experienced attackers and can indiscriminate or target specific victims by influencing the patient health or records as indicated in Table 1. As such, they are normally driven by financial benefits or other illegal activities such as extortion (ISE, 2016).
Terrorism/Terrorist Organisations	Driven by causing fear or harm to either as specific victim or random individuals by attempting to compromise their health. Research conducted by the Independent Security Evaluators (ISE) (ISE, 2016) indicate that such attackers do not demonstrate high skills as those from organized crime or state-sponsored attackers
Nation States (State-Sponsored Attackers)	Their motivations and level of sophistication differs from the group of adversaries mentioned within this table. From Table 1, it can be noted that state-sponsored attackers are indiscriminate, with the probability of conducting mass exploitation. In addition to being highly motivated to going for their targets, state-sponsored attackers are better funded and hence can exploit the most expensive and arduous attack vectors to achieve their goals (Cordey, 2020)

With the global spread of SARS-CoV-2 virus that causes COVID-19, the uptake and influence of e-Health has been significant. For example, in the year 2020, there was rapid development of government sponsored COVID-19 contact tracing applications that were introduced to help slow the spread of the virus by supporting manual contact tracing. In addition to this, and even more recently, there have been current improvements within some healthcare sectors so as to minimise the risk to exposure of COVID-19. For instance, earlier this year, the healthcare sector in Ontario, Canada launched a pilot project that aims to improve remote monitoring of high-risk patients with the intention of reducing unnecessary visits to clinics thus minimising the risk of being exposed to the virus (Canadian Health Technology, 2021). With such digital interactions, the risk of cyber threats against the healthcare sector, which is one of the most vulnerable sectors to cyber-attacks (Irwin, 2021), increases even more during the pandemic.

From Table 1, it can be noted that there are diverse cyber-attackers; nevertheless, the chapter aims to dive deep into state-sponsored attackers, as they have been shown that they can leverage e-Health in the context of cyberwar (Wairimu, 2021). While evidence suggests that state-sponsored attacks have been carried out before, for example, the 2007 Estonia cyber-attacks that lasted for 22 days (Ottis, 2008) (termed as the first cyberwar (Kaiser, 2015)), the attack against the Iranian nuclear enrichment facilities using the first cyberweapon named Stuxnet (Langner, 2011), and the interference of the Ukrainian power grid in 2015 (Case, 2016); the interests of state-sponsored attackers have widened to that of targeting the healthcare sector and medical research institutions, and most especially during the COVID-19 pandemic (Cordey, 2020).

1.1   Research question

Cyber security issues within the healthcare sector have become of high concern in recent times due to the persistent threats and cyber-attacks. In particular, and more precisely during the COVID-19 pandemic, there have been a number of cyber-attacks emanating from not only opportunistic attackers, but from state-sponsored attackers that target the sector with the aim of espionage, subversion or propaganda. In his paper, Jan Kallberg explains how a strategic cyber-attack against a targeted society's critical infrastructure can knock out one or all of the five pillars identified by Dwight Waldo, that is, legitimacy, authority, institutional knowledge, bureaucratic control, and confidence (Kallberg, 2016). Hence, this could not only develop a belief that the government is incapable of running the country, but the citizens trust towards the government or the healthcare organisations can erode with every successful cyber-attack. To explore this, the research examines the concept of e-Health as a critical infrastructure within society, and its potential abuse in the context of cyberwar in relation to privacy. This is because, like information security, privacy has always been an issue of importance due to the nature and sensitivity of medical research and health data. As such, the motivation of this chapter, in addition to the fact that the state-sponsored attacks in the context of the pandemic are well documented, is steered with the following research question:

- *What will be the impact of cyberespionage and weaponization of e-Health data in the context of cyberwar?*

2 Background

Undoubtedly, e-Health is playing a major role in today's society. In particular, during the ongoing pandemic, the influence of e-Health is expected to be significant for a number of reasons. For example, the European Commission acknowledged the use of e-Health applications, i.e., contact tracing applications, in the support of returning to normalcy of the fundamental human rights by reducing the spread of COVID-19 and gradual lifting of lock-downs in 2020-2021 (European Commission, n.d.). Furthermore, the pandemic has caused a surge in the use of Telehealth, which has positively altered the patient and healthcare professional relationship, creating conveniency and preventing further spread of the virus by effecting the physical distance rule between the healthcare professionals and their patients (Wosik *et al.*, 2020). As a result, e-Health supports consumers with improved access and control over their health by emphasising self-management, involvement, and transparency (Erlingsdóttir and Sandberg, 2016), while at the same time providing healthcare professionals with an opportunity to make clinical decisions and to improve consumers' welfare (Gaddi, Capello and Manca, 2013; Kreps and Neuhauser, 2010).

Nevertheless, the pandemic has not only caused a public health scare, but also major worries in the cybersecurity domain. Generally, healthcare sectors across the globe have become a primary target for cyber-attackers due to the lack of stringent cybersecurity measures, ground-breaking medical research data, and vast patient health information (PHI) that is considered of high value in the dark web. Additionally, with the threat of ransomware attacks, it is regarded by bad actors that, due to the critical nature of healthcare services, in conjunction with the possibility of either reputational and legal damage (or both), the sector is more likely to meet up ransom demands (Bernard, Bowsher and Sullivan, 2020). For instance, in 2018, the ransom demands were approximately $5,000 and increased from this value to about $200,000 in 2020 during the pandemic (Newman, 2020). Hence, with such trends, it is recognized that the number one leading motivation is normally financial gain as highlighted by (Coventry and Branley, 2018; Martin *et al.*, 2017).

However, more recently, the sector has become a target for state-sponsored attackers who are motivated by information acquisition or cyber espionage - that is the theft of confidential information related to public health activities, intellectual property and innovative research concerning COVID-19 data (which involves vaccines, trials and treatment data) (Cordey, 2020) through Advanced Persistent Threats (APT) techniques, with an effort to obtain a competitive edge over the rival state. In fact, Bernard, Bowsher and Sullivan (2020) mentions that APT actors have constantly targeted pharmaceutical companies and e-Health (e.g., medical devices) with the aim of obtaining sensitive and intellectual property. For example, an advisory published in July 2020 by the National Cyber Security Centre (UK) highlights that the US, UK and Canadian governments accused a group known as APT 29 or Cozy Bear (that is almost certainly linked to the Russian Intelligence), for targeting and attacking organisations concerned with developing COVID-19 vaccines with the aim of gaining sensitive research data and intellectual property (NCSC, 2020).

In addition, and with comparison to the other critical infrastructures (for example, energy and transport), the healthcare sector has become a preferred target on account of its pre-eminent nature, and its extensive impact when hit by a cyber-attack (Bernard, Bowsher and Sullivan, 2020). Examples of these extensive impact is the disruption of the NHS (UK) systems as a result of the 2017 untargeted WannaCry malware attack; this was attributed to the use of legacy systems that were no longer supported and that were vulnerable (Ghafur *et al.*, 2019), and the Singapore Health Services (SingHealth) cyber-attack that led to massive data exfiltration of approximately 1.5 million patients (The Committee of Inquiry, 2019). In the paper, "Cyber war is inevitable (unless we build security in)", McGraw argues that information and communication technology (ICT) integrated systems (in this case e-Health) not only harbour a lot of vulnerabilities that increase cyber threats, but our growing dependence on them is a key factor that makes cyber war against such systems unavoidable (McGraw, 2013). As such, it can be deduced that our over-reliance on e-Health, and especially during a pandemic, makes a nation and the general population more susceptible to state-sponsored cyber-attacks.

In essence, e-Health, which is deemed as a critical infrastructure due to its importance in the functioning of the society (as aforementioned), can destabilise the population and at the same time put the national security at risk when targeted at a strategic level, as it is often, among other critical infrastructure, considered as a preferred military target (Walker-Roberts, Hammoudeh and Dehghantanha, 2018).

3 Privacy in healthcare

In the Health Insurance Portability and Accountability Act (HIPAA), and the General Data Protection Regulation (GDPR), the privacy of patients, especially in regards to their health data, is deemed as a core precept. Generally, providing health data for the purposes of patient care (e.g., for proper diagnosis and prevention of unnecessary drug interaction) and for other extensive uses within a healthcare system, for example, clinical research is regarded as necessary, and at the same time, protecting this information is critical as its leakage can lead to unintended consequences to either the patient or the organisation. For example, an organisation can lose intellectual property on their ongoing clinical research or patients health information can be stolen through data exfiltration. Because of this and for many other reasons, privacy is considered as a critical element in the healthcare sector. In fact, the NIS directive highlights the need for EU Member States to govern their critical sectors, one of them being the healthcare sector, with the intention of maintaining the reliability and security of the network and information systems thus preventing threats that can disrupt the society (Europa, 2016). However, with the advances in e-Health, the notion of privacy in healthcare arises due to the inherent vulnerabilities in its cybersecurity infrastructure. For example, with the rapid development of COVID-19 contact tracing apps, vulnerabilities have been discovered (Hatamian *et al.*, 2021) that can be explored to provide real data on the state of COVID-19 within a state and how they are handling the cases.

While it is acknowledged that there has been major improvement in the healthcare organisations attributed to e-Health, Coventry and Branley (2018) state that its security posture is wanting; in fact, it can be argued that the privacy of a patient can be based on the security measures implemented, which more than ever seems to be not the case due to the rising number of cyber-attacks against the healthcare. This has been attributed to an increase in inter-connectivity, which exposes the sector to not only common, but also to new vulnerabilities that weaken the security posture of the healthcare system thus risking health data breach and manipulation of health devices (Williams and Woodward, 2015). Additionally, taken in isolation, disruptive technologies introduced in e-Health tend to introduce unanticipated vulnerabilities that create more cyber threats. According to Liff (2012), attacks that use these vulnerabilities in computer networks can be exploited in cyberwar. This can result to creating panic in the society (through massive exposure of patient records, and disruption of critical health infrastructure at a large scale), loss of trust with the authorities and damage of reputation to the organisation or health professional.

4 State-sponsored attackers

Unlike other cyber-attackers outlined in Table 2, state-sponsored actors portray different motivations and demonstrate a high level of sophistication when it comes to launching a cyber-attack. Such attacks are ascribable to a state-affiliated agency or the government, hence, these actors are better funded and would normally go for costly and arduous attack vectors (Kävrestad and Huskaj, 2021) in addition to launching organised attacks over a longer duration while evading detection. Furthermore, they target military infrastructures, society, CII (critical information infrastructure), civilian infrastructures, among others (Jayakumar, 2020), through a number of attack vectors, for example, long-term social engineering (Kävrestad and Huskaj, 2021).

In the current threat landscape where state-sponsored attackers are targeting and hitting healthcare organisations with cyber-attacks, the consequences and the impact can be vast and devastating. For example, at a strategic level, a cyber-attack directed on e-Health could compromise the integrity of data systems, privacy of patients (through the exposure of sensitive personal and health data of key personnel within the government or the military), mass disruption of critical facilities, and cyber espionage (stealing of important research material or intellectual property. For example, ground-breaking COVID-19 research data). In addition, they can access and amass patient records (both PHI and PII) of targets or a groups of individuals for the purposes of individual or mass exploitation (ISE, 2016).

4.1 Cases of state-sponsored cyber-attacks

While there have been a number of cyber-attacks perpetrated since COVID-19 was declared a pandemic, for example the Ransomware attack at the Champaign-Urbana Public Health District in Illinois (Bergal, 2020), this research highlights attacks directed towards healthcare organisations by state-sponsored attackers or APT groups. With an in-depth description of COVID-19 related cyber-attacks provided by Lallie *et al.*, (2021), a table is constructed (See Table 3), in this case, with only COVID-19 related state-sponsored cyber-attacks against the healthcare sector and its related organisations. Furthermore, a detailed description is provided in each case.

Table 3: Overview of State-Sponsored Attacks against Healthcare Organisations during the pandemic. The table shows the group behind the attacks, together with the description of how they attempted to conduct the attack.

Adversary	Description
APT Group from India	In the second month of 2020, a technology firm in China identified phishing campaigns directed to Chinese medical organisations with the aim of stealing sensitive information (scientific research) through phishing emails. The attackers are said to have been using malicious documents to lure unsuspecting people so as to gain access to this information (Caiyu, 2020).
Hades Group - Linked to Fancy Bear (a Russian cyberespionage APT group)	Disinformation campaign spread through malicious documents concealed as documents originating from the Centre for Public Health of the Ministry of Health of Ukraine. The group hid a C\# backdoor Trojan within the documents and sent it to their targets in Ukraine (Cimpanu, 2020).
Iranian-linked Group	Targeted a US based biopharmaceutical company known as Gilead Science Inc. The group aimed at compromising staff email accounts by impersonating journalists. It is noted that malicious access to an email of any staff within a Western pharmaceutical company such as Gilead, would have given the Iranian government the necessary information and put them on a forefront in developing treatments and counteracting the virus (Stubbs and Bing, 2020).
Vietnamese Threat Actors (APT 32)	Attempted cyberespionage with the aim of gathering intelligence concerning COVID-19 crisis through spear phishing emails sent to the Government Health Ministries, that is, the Chinese Ministry of Emergency Management and the Wuhan Government (Fireeye, 2020).
Chinese-Linked Attackers	Targeted Moderna (a pharmaceutical and biotechnology company based in the US) with the aim of gathering intelligence concerning COVID-19

Adversary	Description
	research data through reconnaissance (Bing and Taylor, 2020).
North Korean-Linked Attackers	Targeted AstraZeneca Plc (a British-Swedish pharmaceutical and biotechnology company based in the UK) through social engineering attacks with aim of gaining access into victims' computers researching on COVID-19 (Stubbs, 2020).
APT 29 (Cozy Bear), APT 10 (Stone Panda) and Lazarus Group	Targeted a number of Indian Pharmaceutical and Biotechnology companies, for example, Bharat Biotech, Serum Institute among others, with the aim of stealing research data concerning COVID-19 through a massive global campaign (Ahaskar, 2020).

5   Attack vectors

The integration of ICT in health and its massive inter-connectivity has opened doors to new vulnerabilities (Coventry and Branley, 2018) that give rise to a wider attack surface. In addition, the innovation of new digital technologies that were rapidly developed and deployed to combat the spread of the virus, for example, COVID-19 contact tracing applications, have been shown to harbour both security and privacy vulnerabilities (Hatamian *et al.*, 2021; Wairimu and Momen, 2020).   Some of these security and privacy vulnerabilities are: insecure communication protocols, tracking of user's location, and violation of the principle of least privilege. On top of these, the healthcare sector has intersected with a number of organisations, for example, Health Insurance Companies (Walker-Roberts, Hammoudeh and Dehghantanha, 2018) and COVID-19 research centres, which further enlarges the attack surface that state-sponsored attackers can take advantage of.

With an enlargement of the attack surface, comes the increase of attack vectors that need to be addressed to prevent massive disclosure of information for the sake of social disruption, disinformation campaigns, or holding critical and sensitive information to ransom through ransomware attacks, for example, the Irish Health System that was majorly disrupted by foreign actors (BBC, 2021) through a ransomware attack, and whose Health Service Executive (HSE) is still recovering months later after the attack (McNamee, 2021).

The following are some of the attack vectors identified together with their descriptions:

1. **Phishing** - During the COVID-19 pandemic, there have been major phishing campaigns. For instance, the global phishing campaigns that targeted the COVID-19 cold chain (Bisson, 2020). State-sponsored attackers use this method to gain access to sensitive COVID-19 information by stealing victims' credentials. In the above example, a victim was lured to open an attachment that led to the attackers learning the plans aligned by the organization to assist in distributing vaccines, which was part of the COVID-19 cold chain.

2. **Unpatched vulnerabilities** - State-sponsored attackers can exploit unpatched vulnerabilities with the intention of gaining access to critical sensitive information regarding COVID-19. Furthermore, such exploitation of web-based vulnerabilities could result to disinformation campaign that can lead to mass confusion and lack of trust for the government.

Kävrestad and Huskaj (2021) identified other attack vectors that state-sponsored attackers can leverage based on five interviews conducted independently with security professionals working within civilian organizations. These are as follows:

1. **Zero-day vulnerabilities** - state-sponsored actors are known to be highly skilled, and in addition to exploiting common vulnerabilities, they can exploit zero-day vulnerabilities. Furthermore, and according to the interview they conducted, based on the huge availability of resources, which either comes from a state-agency or the government, state-sponsored attackers can "create and hold zero-day exploits". Nevertheless, even though it is acknowledged that other threat agents can exploit zero-day vulnerabilities, they are normally arduous and expensive and as such a lesser option for other actors. While irrelevant in this case, the example of the Stuxnet malware that hit the Iranian enrichment facilities utilised four zero-day exploits (Baezner and Robin, 2017).

2. **Long term social engineering** - While this might be time consuming for any other threat, the respondents of the interview stated that state-sponsored attackers have the patience that can permit them to use long term social engineering.

3. **Human intelligence** - This involves the use of a human-intelligence approach to target employees within an organization who can be used as attack vectors. Such employees could be targeted for the purposes of spear phishing and intelligence gathering (Kävrestad and Huskaj, 2021).

As noted above, there are a number of attack vectors that can be put to use by state-sponsored actors. Nevertheless, it is noted that they are not limited to the aforementioned attack vectors and as such can use any available vector. However, what sets these actors apart from the rest of the attackers, is that they are highly motivated and well-resourced, and as such can leverage vectors that are arduous and expensive to exploit.

In their paper, Limba *et al.*, (2019) identify and place cyber-attacks against critical infrastructures in five major threat groups. These are: Data manipulation, service unavailability, leakage of personal information, unauthorised access of resources and physical destruction. By using the listed attack vectors, four of these cyber-attacks against e-Health could put the privacy of users at risk, push the agenda of mass confusion or fear, lead to the surveillance or theft of sensitive research data, or possibly lead to irreversible damage. These are:

1. **Data manipulation** - During the pandemic, COVID-19 data could be manipulated to give an idea that the government is not managing the spread of the virus. This can be used to spread propaganda within a targeted state thus making the citizens lose confidence with the relevant authorities.

2. **Leakage of personal information:** A state-sponsored actor can gain access to e-Health data centres with the aim of gaining access to PII, including the health data of key personnel within the government.

3. **Unauthorised access of resources:** Cyberespionage has been increasing during the pandemic. Attackers gain access and steal sensitive medical data. For example, a Russian group (APT 29) attempted to steal COVID-19 research data from Canada, the UK and US (NCSC, 2020).

4. **Service unavailability:** Disruption of critical services when hospitals are still struggling during the pandemic has been noted. While there is no suspected actor, the attack at Brno University Hospital in the Czech Republic led to the cancellation of urgent

surgical interventions and failure in accessing sensitive patient data (Botek, 2020).

6   Impact of cyberwar against e-health

Sevis and Seker (2016) state that attackers compromise critical systems with the intention of pilfering, damaging or taking control of critical information. This is supported by Limba et al., (2019) as identified in the aforementioned five major threat groups. In the context of e-Health, patient records contain extensive information, and unlike financial data, resetting certain identifiers, for example, name, address and SSN, remains impossible (Martin *et al.*, 2017). This makes it a potential target for attackers at different levels as identified in Table 1. Additionally, a patient record contains the full medical history of an individual, which includes the type of medication they are on, and if they have a medical device to support their health or not. This information can be used to target a patient's health thus causing harm.

To highlight the impact of cyberwar against e-Health, a comparison is made between a non-state sponsored (e.g., Individual/Small Group) and state-sponsored attacker. Hence, based on the identified attack vectors, the exploitation of e-Health is conducted for several motives and with different outcomes. This could range from a disgruntled employee, accidental data breach, to low-level malicious data breaches. With the health data containing an extensive source of valuable information, Martin et al., (2017) identifies that financial gain is the key motive for compromising healthcare systems. As such, a cyber-attack launched by non-state sponsored attackers would have the following consequences and impacts listed in Table 4.

Table 4: Consequences and impact of low level, non-state sponsored attacks against e-Health.

Impact	Consequences
Active surveillance - collecting patient records, which contains both PII and PHI.	The disclosure of patient's PII and PHI could result in people being targeted for medical identity theft or medical fraud insurance (Coventry and Branley, 2018). At the same time, opportunistic attackers have taken advantage of the COVID-19 pandemic to target victims.
Personal attacks derived from PHI	Unauthorized access to PHI could lead to blackmailing or cyberbullying due to sensitive information being documented. This could result in physiological and

Impact	Consequences
	psychological problems or financial harm.
Disruption of medical services	While this might have an indirect impact on privacy, the disruption of medical services could result in cancellation of appointments. Further, this could cause indirect deaths associated with cyber-attacks against critical services, for example in Dusseldorf's University Clinic in Germany (Tidy, 2020).

However, in an age where global awareness of cyberwarfare has increased sharply (Arquilla and Ronfeldt, 1993), cyber-attacks could not only be driven by political or financial gain, but by the ability to take lives (Coventry and Branley, 2018) and advance the interest of the particular nation state that has initiated the attack (Ablon, 2018). As such, weaponization of health data and patients' records, in addition to cyberespionage of COVID-19 research data can have severe consequences and impacts such as those listed in Table 5.

The exploitation of e-Health within the digital sphere with the resources and skills of a state-sponsored attacker can cause a ripple effect that can be experienced in the physical sphere as indicated in Table 5.

Table 6: Consequences and impact of weaponizing PHI and PII, and cyberespionage in the context of cyberwar against e-Health

Impact	Consequences
Active Reconnaissance - collecting COVID-19 research data and patients records for enemy intelligence	During the COVID-19 pandemic, there have been cases of reconnaissance with the aim of identifying vulnerabilities and exploiting them to gain sensitive data. One of the examples is the Chinese-Linked Attackers (See Table 3) that targeted Moderna. This can be used to put the enemy state at a competitive edge. In addition to this, due to the disclosure of PII from health data, key people can be targeted (either within the government or military), e.g., The Trident Juncture 18 (Hughes, 2020), and Singapore's Prime Minister's private and outpatient medical information, including that of other people (The Committee of Inquiry, 2019).

Impact	Consequences
Personal attacks derived from PHI	Disclosed COVID-19 data can be used for intimidation purposes. For example, a state actor can intimidate an enemy state by trying to expose patients who have had the virus. Furthermore, e-prescriptions and personal medical records can be altered (Gross, Canetti and Waismel-Manor, 2015) with nefarious intentions of putting the patients' health and safety at risk. Disclosure of famous people's medical files - for example, the case medical files disclosed from the World Anti-Doping Agency (BBC, 2016).
Mass disruption of medical services	There is a possibility of data breach (e.g., research data), leading to disruption of medical facilities and disruption of care and emergency services. Moreover, the disruption to medical services can lead to mass interruption of appointments (example, the WannaCry NHS attack) leading to public unrest. This can further cause the populations' trust towards the government and the healthcare organisations to erode.
Disinformation Campaigns	During the pandemic, there have been disinformation campaigns aimed at spreading conspiracies and demeaning governments. For example, the US claimed that Russian actors spread conspiracy theories on the origin of the virus through fake social media accounts (Glenza, 2020). This can lead to reputational damage of the targeted state.

Nevertheless, the exploitation can have further impact on the privacy of patients and the organisation as highlighted in Table 6.

Table 6: Impact on privacy of a patient and organisation in the physical sphere when sensitive data from the e-Health digital sphere is accessed by state-sponsored cyber-attacker.

e-Health digital sphere	Physical sphere
PII - This contains data that could be used to potentially **identify** a healthcare consumer or perpetrate identity theft.	The impact of disclosing such data would be creating a database of targets by accessing their names, addresses, locations, etc. For example, in 2015, Anthem, a healthcare provider in the US, sustained a data breach that led to the exfiltration of 78.8 million records of PII by state-sponsored attackers (Chinese-linked hackers); it was believed that the records would be used to carry out identity theft (Johnson *et al.*, 2017).
PHI - This contains an entire background of a person's medical history	The impact of disclosing such data would result in learning the behaviour of an individual; insurance information, location, medical history (including whether they have had COVID-19 and are vaccinated or not), possible allergies, etc. For example, in the public report regarding the cyber-attack against SingHealth, the Cyber Security Agency of Singapore noted that the attackers had a clear goal as the health data accessed contained, along with health information of other patients, that of the Prime Minister of Singapore (The Committee of Inquiry, 2019). With such information, an attacker can plan to harm the health of the said targeted individual.
System Security Data	The impact of this would be the disclosure of staff credentials that would lead to further leakage of patients' data or ground-breaking research data, e.g., COVID-19 data. Furthermore, there can be possible privilege escalation with the intent of taking control over the entire critical infrastructure information. For example, in the case of Anthem where the attackers got hold of credentials that they used to further gain access into the network (Johnson *et al.*, 2017).

7   Mitigations

Having established the impact of exploiting patients' records and cyberespionage in the context of cyberwar, the situation highlights a dire need to improve the security and privacy of e-Health. Research conducted by ISE identifies that healthcare organisations devalue the motivation and sophistication of state-sponsored attackers and only address the low-level attackers, for example, Individual/Small Groups (ISE, 2016). As such, it is imperative for healthcare organisations to acknowledge state sponsored attackers by understanding their motivation and recognising their profiles. This goes a long way towards ensuring that measures are taken that can prevent such attacks against healthcare.

While there are no well-defined strategic or technical measures that can be implemented to defend against cyber-attacks from state-sponsored attackers, certain measures can be taken to mitigate cyberwar in the context of e-Health. For instance, healthcare organisations are now investing in cyber and information security after WannaCry, for example the NHS(UK) and HHS (US). Given that the healthcare sector implements existing laws (e.g., HIPAA (Arquilla and Ronfeldt, 1993) and invests in the current standards (e.g., ISO/IEC 27001:2017) and frameworks (e.g., NIST-CSF or NIST-PF); would these be enough to prevent cyberwar in the context of e-Health?

It can be argued that these laws, standards, and frameworks are rather irrelevant, but in the context of cyberwar and information security in healthcare, a number of them can be useful. For example, ISO/IEC 27032:2012 that describes guidelines for cybersecurity, provide controls for addressing cyber risks, including controls for cyber organised criminals (ISO, 2012). Further, this standard highlights the guidance required for improving the cybersecurity of critical information infrastructure protection. Hence, this standard can play an important and urgent role when mitigating the threat of state sponsored attackers.

In addition to ISO/IEC 27032:2012, ISO/IEC 27799:2016 could be implemented in this context. This standard describes specific guidelines for information security management in health using ISO/IEC 27002 (ISO, 2016). This is a special type of standard that focuses entirely on the privacy and security of e-Health by ensuring best practices are followed within the healthcare sector. By doing so, health information data, such as PHI, medical research data and other sensitive data concerned with system security is protected from malicious actors, which include the state sponsored attackers.

However, while these standards are highly recommended for better privacy and security practices, there needs to be implementation of other cybersecurity measures to support the above. According to McGraw (2013), one way to prevent this is to build security in the system that factors in skilled and resourceful attackers with high levels of intent in consideration. This could be done by applying Article 25 of the GDPR, which ensures data protection by design and by default, and Article 32, which ensures appropriate levels of security when processing personal data.

Furthermore, calculating possible risks by cyber-mapping all hardware and software within a critical infrastructure could protect critical infrastructure like e-Health from cyber threats (Cohen, 2019). Identifying, calculating and treating risks within the healthcare sector could play a part in the reduction of privacy threats. During this process, it is imperative to consider the motivations and skills of a state-sponsored attacker, so as to identify an appropriate approach and utilise the right risk metrics. According to the interviews conducted by Kävrestad and Huskaj (2021), this is one key aspect that two respondents highlighted. Additionally, healthcare organisations can also go for high privacy impact assessments, which can be used to prevent privacy risks, not only in the context of non-state sponsored attackers, but also in the context of state sponsored attackers. At the same time, healthcare organisations can apply ISO/IEC 27005: 2013, which specifies general rules for information security risk management.

In addition, improving the identification and management of highly advanced cyber incidents and attacks against critical infrastructures, for example, in the case of the European collaborative early warning system ECOSSIAN (Kaufmann *et al.*, 2015), is also imperative in preventing the impact of cyberwar in e-Health. Furthermore, in the study by Kävrestad and Huskaj (2021), two respondents also highlighted the importance of having in place detection and logging systems that can be used to detect malicious access from state-sponsored cyber-attackers.

Other than the above-mentioned mitigations, there are some practical approaches that would be implemented to avoid cyber-attacks against healthcare, both at the level of state-sponsored and non-sponsored attackers. For instance, the need to educate the users who are the weakest links and who can be targeted through the human-intelligence approach or long-term social engineering as identified by Kävrestad and Huskaj (2021). In addition, patching of identified vulnerabilities is essential. As mentioned, state-sponsored attackers can leverage unpatched vulnerabilities to launch an attack, as in the case of the untargeted WannaCry attack that crippled the NHS (UK). Above all, IT specialists within healthcare should stay informed about threats and vulnerabilities, as the cybersecurity landscape within the healthcare sector is continuously evolving.

8 Discussion

Regardless of the motivation, the impact and consequences of hitting a healthcare organisation with a cyber-attack can be dire. However, differences can be noted when each attack is taken in isolation. For example, low-level skills, non-sponsored attackers tend to compromise e-Health with the intention of financial gain. This is so because patient records contain PHI, which is considered highly valuable as it can be used to obtain health services through medical identity theft and insurance fraud (Coventry and Branley, 2018), and PII, which holds financial data etc. In addition to this, there is normally disruption of medical services.

However, when it comes to highly skilled and sophisticated state sponsored attackers, the consequences and impacts can be devastating. It can be seen from Table 5 that state sponsored attackers tend to have broad motivations when they compromise e-Health. For example, compromising patient records can lead to the targeting of specific people, e.g., certain people within the government. Furthermore, deriving PHI from the records can lead to either disclosure of the medical history of notable people, or alterations of prescriptions, which can be used to cause harm or irreversible damage to a patient's health. Also, stealing research data relating to COVID-19 can give a nation a competitive advantage. Furthermore, when state sponsored attackers compromise e-Health, the impact is felt on the physical sphere. For example, targeting a system's security data can be used access ground breaking research data concerning COVID-19. As indicated earlier, access to such sensitive data could put a nation ahead of its enemy state.

While some strategic cyber-attacks are directed towards e-Health, some of the attacks experienced are because of cyber-collateral damage (Romanosky and Goldman, 2016) for example, the WannaCry cyber-attack which paralysed e-Health across the NHS (UK) resulting in cancellation of surgeries, hospital diversion of emergencies and unavailability of patient records in both England and Scotland (Mattei, 2017). Initial investigations indicate that the NHS was not the specific target (Morse, 2018) hence showing that cyber-collateral damage can have adverse effects on e-Health in the context of cyberwar. Further, according to Fritsch and Fischer-Hübner (2018), "the future Battlefield of Things will be the weaponization of civilian or dual-use infrastructure." This suggests that through interlinking of these infrastructures, healthcare organisations can be caught in the crossfire thus having a destructive impact on an entire nation (Walker-Roberts, Hammoudeh and Dehghantanha, 2018) as highlighted in Table 5.

To prevent direct and indirect possible state-sponsored attacks against e-Health, which could lead to the weaponization of PHI and PII, and cyberespionage of sensitive data, it is recommended that healthcare sectors together with the relevant stakeholders, play part in ensuring the protection of critical information infrastructures. This can be done by implementing effective standards identified in Section 7, for example, ISO/IEC 27032:2012 and ISO/IEC 27799:2016. In addition to this, risk assessments should be conducted, taking into account the profiles and motivations of sophisticated state sponsored attackers. On top of these, understanding and being aware of matters concerning threats and vulnerabilities is essential in the healthcare sector. These safeguards would aid in creating a mitigation program that would help the sector stay one step ahead of both state-sponsored and non-state-sponsored attackers.

9 Conclusion

The healthcare sector has been a preferred target for cyber-attackers over the years. This has mostly been attributed to financial gain due to extensive personal health information and personally identifiable information. However, it has been shown that the sector has also become a target for state-sponsored attackers. While this has occurred before in the healthcare sector, for example, the cyber-attack on Sing Health (Singapore Health Services), cyber-attacks perpetrated by state-sponsors have been experienced more during the COVID-19 pandemic as outlined in Table 3. The major reason for these attacks during the pandemic has been linked to cyberespionage of COVID-19 research data as they would put an enemy state in a competitive edge.

In addition to cyberespionage, state-sponsored attackers can compromise e-Health data with the aim of targeting key people within the government or famous people. Such data can be weaponized with the aim of causing harm to an individual or creating panic and disturbance within the society. As such, the question of cyberespionage and weaponization of e-Health data in the context of cyberwar is one to ponder on. As noted in Table 5, the consequences of weaponizing PII and PHI, and cyberespionage of e-Health data can have have broad and highly devastating consequences. Apart from this, such attacks can lead to a number of privacy breaches within the physical sphere as indicated in Table 6.

Hence, to prevent this, several mitigations highlighted in section 7 need to be implemented to avoid the imaginable cyberwar. Of essence is the need to conduct risk assessments that take into consideration the capabilities and motives of state-sponsored attackers.

Acknowledgements

This work was funded by the DigitalWell Research Project from Region Värmland.

References

Ablon, L. (2018) 'Data Thieves', The Motivations of Cyber Threat Actors and Their Use and Monetization of Stolen Data.

Ahaskar, A. (2020) Indian pharma companies and hospitals targeted by Chinese, Russian and Korean hackers group. Available at: https://www.livemint.com/technology/tech-news/indian-pharma-companies-and-hospitals-targeted-by-chinese-russian-and-korean-hackers-groups-11614618146968.html (Accessed: 09 September 2021).

Arquilla, J. and Ronfeldt, D. (1993) 'Cyberwar is coming!', Comparative Strategy, 12(2), pp. 141-165.

Baezner, M. and Robin, P. (2017) Stuxnet: ETH Zurich.

BBC (2016) Wiggins and Froome medical records released by 'Russian hackers'. Available at: https://www.bbc.com/news/world-37369705 (Accessed: 10 September 2021).

BBC (2021) Cyberattack 'most significant on Irish State'. Available at: https://www.bbc.com/news/world-europe-57111615 (Accessed: 09 September 2021).

Bergal, J. (2020) Hospital Hackers Seize Upon Coronavirus Pandemic. Available at: https://www.pewtrusts.org/en/research-and-analysis/blogs/stateline/2020/04/13/hospital-hackers-seize-upon-coronavirus-pandemic (Accessed: 08 September 2021).

Bernard, R., Bowsher, G. and Sullivan, R. (2020) 'Cyber security and the unexplored threat to global health: a call for global norms', Global Security: Health, Science and Policy, 5(1), pp. 134-141.

Bing, C. and Taylor, M. (2020) Exclusive: China-backed hackers 'targeted COVID-19 Vaccine Firm Moderna'. Available at: https://www.reuters.com/article/us-health-coronavirus-moderna-cyber-excl-idUSKCN24V38M (Accessed: 09 September 2021).

Bisson, D. (2020) Global Phishing Campaign Sets Sights on COVID-19 Cold Chain. Available at: https://www.tripwire.com/state-of-security/security-data-protection/global-phishing-campaign-sets-sights-on-covid-19-cold-chain/ (Accessed: 09 September 2021).

Botek, A. (2020) Brno University Hospital Ransomware Attack (2020). Available at: https://cyberlaw.ccdcoe.org/wiki/Brno_University_Hospital_ransomware_attack_(2020) (Accessed: 09 September 2021).

Caiyu, L. (2020) Cyberattack from India targets Chinese medical facilities amid coronavirus fight: experts. Available at: https://www.globaltimes.cn/content/1178731.shtml (Accessed: 08 September 2021).

CanadianHealthTechnology (2021) Project Improves Remote Monitoring of Patients. Available at: https://www.canhealth.com/2021/03/24/project-improves-remote-monitoring-of-patients/ (Accessed: 08 September 2021).

Case, D. U. (2016) 'Analysis of the cyber attack on the Ukrainian power grid', Electricity Information Sharing and Analysis Center (E-ISAC), 388.

Cimpanu, C. (2020) State-sponsored hackers are now using coronavirus lures to infect their targets. Available at: https://www.zdnet.com/article/state-sponsored-hackers-are-now-using-coronavirus-lures-to-infect-their-targets/ (Accessed: 08 September 2021).

Cohen, J. (2019) Protecting Critical Infrastructure From Cybersecurity Threats. Available at: https://securityboulevard.com/2019/10/protecting-critical-infrastructure-from-cybersecurity-threats/ (Accessed: 12 September 2021).

Cordey, S. (2020) 'The Evolving Cyber Threat Landscape during the Coronavirus Crisis'.

Coventry, L. and Branley, D. (2018) 'Cybersecurity in healthcare: a narrative review of trends, threats and ways forward', Maturitas, 113, pp. 48-52.

Erlingsdóttir, G. and Sandberg, H. (2016) 'eHealth opportunities and challenges: a white paper'.

Europa (2016) NIS Directive. Available at: https://eur-lex.europa.eu/eli/dir/2016/1148/oj (Accessed: 08 September 2021).

EuropeanCommission (n.d.) e-Health and COVID-19. Available at: https://ec.europa.eu/health/ehealth/covid-19_en (Accessed: September 2021).

Fireeye (2020) Vietnamese Threat Actors APT32 Targeting Wuhan Government and Chinese Ministry of Emergency Management in Latest Example of COVID-19 Related Espionage. Available at: https://www.fireeye.com/blog/threat-research/2020/04/apt32-targeting-chinese-government-in-covid-19-related-espionage.html (Accessed: 09 September 2021).

Fritsch, L. and Fischer-Hübner, S. (2018) 'Implications of Privacy & Security Research for the Upcoming Battlefield of Things', Journal of Information Warfare, 17(4), pp. 72-87.

Gaddi, A., Capello, F. and Manca, M. (2013) eHealth, care and quality of life. Springer.

Ghafur, S., Kristensen, S., Honeyford, K., Martin, G., Darzi, A. and Aylin, P. (2019) 'A retrospective impact analysis of the WannaCry cyberattack on the NHS', NPJ digital medicine, 2(1), pp. 1-7.

Glenza, J. (2020) Coronavirus: US says Russia behind disinformation campaigns. Available at: https://www.theguardian.com/world/2020/feb/22/coronavirus-russia-disinformation-campaign-us-officials (Accessed: 10 September 2021).

Gross, M. L., Canetti, D. and Waismel-Manor, I. (2015) 'The Psychological & Physiological Effects of Cyberwar', Binary Bullets: The Ethics of Cyberwarfare, pp. 157-76.

Hatamian, M., Wairimu, S., Momen, N. and Fritsch, L. (2021) 'A privacy and security analysis of early-deployed COVID-19 contact tracing Android apps', Empirical Software Engineering, 26(3), pp. 1-51.

HHS (2021) Breach Portal: Notice to the Secretary of HHS Breach of Unsecured Protected Health Information. Available at:

https://ocrportal.hhs.gov/ocr/breach/breach_report.jsf (Accessed: 08 September 2021).

Hughes, O. (2020) Norway Healthcare Cyber-Attack 'Could be the biggest of its kind'. Available at: https://www.digitalhealth.net/2018/01/norway-healthcare-cyber-attack-could-be-biggest/ (Accessed: 10 September 2021).

Irwin, L. (2021) The 5 most Vulnerable Sectors to Cyber Attacks. Available at: https://www.itgovernance.eu/blog/en/the-5-most-vulnerable-sectors-to-cyber-attacks (Accessed: 08 September 2021).

ISE 2016. Securing Hospitals: A Research Study and Blueprint.

ISO (2012) 'ISO/IEC 27032:2012 - Information Technology - Security Techniques - Guidelines for Cybersecurity', ISO/IEC-The standard was published in October.

ISO (2016) ISO 27799:2016 - Health Informatics - Information Security Management in Health using IOS/IEC 27002. Available at: https://www.iso.org/standard/62777.html (Accessed: 11 September 2021).

Jayakumar, S. (2020) 'Cyber Attacks by Terrorists and other Malevolent Actors: Prevention and Preparedness'.

Johnson, D. L., Tan, K., Lam, J. and Dass, A. (2017) 2015 Anthem Data Breach. Available at: https://asamborski.github.io/cs558_s17_blog/2017/04/04/anthem.html (Accessed: 10 September 2021).

Kaiser, R. (2015) 'The birth of cyberwar', Political Geography, 46, pp. 11-20.

Kallberg, J. (2016) 'Strategic cyberwar theory-A foundation for designing decisive strategic cyber operations', The Cyber Defense Review, 1(1), pp. 113-128.

Kaufmann, H., Hutter, R., Skopik, F. and Mantere, M. (2015) 'A structural design for a pan-European early warning system for critical infrastructures', e & i Elektrotechnik und Informationstechnik, 132(2), pp. 117-121.

Kävrestad, J. and Huskaj, G. 'How the Civilian Sector in Sweden Perceive Threats From Offensive Cyberspace Operations'. 2021: Academic Conferences International Limited, 499-XII.

Kreps, G. L. and Neuhauser, L. (2010) 'New directions in eHealth communication: opportunities and challenges', Patient education and counseling, 78(3), pp. 329-336.

Lallie, H. S., Shepherd, L. A., Nurse, J. R. C., Erola, A., Epiphaniou, G., Maple, C. and Bellekens, X. (2021) 'Cyber security in the age of covid-19: A timeline and analysis of cyber-crime and cyber-attacks during the pandemic', Computers & Security, 105, pp. 102248.

Langner, R. (2011) 'Stuxnet: Dissecting a cyberwarfare weapon', IEEE Security & Privacy, 9(3), pp. 49-51.

Liff, A. P. (2012) 'Cyberwar: a new 'absolute weapon'? The proliferation of cyberwarfare capabilities and interstate war', Journal of Strategic Studies, 35(3), pp. 401-428.

Limba, T., Plėta, T., Agafonov, K. and Damkus, M. (2019) 'Cyber security management model for critical infrastructure'.

Martin, G., Martin, P., Hankin, C., Darzi, A. and Kinross, J. (2017) 'Cybersecurity and healthcare: how safe are we?', Bmj, 358.

Mattei, T. A. (2017) 'Privacy, confidentiality, and security of health care information: lessons from the recent wannacry cyberattack', World neurosurgery, 104, pp. 972-974.

McGraw, G. (2013) 'Cyber war is inevitable (unless we build security in)', Journal of Strategic Studies, 36(1), pp. 109-119.

McNamee, M. S. (2021) HSE cyber-attack: Irish health service still recovering months after hack. Available at: https://www.bbc.com/news/world-europe-58413448 (Accessed: 09 September 2021).

Morse, A. (2018) 'Investigation: WannaCry cyber attack and the NHS', Report by the National Audit Office. Accessed, 1.

NCSC (2020) Advisory: APT 29 Targets COVID-19 Vaccine Development. Available at: https://www.ncsc.gov.uk/news/advisory-apt29-targets-covid-19-vaccine-development (Accessed: 08 September 2021).

Newman, L. H. (2020) Ransom Hits Dozens of Hospitals in an Unprecedented Wave. Available at: https://www.wired.com/story/ransomware-hospitals-ryuk-trickbot/ (Accessed: 08 September 2021).

Ottis, R. 'Analysis of the 2007 cyber attacks against estonia from the information warfare perspective'. 2008, 163.

Romanosky, S. and Goldman, Z. (2016) 'Cyber collateral damage', Procedia Computer Science, 95, pp. 10-17.

Sevis, K. N. and Seker, E. 'Cyber warfare: terms, issues, laws and controversies'. 2016: IEEE, 1-9.

Stubbs, J. (2020) Exclusive: Suspected North Korean hackers targeted COVID vaccine maker AstraZeneca - sources. Available at: https://www.reuters.com/article/us-healthcare-coronavirus-astrazeneca-no-idUSKBN2871A2 (Accessed: 09 September 2021).

Stubbs, J. and Bing, C. (2020) Iran-linked hackers recently targeted coronavirus drugmaker Gilead - sources. Available at: https://www.reuters.com/article/us-healthcare-coronavirus-gilead-iran-ex-idUSKBN22K2EV (Accessed: 08 September 2021).

TheCommitteeofInquiry (2019) Public Report of the Commission of Inquiry into the Cyber Attack on Singapore Health Services Private Limited's Patient Database on or around 27 June 2018. Available at: https://www.mci.gov.sg/-/media/mcicorp/doc/report-of-the-coi-into-the-cyber-attack-on-singhealth-10-jan-2019.ashx (Accessed: 08 September 2021).

Tidy, J. (2020) Police launch homicide inquiry after German hospital hack. Available at: https://www.bbc.com/news/technology-54204356 (Accessed: 09 September 2021).

Wairimu, S. and Momen, N. 'Privacy Analysis of COVID-19 Contact Tracing Apps in the EU'. 2020: Springer, 213-228.

Wairimu, S. 'e-Health as a Target in Cyberwar: Expecting the Worst'. 2021: Academic Conferences International Limited, 549-XVI.

Walker-Roberts, S., Hammoudeh, M. and Dehghantanha, A. (2018) 'A systematic review of the availability and efficacy of countermeasures to internal threats in healthcare critical infrastructure', IEEE Access, 6, pp. 25167-25177.

Wickström, G., Regner, Å. and Micko, L. (2017) 'Vision eHealth 2025—Common starting points for digitization in social services and health and medical care', Affairs. Available online: https://www. ehalsomyndigheten. se/globalassets/dokument/vision/vision-for-ehealth-2025. pdf (accessed on 10 December 2019).

Williams, P. A. H. and Woodward, A. J. (2015) 'Cybersecurity vulnerabilities in medical devices: a complex environment and multifaceted problem', Medical Devices (Auckland, NZ), 8, pp. 305.

Wosik, J., Fudim, M., Cameron, B., Gellad, Z. F., Cho, A., Phinney, D., Curtis, S., Roman, M., Poon, E. G. and Ferranti, J. (2020) 'Telehealth transformation: COVID-19 and the rise of virtual care', Journal of the American Medical Informatics Association, 27(6), pp. 957-962.

Author biography

Samuel Wairimu is a PhD student in Computer Science in the Department of Mathematics and Computer Science at Karlstad University, Sweden. He received his Master's in Cybersecurity from the University of Chester, UK in 2018. His main research areas are cybersecurity, cyberwarfare, information security and privacy, and security and privacy in e-Health.

Chapter Six

Pandemic Information Warfare: Cyberattacks, Disinformation and Privacy during the COVID-19 Pandemic

Brett van Niekerk and Trishana Ramluckan

University of KwaZulu-Natal, South Africa
vanniekerkb@ukzn.ac.za
ramluckant@ukzn.ac.za

Abstract: At the end of 2019 a new coronavirus was detected in China and was reported to the World Health Organization; it subsequently spread to almost all countries around the world by April 2020. During this time cybercriminals, governments, and other malicious actors leveraged the fear generated by the disease to promote scams, propaganda, and to further spread confusion and chaos. This article conducts exploratory research and thematic analysis to investigate the trends of online malicious actions during the initial stages of a global pandemic (from March to May 2020) through the lens of information warfare and with reference to international humanitarian law. The results illustrate greater reporting on cyberattacks compared to disinformation, and the incidents tend to align with the increasing infections at the beginning of the pandemic.

Keywords: Cyberattack, cyber law, cybersecurity, disinformation, fake news, pandemic, privacy

1 Introduction

On the 31st of December 2019 the World Health Organization (WHO) was notified of a new respiratory coronavirus disease in China; on the 30 January 2020 it was declared a "Public Health Emergency of International Concern" (WHO, 2020). This new disease was named COVID-19 on the 11 February 2020 (WHO, 2020), and it affected nearly every country with over 2 million cases reported globally by 17 April 2020 (European Centre for Disease Prevention and Control, 2020).

As with other disasters, scams and other online malicious activity become prevalent. Historical examples of such scams include illegitimate donation requests after the 2015 terror attacks in France (Singletary, 2015) and the Australian bush fires in January 2020 (Elsworthy, 2020). The media have always benefitted from major world events and crises, and terrorism has thrived on media attention of their actions (Ramluckan & van Niekerk, 2009). With the growing prevalence of the Internet, and in particular social media, major world events have been reflected, or shaped by online activity. Examples include the alleged interference in the 2016 US presidential elections, events in Europe through online influence operations (van Niekerk, 2018), and cyberattacks as an alternative to armed conflict, which still projected national power as is evidenced by the Stuxnet disruption of the Iranian nuclear program (Zetter, 2014) and reported US cyberattacks in retaliation for the downing of an unmanned aerial vehicle (Doffman, 2019). The repercussions of the alleged election interference are still being felt at the time of writing, with the term 'fake news' subsequently becoming common lexicon. The US efforts to counter online influence operations by ISIS and Russia reportedly fell short of what was termed an Information War by Stengel (2019). In Ukraine, the use of influence operations and cyber-attacks to support the Russian intervention in Crimea illustrates how effective these tools can be in shaping regional power dynamics. However, the concept of fake news can be used by politicians to dismiss criticism, and in Zimbabwe this was taken further when a journalist was arrested for criticizing then-President Robert Mugabe under the guise of cyber-security (van Niekerk, 2018).

This chapter aims to analyse events reported in the news through the lens of information warfare (IW). The concept of information warfare is particularly useful as it incorporates a number of 'pillars' that will allow for the consideration of cyber-attacks, cyber-security, privacy, and disinformation. Online activities of both state and non-state actors, and government responses will be considered, with the news reports of incidents providing specific cases. Humanitarian aspects will also be considered, in particular the rights to privacy and freedom of expression. The chapter involves exploratory research, using thematic analysis of news reports to investigate trends in the reporting of incidents. The following section will further define and discuss IW; this is followed by a discussion of the range of incidents. These are then analysed based on the IW models, and further discussed.

2 Information warfare

Information Warfare (IW) can be described as "All actions taken to defend the military's information-based processes, information systems and communications networks and to destroy, neutralize or exploit the enemy's similar capabilities within the physical, information and cognitive domains" (Brazzoli, 2007:219). However, some authors also extend this to the corporate environment (Hutchinson and Warren, 2001), and the concept of Information Operations (IO) as an evolution of IW, where IW is considered operations during wartime, and IO extends these activities to peacetime. Traditionally, the concept of CIA – the confidentiality, integrity, and availability of information – is the basis for information security and cybersecurity (Denning, 1999). However, other attributes of information are also proposed: possession, control, authenticity, utility, non-repudiation, relevancy, accuracy, and timeliness (Denning, 1999; Parker, 2002; Poisel, 2004; Waltz, 1998). These attributes are also applicable to the IW scenario, and the relationships amongst these attributes are shown in Table 1.

Table 1: Relationship of information criteria

The below:	Is relevant to:										
	Confidentiality	Integrity	Availability	Possession	Control	Authenticity	Utility	Non-	Relevancy	Accuracy	Timeliness
Confidentiality	■			green							
Integrity		■				green		green	green		
Availability			■	yellow		green					green
Possession	green		yellow	■	green		yellow			yellow	
Control	green		yellow		■						yellow
Authenticity		green				■		yellow		yellow	
Utility			green	yellow			■				
Non-repudiation		green				yellow		■			
Relevancy		green							■		
Accuracy		green			yellow					■	
Timeliness			green	yellow							■

In Table 1 the green indicates full relevance and yellow indicates partial relevance. These attributes are those that need to be protected or maintained, and therefore can be considered as a defensive model.

An offensive perspective to IW includes actions such as deny, destroy, degrade, disrupt, corrupt and exploit. The destruction, denial, disruption or degradation of information services or data will negatively impact availability. Corruption can affect the integrity through the modification of existing data, fabrication of false information, or changing the context or perceptions in which the information is viewed. Exploitation includes the compromise of systems to intercept and/or facilitate the theft of information (Hutchinson & Warren, 2001; Pleeger & Pfleeger, 2003; Waltz, 1998).

A number of sub-disciplines exist in IW, in part aligning to the three domains mentioned in the above quote. These include cyber operations (also known as computer network operations), psychological operations, electronic warfare, as well as intelligence and military command and control aspects (Brazzoli, 2007). For the purposes of this article, cyber operations and psychological operations are the two focus areas. Cyber operations are as the name suggests; however, the concept of psychological operations warrants some further description: in the contemporary context with mass online communication, it can be considered to be influence operations. Whilst influence operations can be considered to be benign (such as awareness campaigns), the focus in this article will be the malicious application: misinformation, disinformation, malinformation, colloquially called 'fake news' (Wardle and Derakhshan, 2018).

When considering disinformation, cyber-incidents, and the relevant responses, it is important to do so with reference to human rights such as the rights to privacy and freedom of speech as defined by the Universal Declaration of Human Rights (United Nations, 1948). However, there may be limitations based on national and social security or where the rights of others may be infringed. For example, in South Africa the rights to freedom of expression are not absolute and does not include incitement of violence or hatred or propaganda for war (Vermeulen, 2021). While these are not traditionally aspects of IW, they will be treated as such for the purposes of this chapter in order to assess them.

3   Methodology

This article is exploratory research, to assess the news stories through an information warfare lens. This will aid in identifying the prevalence of cybersecurity and disinformation activities related to the COVID-19 pandemic, as well as the related human rights.

Relevant online news stories were collected from Google News from March to May 2020 (3 months). These were filtered so that there were no repeats of a specific incident unless each article provided unique information. In total, 110 documents were collected, of which 89 were retained and 21 were rejected. Those rejected were either duplicates or marketing related stories that provided information in general around attacks, without mentioning specific incidents.

Thematic analysis was performed on the documents based on the major information warfare categorizations and themes described above. For the purposes of this chapter, the following themes will be used, as discussed in the above section: IW areas include cyber, disinformation, and human rights; IW domains include virtual, physical and cognitive; defensive IW themes include confidentiality, integrity, availability and freedom of speech; and offensive IW themes include corrupt/dceive, destroy/deny, disrupt/degrade, and exploit/steal. In addition, state activity in relation to the above themes is considered in order to gain insights on the activity conducted by states versus those of non-state actors. The following section provides an overview of the incidents described in the news stories considered. Thereafter, an analysis and discussion are provided on the information warfare themes that are present.

3.1 Online activities and concerns during the pandemic

This section is divided into three parts: the first has a focus on cyberattack trends and cybersecurity in relation to the pandemic; the second considers disinformation and propaganda related to the pandemic; and the third discusses the impact on human rights based on the efforts to mitigate fake news and provide contact tracing.

3.2 Cyberattacks and cybersecurity

Cyberattacks were seen to spike during the pandemic. Reports indicate that South Africa experienced a tenfold increase in affected devices immediately after the announcement of a state of disaster in March 2020 (van der Merwe, 2020); approximately 9,100 malicious files related to the coronavirus were detected in India in a three-month period, with 19 million similar attacks across Asia (Deasi, 2020). The UK's National Cyber Security Centre's dedicated reporting service for coronavirus related scams received 5,151 reports and took down 83 online scams in the first 24 hours; in the first two weeks 160,000 reports and 300 take-downs of malicious websites were reported (Scroxton, 2020b; Scroxton, 2020c). Muncaster (2020) cites a report by VMWare Carbon Black indicating that attacks against the financial sector increased 237% during the pandemic, with 27% of attacks in 2020 affecting either the financial or health care sectors. Analysis by Bitdefender shows the retail and transportation sectors being the most affected, with the top countries illustrated in Table 2 (Arsene, 2020). The attacks appear to follow the growing trends of infections and news reporting in the countries (Arsene, 2020; Muncaster, 2020). Research by Palo Alto Networks indicted a 569% increase in the registration of malicious Internet domains (Szurdi, Chen, Starov, McCabe and Duan, 2020).

Reasons for the increase in cyberattacks include the fact that organizations were forced to rapidly implement remote working giving rise to a sharp spike in the uptake of collaboration tools and virtual private networks (VPNs), expanding the threat surface dues to rushed implementations; and the anxiety and need for information making people more susceptible. Malware was reported for have been found on 45% of home office networks, with these networks over three times more likely to be infected compared to corporate networks (Waldman, 2020b); and attacks against business through the VPNs became prevalent, with a report indicting 22 million attacks globally in the space of seven days (Monzon, 2020; Palmer, 2020). Vulnerabilities and stolen logins of popular collaboration software was being sold and traded over the Internet (O'Donnell, 2020d; Prior, 2020; Scroxton, 2020a). The names of the software were used as a lure in distributing cyber-threats, and the software was reported to be targeted by intelligence services (Staff Reporter, 2020; Walcott, 2020).

Table 2: Top affected countries from COVID themed attacks, source: Arsene (2020)

Rank	March	April
1	US	US
2	Italy	South Africa
3	UK	Italy
4	Spain	Canada
5	South Africa	UK

As mentioned above, the healthcare sector exhibited an increase in attacks. Multiple warnings from Microsoft, Interpol, the Czech Republic government, and a joint UK and US statement were issued indicating the likelihood of hospitals, research facilities and governments being targeted by cyber-criminals and state-backed cyber-espionage (Interpol, 2020; Lopatka and Muller, 2020; Osborne, 2020; Waldman, 2020a). Despite this, hospitals and health departments in the Czech Republic, US, India, and Germany were affected by cyberattacks (Cimpanu, 2020a; CISOMag, 2020; Matthews, 2020). These attacks included ransomware and denial-of-service attacks affecting availability, website defacements affecting information integrity, phishing and scam campaigns, and breaches of patient information affecting confidentiality (Cimpanu, 2020a; CISOMag, 2020; Lopatka and Muller, 2020; Matthews, 2020; McCabe, Ray and Cortes, 2020; Montalbano, 2020d; Osborne, 2020; Seals, 2020). In extreme cases a hospital had to cancel surgeries, and US government agencies paid money to scammers based on fraudulent medical equipment scams (Cimpanu, 2020a; Montalbano, 2020d). The WHO was particularly affected, experiencing a spike in cyberattacks, a breach of 450 active email addresses, and targeting of senior officials (Asokan, 2020; Gallagher, 2020; Vijayan, 2020b). Iran and China were specifically mentioned as perpetrators of state-backed incidents (Cimpanu, 2020b; Menn, Bing, Satter and Stubbs, 2020).

Concerns over Zoom's security were prevalent, with numerous issues being highlighted due to the rise of what became known as 'zoombombing', where meetings were invaded and the attendees exposed to offensive content; the company since took measures to update the security (Culafi, 2020; Mehta, 2020; Whittaker, 2020). In addition to collaboration technology, COVID-19 tracking and tracing mobile applications were also found to have vulnerabilities (Montalbano, 2020e; Scroxton, 2020f). These vulnerabilities in collaboration software and tracing applications raise privacy concerns, which will be discussed below.

Initially there were concerns that pandemic related scams and 'lures' for attacks were passing through email protections (Montalbano, 2020a). The lures were observed being used by criminal groups, advanced persistent threats, nation-state mobile malware in Syria, alleged Chinese cyber-espionage, and for attacks against industrial control systems (Del Rosso, 2020; Lakshmanan, 2020; Mercer, Rascagneres, and Ventura, 2020; Montalbano, 2020b; O'Donnell, 2020a; O'Neill, 2020; Olson, 2020). In addition, scams based on stimulus payments were used as lures (Sheridan, 2020), and there were accusations that the pandemic was used to rush the awarding of irregular tenders for cybersecurity services in South Africa (Selisho, 2020a). Legitimate reporting tools showing the spread of the virus were copied and 'weaponized' to lure people into providing details or installing malware (Barth, 2020), and websites attempted to sell fake vaccines (O'Donnel, 2020b).

In response to the attacks, volunteer cyber security groups organized themselves to help protect infrastructure and services against the attacks (Brewster, 2020), and domain registrars were pressured by governments to combat scams based on the pandemic (Vijayan, 2020a). To allow effective response to the pandemic, the UN Under-Secretary General called for a cease to cyber-attacks (Hochschild, 2020).

4   Disinformation, fake news, and propaganda

As described in the introduction, when there is a crisis there is invariably some form of disinformation that accompanies it; however, in this instance the crisis is global rather than local or regional, resulting in some interesting disinformation and propaganda. One of the most prevalent fake news or disinformation messages that was being circulated was that the pandemic was the results of biological warfare. Whilst some pointed to the research center in Wuhan as the origin of the pandemic, there was similar disinformation being spread from Russia, China and Iran in claiming the pandemic was the result of biological warfare from the United States (Glez, 2020; Swan, 2020). Other 'fake news' items include fear-mongering over transmission by mosquito and parcels from China, fake remedies, and false claims of immunity based on age and/or race (Glez, 2020). Another example of disinformation is a report indicating high numbers of casualties in India, falsely using the John Hopkins University logo in order to give the report legitimacy (The Economic Times, 2020).

Disinformation circulated in South Africa included manipulated images purporting to show TV announcements that the national funding body for university students will stop paying allowances (Samuels, 2020) and an early lifting on the ban on alcohol sales in the country (Cilliers, 2020). Far-fetched conspiracy theories, such as claiming Bill Gates and TV personality Trevor Noah were involved in planning to test vaccines in Africa and used a fund-raising tennis match hosted in South Africa as a cover to arrange for the testing. This conspiracy became more prevalent when a small South African political party formally raised questions related to this to the national president, and some of the media houses reported on the claims, fuelling the rumours with some sense of legitimacy (Le Roux, 2020). Another strange conspiracy theory that was prevalent globally was that the new 5G towers for mobile devices were spreading the virus, resulting in some of the mobile phone towers being attacked (Gold, 2020; O'Halloran, 2020).

Nation-state propaganda was seen, with China being singled out for the use of over 10,000 autonomous 'bots' and compromised user accounts to push pro-Chinese propaganda on social media, targeting countries that received aid or equipment from China, such as Italy (Allen-Ebrahimian, 2020; Kao and Li, 2020). This propaganda was conducted in parallel with more conventional diplomatic and corporate assistance, notably including a telecommunications company bidding for 5G contracts in some of the targeted countries (Brattberg and Le Corre, 2020). Brattberg and Le Corre (2020) contend that the sometimes-strong diplomacy and propaganda might have an adverse effect against China's image, as many European countries were actively attempting to counter the online propaganda and disinformation, in addition to sometimes poor quality supplies. State presidents have also been criticized for making false public statements regarding the pandemic, apparently in an attempt to benefit from local politics; both the US and Brazilian presidents are attributed to making incorrect and sometimes dangerous statements (Friedman, 2020; McCarthy, 2020). Disinformation, fake news and propaganda, in an information warfare context, target information integrity at a cognitive level, providing numerous alternatives to the 'truth', impeding or influencing decision making. Where internal politics have always played a part in local crises, the scope of a pandemic has brought more blatant international politics and disinformation attempts to the fore. In addition, concerns were raised that the pandemic would make people vulnerable to extremism as they were vulnerable and extremist disinformation may become appealing (McDonald-Gibson).

In attempt to counter the spread of disinformation, governments are placing pressure on social media companies: in the UK it was indicated that social media companies were not doing enough to address pandemic related disinformation (Gold, 2020; Skelton, 2020), and in South Africa it was reported that new legislation put pressure on social media companies to remove posts containing disinformation immediately after they were identified (de Wet, 2020a). Efforts made by the social media companies include Twitter's labelling of potential pandemic disinformation (Seitz, 2020) and deleting malicious accounts that were controlled by state actors (Kao and Li, 2020). Facebook notified users who posted misinformation related to the pandemic (Perrigo, 2020) and stopped forwarding of messages containing pandemic information to large number of recipients (Montalbano, 2020c). YouTube and other social media organizations were collaborating with mobile providers in an attempt to hinder the propagation messages related to the 5G conspiracy theory mentioned above (Gold, 2020), and the WHO released a fact-checking document related to the 5G disinformation (O'Halloran, 2020).

Nations, particularly in Southern Africa, instituted legislation criminalizing the distribution or generation of pandemic related disinformation (Hodgson, Farise, and Mavedzenge, 2020). For example, under the new legislation in South Africa, the administrators of WhatsApp groups could potentially be held criminally liable under certain circumstances for disinformation on their groups even if they did not post it (de Villiers, 2020). In a similar situation the broadcast regulator in the UK was investigating a news anchor for challenging the refuting of the 5G disinformation in the media (O'Halloran, 2020). Concerns were raised that this legislation was excessive and could be maliciously used to hinder freedom of speech (Hodgson, Farise, and Mavedzenge, 2020; Moyo, 2020). These ethical and legal concerns are discussed in more detail in the next section.

5   Privacy and freedom of speech

The unprecedented scale of the pandemic and the technology-based initiatives to manage the spread of the virus raised concerns over surveillance and privacy. In particular, a mobile phone application used in the UK for contact tracing was alleged to be designed in such a way that human rights and privacy of the individuals was inadequately protected (Scroxton, 2020d). Apple and Google collaborated to include functionality in their mobile phone operating systems that would allow for contact tracing. While there were claims that privacy would be protected, concerns were raised in that the functionality is embedded in the operating system and cannot be uninstalled like a traditional application, therefore this tracing functionality could potentially be repurposed to collect data outside of the contact tracing (Estes and Ghaffary, 2020; Higginbotham, 2020). In South Africa the government reportedly intended to use mobile phone locations, amongst other personal information, as part of tracking and tracing, and those being tracked might not initially be notified; however, the mobile operators claimed that they had not consented to provide the data as it could be considered illegal (de Wet, 2020b; Staff Writer, 2020).

Privacy concerns do not stop at the explicit collection of personal data. Due to 'zoomboming', the video conferencing tool was banned by education departments in New York City and Singapore after incidents occurred (Feiner, 2020; Geddie, 2020). This not only infringes on privacy, but also exposes the participants to undesirable content, and this is more problematic when minors are involved. Both the US and South African governments had meetings disrupted by 'zoombombing' (O'Donnell, 2020e; Selisho, 2020b). The fact that government meetings were affected also raises the possibility of espionage, where hackers could gain access to sensitive meetings to obtain information rather than disrupt them, as was indicated in Walcott (2020). In South Africa the orders to deploy the South African National Defence Force to aid in enforcing the lockdown in the country were leaked on social media, as well as orders to deploy additional troops (Gerber, 2020; Mahlakoana, 2020). Whilst the breach of military movements through social media is not new, these incidents reinforce the impact of hyper-connectivity on the military.

As described in the previous section, the government regulations targeting the posting and distribution of disinformation and fake news was considered as excessive in some instances. Moyo (2020) provides examples in Zimbabwe where legislation meant to prevent disinformation was also used in targeting journalists, effectively suppressing a free press. Hodgson, Farise, and Mavedzenge (2020) extend these concerns to the similar legislation in South Africa and eSwatini, claiming that the penalties for accidentally or unknowingly distributing 'fake news' is excessive. Possible challenges in the implementation of the laws is that it may be difficult to prove that the individual knew the content was fake news at the time and intentionally distributed it for malicious purposes (de Villiers, 2020). The example of the UK media regulator investigating someone for challenging the response (O'Halloran, 2020) can also be claimed to be excessive; an opinion about a response is not necessarily equivalent to the generation or distribution of fake news for malicious intent.

The concerns raised relating to both privacy and freedom of speech are referring to the trade-off between human rights for individuals versus public safety. Adams (2020) raises the concerns over tracing technologies remaining in place after the pandemic, arguing the range of technologies employed can also be used for mass surveillance; in a similar manner the concerns over embedding tracking functionality into a mobile device's operating system may allow for surveillance (Higginbotham, 2020). A concern raised around the tracing in South Africa was that retrospective approvals and consent from the subjects were not obtained, however based on the South African privacy legislation consent is not required if the collection is for the public good and/or allows the government to perform its duties (Staff Writer, 2020). In comparison, it was claimed that that the European General Data Protection Regulation (GDPR) was insufficient to deal with the privacy and security implications of contact tracing (Scroxton, 2020e). Amnesty International provided suggestions for managing the tracing with respect to privacy, including ensuring the necessity and proportionality of the data collected; time limiting the use, storage and collection of the data to what is required by the pandemic; adequate accountability procedures; managing the risk of algorithmic bias that could result in discrimination; and ensuring any collection, storage and sharing of data is based on law (Jordaan 2020). However, a question raised by Steinmetz (2020) takes the issue of privacy beyond the government collection and interrogates who has the right to know if someone is infected with the virus; this appears to follow those who may have been in contact or could be exposed in a workplace. One of the concerns raised is that of stigmatization (Steinmetz, 2020). An informal online poll was conducted, and the majority of the respondents indicated that they would not participate in government tracing due to privacy concerns (O'Donnell, 2020c).

6   Results and discussion

This section presents the results of the thematic analysis of the 89 documents for themes of IW areas, defensive IW, offensive IW, and the IW domains. The prevalence of state actions related to the various IW themes is then discussed.

6.1   IW areas

Figure 1 presents the percentage composition of the IW areas, and Figure 2 presents the monthly distribution of the theme occurrence.

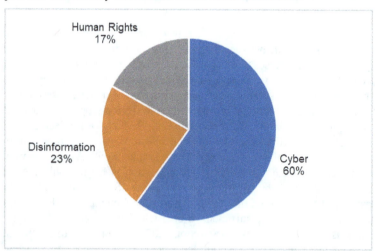

Figure 1: Percentage of IW Areas

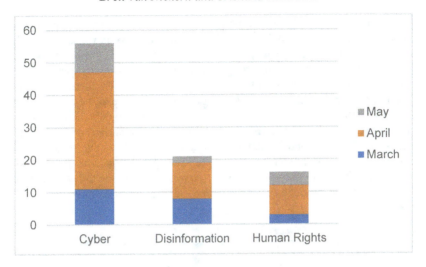

Figure 2: Number of theme occurrences for IW areas per month

As is evidenced from these figures, cyber is the dominant theme, followed by disinformation. A reason for cyber receiving more attention is that there are 'tangible' affects, such as system outages or financial loss. By comparison, disinformation can be more subtle, and the effects are not as noticeable or are more gradual. Human rights aspects usually only received attention when concerns were raised against government efforts to contain or manage the spread of the virus (e.g. track and trace) or disinformation.

The monthly distribution of the three areas shows that April had the highest proportion of reports (based on the number of incidents). This particular spread of cyber and disinformation is consistent as the activity 'followed' the increase in national reported cases, therefore more activity can be expected in April when more nations were entering lockdowns and the experiencing the initial spread of the virus. The malicious activity fed off the confusion and fear resulting from the initial lockdowns. Therefore, there were fewer reports for cyber and disinformation in May compared to March, as the situation was becoming more 'normalized' in May. In contrast, human rights reports were slightly higher in May compared to March, which is due to the fact that this follows the government responses to curb the spread of the virus as well as disinformation, which lagged the actual spread of the virus.

Figure 3 presents the percentage composition of the defensive IW themes, and Figure 4 presents the monthly distribution. Confidentiality and integrity form the bulk of the reports. Given the reports of cyber-attacks and scams, confidentiality is an obvious target as cyber-criminals attempt to gain access to account information, and reports of espionage attempts on vaccine research were also noticeable. Integrity is related more to the disinformation, where the activity was aimed at distorting human perception to either escalate fear or sway opinion in favour of certain countries; however, there were also reports of website defacements. Availability relates more to the ransomware or DDoS attacks which can affect operations or access to data. Of the human rights aspects, privacy was prevalent as these concerns were raised related to track and tracing and infection notifications, which many nations and organizations were implementing. Freedom of speech concerns only related to nations that were outlawing disinformation, sparking the debate; as these were in the minority, the freedom of speech discussion was limited.

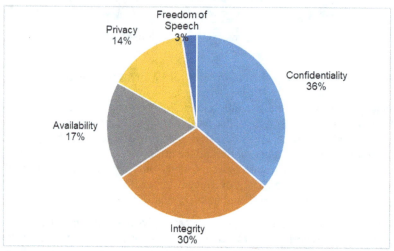

Figure 3: Percentage of defensive IW themes

In general, the monthly distribution follows the same trends as before, with the majority of reports falling in April and there being a decline in May. Freedom of speech is the main exception in that the only reports occurred in April, due to the attempts to outlaw disinformation in some countries. Availability has a higher occurrence in May compared to March; this can be attributed to changing in cyber-attack patterns. Integrity had a larger occurrence in March compared to the other themes, with a bigger reduction in prevalence in May. This can be explained by the initial surge in disinformation, which abated earlier that the other IW areas.

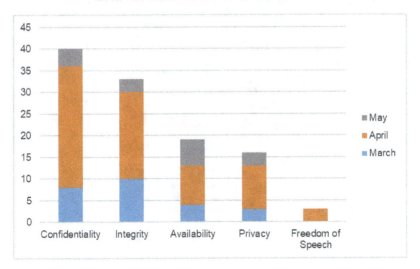

Figure 4: Number of occurrences for defensive IW themes per month

6.2 Offensive concepts

Figure 5 presents the percentage composition of the offensive IW themes, and Figure 6 presents the monthly distribution. The two prevalent themes are exploit/steal and corrupt/deceive. Exploit/steal aligns to the cyber-attacks such as scams and espionage (this relates to the defensive themes of confidentiality). Corrupt/deceive aligns more to the disinformation activity, but also to the website defacements, just as its defensive theme counterpart of integrity does. Disrupt/degrade and destroy/deny are relevant to availability, in particular the ransomware and DDoS attacks. There are no explicit offensive counterparts to the human rights concerns, thus the percentages do not correspond exactly. The monthly distribution of the offensive IW themes corresponds to those of their defensive IW counterparts.

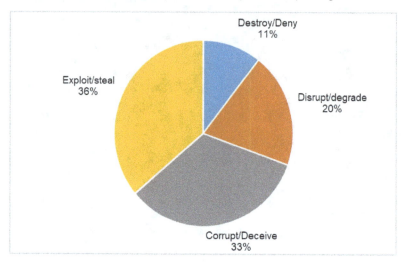

Figure 5: Percentage of Offensive IW Themes

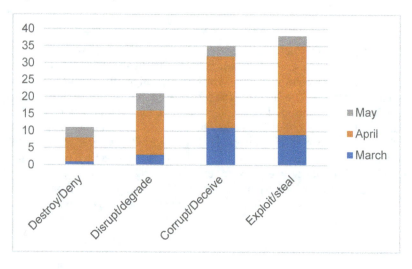

Figure 6: Number of Occurrences for Offensive IW Themes per month

6.3 Domains

Figure 7 presents the percentage composition of the IW domains, and Figure 8 presents the monthly distribution. As is evident from the figures, incidents that focused on the virtual domain were prevalent, followed by the cognitive domain. The same trends can be seen as before, with the majority of the reported incidents occurring in April, and the limited effects in the physical domain only occurred in April. The number of the cognitive domain incidents occurring in March was a greater than that of the virtual domain; this implies there was an initial surge in disinformation and/or social engineering scams, With the domains a single incident may contribute to multiple domains, for instance emails in the virtual domain are used to deliver social engineering in the cognitive domain, or misinformation is used to impact the physical domain due to protests.

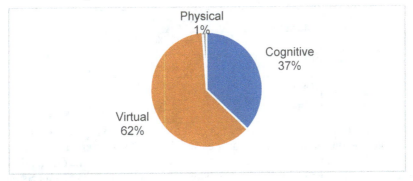

Figure 7: Percentage of IW Domains

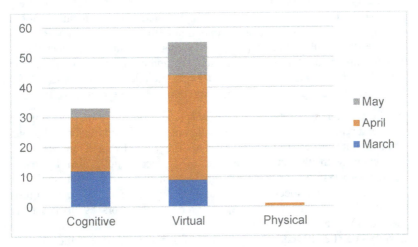

Figure 8: Number of Occurrences for IW Domains per Month

153

6.4 Prevalence of State Actions

Of the 89 documents considered, 16 related to actions by states, accounting for 18% of the total. This is not a large proportion of the reported events; however, this does not indicate the impact of the state actions. In addition, state actors could remain hidden amongst the noise generated by the non-state actors and ultimately remain undetected, and therefore are not reported. Table 3 illustrates the prevalence of state actions per month, showing a similar trend as above with a peak in April.

Table 3: Prevalence of state actions per month

Month	State actions	
	No	% of total
March	4	20
April	9	16,36
May	3	21,43

Table 4 indicates the prevalence of state information activity for the various categorisations of information warfare used above. The most prevalent relates to freedom of speech, with states enacting laws to criminalise the distribution of disinformation. Combining the freedom of speech with privacy aspects of state contact tracing of suspected infections makes human rights the most prevalent (in terms of percentage) IW area. However, it is evident that there were an equal number of reports of cyber activity and disinformation; although the prevalence of disinformation in terms of percentage of the total is more than double that for the cyber activities. Disinformation included apportioning blame for the origin of the virus and propaganda to enhance the nation's own reputation. Cyber activities included malicious code for surveillance and espionage activities targeting research facilities.

By comparison, non-state actors usually spread disinformation regarding the virus and remedies, or other needless attempts to cause confusion and panic. The non-state cyber activities made use of the existing fear as a lure, primarily for scams with the main objective of financial theft, also by using ransomware. As non-state actors do not implement broad laws, but their acts tend to target unsuspecting individuals or organisations, there is limited discussion on the human rights aspects on non-state actors, as this is usually viewed through the lens of criminality. However, ransomware attacks on hospitals can be viewed through the lens of human rights due to the potential implications.

Table 4: Prevalence of state actions for each IW theme

IW Theme		State actions	
		No	% of total
IW areas	Cyber	6	10,71
	Disinformation	6	28,57
	Human Rights	5	31,25
Defensive concepts	Confidentiality	6	15
	Integrity	6	18,18
	Availability	1	5,26
	Privacy	3	18,75
	Freedom of Speech	3	100
Offensive concepts	Destroy/Deny	0	0
	Disrupt/degrade	1	4,76
	Corrupt/Deceive	6	17,14
	Exploit/steal	6	15,79
IW Domains	Cognitive	7	21,21
	Virtual	6	10,91
	Physical	0	0

7 Discussion

A consistent trend visible amongst the data is a 'peak' of reported incidents in April, which is consistent with the views of Arsene (2020) and Muncaster (2020), who indicated that the incidents appeared to follow the rise in infections. This trend can be explained by malicious actors using the uncertainty surrounding the pandemic and the emerging sources of information as lures or points to create more panic, similar to the examples in literature of themed scams leveraging off disasters. The information attributes of timeliness and relevancy from Table 1 are applicable in that malicious actors are timely in terms of the events they are themed around (relevance); if the scams or disinformation are spread too late the effectiveness may be diminished due to the target population being alerted to check for scams and the legitimacy of information.

There appears to be a greater number of cyber-incidents reported by the new media compared to disinformation, and limited discussion on human rights. The differences do not necessarily indicate there were more cyber-incidents than disinformation, but rather that they were reported more. The difference can be accounted for due to the current 'hype' around cyber-attacks resulting in them receiving more attention, or that disinformation is designed to be more difficult to detect and most of it could go unnoticed or reside in private chats, so it is not publicly available.

Human rights concerns were raised with governments' responses rather than the actions of malicious actors. In particular there were privacy concerns over the track and trace applications and concerns over governments abusing legislation meant to curb disinformation. In contrast to this, it can be posited that disinformation is also a breach of human rights as it is degrading the safety and security of individuals and societies. In addition, cyber-incidents that affected confidentiality or hospitals did not raise equivalent discussion on human rights concerns. This could indicate a mistrust of governments and the effectiveness of their responses during the pandemic.

The offensive and defensive IW models illustrate more reports on exploit/steal affecting confidentiality, associated with cyber-incidents. Often the information quality of authenticity is applicable, as scams and incidents masquerade as a legitimate source. Actions taken to corrupt information or create deception (affecting integrity) are also prevalent. These relate to both disinformation as well as the social engineering techniques used in scams. Authenticity is again applicable, as is accuracy where the scams and disinformation have sufficient accuracy to be believable but lack key elements of truth. Ransomware attacks disrupt or degrade the use of information and affect availability; here the victims do not necessarily lose possession of the data, but they lose control as the data still resides on the machines, but it is inaccessible and at the mercy of the cyber-criminals.

State activity is limited in terms of quantity compared to the non-state activity. The apparent objectives differ, with states focussing on propaganda to place blame or enhance their image, conducting espionage on vaccine development or related medical research, or surveillance of their population using the pandemic information as a lure. Non-state activity constitutes general misinformation, scams and ransomware for financial gain. Non-state activity could potentially be increasing the 'noise', thereby allowing states to operate more effectively among the existing disinformation, scams and criminal cyber-incidents. The state activity appears more targeted based on the incident descriptions above, whereas the non-state activity was more indiscriminate. The categorisation of the various IW themes proved useful in comparing state activity to the non-state activity.

From the results obtained, the IW models can be seen to be relevant and a suitable basis with which to classify the reported malicious online activity during the pandemic. The categories of the models can adequately describe the techniques and/or effects of the malicious actions. Where this research was exploratory to assess the suitability of the models and the prevalence of reported malicious activity, it did not delve into the reasons for the trends and is proposed for future work.

8   Conclusions

As infections of the novel coronavirus began to rise in 2020 and a pandemic was declared, a wave of scams, cyber-incidents, and disinformation became evident. This chapter has described exploratory research using information warfare models to assess the prevalence of reported techniques employed by malicious actors during the early months of the pandemic. The results support the views that the malicious actions 'followed' the infections and national 'lock-downs'. More reports focused on cyber-incidents than on disinformation and propaganda related activities. Related to this, the reported techniques focused on the theft of confidential information, followed by the use of deception in scams and disinformation. Some cyber-incidents, particularly ransomware, affected the availability of data. While some human rights concerns were raised, these focused more on government responses than the malicious actions themselves. State activity was limited in terms of numbers of reports, with a different focus; however, states did actively participate in IW activities during the pandemic. These activities included propaganda, surveillance and espionage. The IW models proved suitable to classify the reports, and to investigate the prevalence and objectives of state activities compared to non-state activity. Future work can focus on more in-depth reasons for the difference in reporting quantities, and more sources over a greater time frame will provide greater insight into the trends of online malicious activity during the pandemic.

References

Adams, R.D. (2020, April 14) Balancing public safety and privacy during COVID-19: The rise of mass surveillance, TechRepublic. [online]
https://www.techrepublic.com/article/balancing-public-safety-and-privacy-during-covid-19-the-rise-of-mass-surveillance/

Allen-Ebrahimian, B. (2020, April 1) Bots boost Chinese propaganda hashtags in Italy, Axios. [online] https://www.axios.com/bots-chinese-propaganda-hashtags-italy-cf92c5a3-cdcb-4a08-b8c1-2061ca4254e2.html

Arsene, L. (2020, April 30) Coronavirus-themed Threat Reports Haven't Flattened The Curve, Bitdefender. [online] https://labs.bitdefender.com/2020/04/coronavirus-themed-threat-reports-havent-flattened-the-curve/

Asokan, A. (2020, April 25) WHO Reports 'Dramatic' Increase in Cyberattacks, BankInfoSecurity.com. [online] https://www.bankinfosecurity.com/who-reports-dramatic-increase-in-cyberattacks-a-14184

Barth, B. (2020, March 18) Spyware disguised as COVID-19 tracker app actually keeps track of users, SC Magazine. [online] https://www.scmagazine.com/home/security-news/mobile-security/spyware-disguised-as-covid-19-tracker-app-actually-keeps-track-of-users/

Brattberg, E., and Le Corre, P. (2020, April 15) No, COVID-19 Isn't Turning Europe Pro-China (Yet), The Diplomat. [online] https://thediplomat.com/2020/04/no-covid-19-isnt-turning-europe-pro-china-yet/

Brazzoli, M. S. (2007) Future Prospects of Information Warfare and Particularly Psychological Operations, In L. le Roux, South African Army Vision 2020 (pp. 217-232). Institute for Security Studies.

Brewster, M. (2020, March 24) All-volunteer cyber civil defence brigade assembles to fight COVID-19 hackers, CBC News. [online] https://www.cbc.ca/news/politics/covid19-cyber-companies-1.5508570

Cilliers, C. (2020, April 12) SABC warns that tweet about alcohol being sold from Monday is fake, The Citizen. [online] https://citizen.co.za/news/south-africa/social-media/2268341/sabc-warns-that-tweet-about-alcohol-being-sold-from-monday-is-fake/

Cimpanu, C. (2020a, March 13) Czech hospital hit by cyberattack while in the midst of a COVID-19 outbreak, Zero Day. [online] https://www.zdnet.com/article/czech-hospital-hit-by-cyber-attack-while-in-the-midst-of-a-covid-19-outbreak/

Cimpanu, C. (2020b, May 13) US formally accuses China of hacking US entities working on COVID-19 research, Zero Day. [online] https://www.zdnet.com/article/us-formally-accuses-china-of-hacking-us-entities-working-on-covid-19-research/

CISOMag (2020, March 27) Hackers Attack Database of India's COVID-19 Patients and Potential Suspects. [online] https://www.cisomag.com/hackers-attack-database-of-indias-covid-19-patients-and-potential-suspects/

Culafi, A. (2020, April 6) Zoom takes new security measures to counter 'Zoombombing', TechTarget. [online] https://searchsecurity.techtarget.com/news/252481257/Zoom-takes-new-security-measures-to-counter-Zoombombing

De Villiers, J. (2020, April 8) WhatsApp group admins may be criminally liable for fake news in SA – under these conditions, Business Insider. [online] https://www.businessinsider.co.za/whatsapp-group-admins-may-be-criminally-liable-for-fake-news-in-sa-under-these-conditions-2020-4

De Wet, P. (2020a, March 27) SA expects WhatsApp to 'immediately' remove fake coronavirus news under new rules, Business Insider. [online] https://www.businessinsider.co.za/ott-fake-news-rules-against-coronavirus-for-whatsapp-2020-3

De Wet, P. (2020b, April 20) The govt can now track cellphone locations back to 5 March: how Covid-19 tracing will work, Business Insider. [online] https://www.businessinsider.co.za/covid-19-cellphone-tracking-rules-in-south-africa-for-contact-tracing-2020-4

Del Rosso, K. (2020, April 15) Nation-state Mobile Malware Targets Syrians with COVID-19 Lures, Lookout.com. [online] https://blog.lookout.com/nation-state-mobile-malware-targets-syrians-with-covid-19-lures

Denning, D. E. (1999) Information Warfare and Security. Addison-Wesley.

Desai, T.L. (2020) 9,100 coronavirus-themed cyberattacks in India between Feb 2-May 2, YourStory.com. [online] https://yourstory.com/2020/05/9100-coronavirus-themed-cyberattacks-india-microsoft

Doffman, Z. (2019, June 23) U.S. Attacks Iran With Cyber Not Missiles -- A Game Changer, Not A Backtrack, Forbes. [online] https://www.forbes.com/sites/zakdoffman/2019/06/23/u-s-attacks-iran-with-cyber-not-missiles-a-game-changer-not-a-backtrack/#3970a285753f.

Elsworthy, E. (2020, February 7) Hundreds of bushfire donation scams circulating — how to tell if you've been duped, ABC News. [online] https://www.abc.net.au/news/2020-02-07/australia-fires-sees-spike-in-fraudster-behaviour/11923174.

Estes, A.C. and Ghaffary, S. (2020, April 10) Apple and Google want to turn your phone into a Covid-tracking machine, Vox. [online] https://www.vox.com/recode/2020/4/10/21216675/apple-google-covid-coronavirus-contact-tracing-app

European Centre for Disease Prevention and Control. (2020) Situation update worldwide, as of 17 April 2020 [online] https://www.ecdc.europa.eu/en/geographical-distribution-2019-ncov-cases.

Feiner, L. (2020, April 6) NYC education department tells principals to stop using Zoom, citing privacy concerns, CNBC. [online] https://www.cnbc.com/2020/04/06/nyc-doe-tells-principals-to-switch-from-zoom-to-google-and-microsoft.html

Friedman, U. (2020, March 27) The Coronavirus-Denial Movement Now Has a Leader, The Atlantic. [online] https://www.theatlantic.com/politics/archive/2020/03/bolsonaro-coronavirus-denial-brazil-trump/608926/

Gallagher, R. (2020, April 21) Hackers Target Top Officials at World Health Organization, Bloomberg. [online] https://www.bloomberg.com/amp/news/articles/2020-04-21/top-officials-at-world-health-organization-targeted-for-hacks

Geddie, J. (2020, April 10) Singapore stops teachers using Zoom app after 'very serious incidents', Reuters. [online] https://www.reuters.com/article/us-zoom-video-comm-privacy-singapore/singapore-stops-teachers-using-zoom-app-after-very-serious-incidents-idUSKCN21S0AH

Gerber, J. (2020, April 22) Defence committee to report Steenhuisen to speaker for tweeting SANDF deployment letter, News24. [online] https://www.news24.com/SouthAfrica/News/defence-committee-to-report-steenhuisen-to-speaker-for-tweeting-sandf-deployment-letter-20200422

Glez, D. (2020, March 17) Top 10 coronavirus fake news items, The Africa Report. [online] https://www.theafricareport.com/24698/top-10-coronavirus-fake-news-items/

Gold, H. (2020, April 6) YouTube tries to limit spread of false 5G coronavirus claims after cellphone towers attacked, CNN. [online] https://edition.cnn.com/2020/04/06/tech/5g-coronavirus-conspiracy/index.html

Higginbotham, S. (2020, May 8) Tracking COVID-19 With the IoT May Put Your Privacy at Risk, IEEE Spectrum. [online] https://spectrum.ieee.org/telecom/security/tracking-covid19-with-the-iot-may-put-your-privacy-at-risk

Hochschild, F. (2020, April 10) To fight Covid-19, cyberattacks worldwide must stop immediately, Vox.com. [online] https://www.vox.com/world/2020/4/10/21216477/coronavirus-covid-19-pandemic-cyberattacks-digital-ceasefire-who-hack-united-nations

Hodgson, T.F., Farise, K., and Mavedzenge, J. (2020, April 5) Southern Africa has cracked down on fake news, but may have gone too far, Mail&Guardian. [online] https://mg.co.za/analysis/2020-04-05-southern-africa-has-cracked-down-on-fake-news-but-may-have-gone-too-far/

Hutchinson, W., & Warren, M. (2001) Information Warfare: Corporate Attack and Defense in a Digital World. Butterworth Heinemann.

Interpol (2020, April 4) Cybercriminals targeting critical healthcare institutions with ransomware. [online] https://www.interpol.int/en/News-and-Events/News/2020/Cybercriminals-targeting-critical-healthcare-institutions-with-ransomware

Jordaan, N. (2020, April 3) Digital tech used to trace Covid-19 patients should not step on human rights: Amnesty International, Times Live. [online] https://www.timeslive.co.za/news/south-africa/2020-04-03-digital-tech-used-to-trace-covid-19-patients-should-not-step-on-human-rights-amnesty-international/

Kao, J., and Li, M.S. (2020, March 26) How China Built a Twitter Propaganda Machine Then Let It Loose on Coronavirus, ProPublica. [online] https://www.propublica.org/article/how-china-built-a-twitter-propaganda-machine-then-let-it-loose-on-coronavirus

Lakshmanan, R. (2020, April 20) COVID-Themed Lures Target SCADA Sectors With Data Stealing Malware, The Hacker News. [online] https://thehackernews.com/2020/04/coronavirus-scada-malware.html

Le Roux, J. (2020, April 17) Wild Covid-19 rumours peddled by fringe political party, Daily Maverick. [online] https://www.dailymaverick.co.za/article/2020-04-17-wild-covid-19-rumours-peddled-by-fringe-political-party/

Lopatka, J., and Muller, R. (2020, April 17) Czech hospitals report cyberattacks day after national watchdog's warning, Reuters. [online] https://www.reuters.com/article/us-czech-cyber-ostrava/czech-hospitals-report-cyberattacks-day-after-national-watchdogs-warning-idUSKBN21Z1OH

Mahlakoana, T. (2020, March 23) SANDF Instructed to be 'Battle Ready' for Coronavirus, Eye Witness News. [online] https://ewn.co.za/2020/03/23/sandf-instructed-to-be-battle-ready-for-coronavirus

Matthews, K. (2020, March 27) Incident of the Week: Health and Human Services Hit with Security Breach, CSHub. [online] https://www.cshub.com/attacks/articles/incident-of-the-week-iotw-health-and-human-services-hit-with-security-breach

McCabe, A., Ray, V., and Cortes, J. (2020, April 14) Malicious Attackers Target Government and Medical Organizations with COVID-19 Themed Phishing Campaigns, Palo Alto Networks. [online] https://unit42.paloaltonetworks.com/covid-19-themed-cyber-attacks-target-government-and-medical-organizations/

McCarthy, T. (2020, April 14) 'It will disappear': the disinformation Trump spread about the coronavirus – timeline, The Guardian. [online] https://www.theguardian.com/us-news/2020/apr/14/trump-coronavirus-alerts-disinformation-timeline

McDonald-Gibson, C. (2020, March 26) 'Right Now, People Are Pretty Fragile.' How Coronavirus Creates the Perfect Breeding Ground for Online Extremism, Time. [online] https://time.com/5810774/extremist-groups-coronavirus/

Mecer, W., Rascagneres, P., and Ventura, V. (2020, April 16) PoetRAT: Python RAT uses COVID-19 lures to target Azerbaijan public and private sectors, Talos. [online] https://blog.talosintelligence.com/2020/04/poetrat-covid-19-lures.html

Mehta, I. (2020, April 3) Zoom is a godforsaken mess — but it can be fixed, The Next Web. [online] https://thenextweb.com/security/2020/04/03/zoom-is-a-godforsaken-mess-but-it-can-be-fixed/

Menn. J., Bing, C., Satter, R., and Stubbs, J. (2020, April 2) Exclusive: Hackers linked to Iran target WHO staff emails during coronavirus – sources, Reuters. [online] https://www.reuters.com/article/us-health-coronavirus-cyber-iran-exclusi/exclusive-hackers-linked-to-iran-target-who-staff-emails-during-coronavirus-sources-idUSKBN21K1RC

Montalbano, E. (2020a, April 1) Top Email Protections Fail in Latest COVID-19 Phishing Campaign, ThreatPost.com. [online] https://threatpost.com/top-email-protections-fail-covid-19-phishing/154329/

Montalbano, E. (2020b, April 3) Spearphishing Campaign Exploits COVID-19 To Spread Lokibot Infostealer, ThreatPost.com. [online] https://threatpost.com/spearphishing-campaign-exploits-covid-19-to-spread-lokibot-infostealer/154432/

Montalbano, E. (2020c, April 8) WhatsApp Axes COVID-19 Mass Message Forwarding, ThreatPost.com. [online] https://threatpost.com/whatsapp-covid-19-mass-message-forwarding/154563/

Montalbano, E. (2020d, April 15) PPE, COVID-19 Medical Supplies Targeted by BEC Scams, ThreatPost.com. [online] https://threatpost.com/ppe-covid-19-medical-supplies-bec-scams/154806/

Montalbano, E. (2020e, April 29) EFF: Google, Apple's Contact-Tracing System Open to Cyberattacks, ThreatPost.com. [online] https://threatpost.com/google-apple-contact-tracing-system-cyberattacks/155287/

Monzon, L. (2020, April 21) Hackers Attacked Businesses 22 Million Times In The Last 7 Days Globally, ITNews Africa. [online] https://www.itnewsafrica.com/2020/04/hackers-attacked-businesses-22-million-times-in-the-last-7-days-globally/

Moyo, T. (2020, April 9) Covid-19 and the suppression of freedom of expression, Daily Maverick. [online] https://www.dailymaverick.co.za/article/2020-04-09-covid-19-and-the-suppression-of-freedom-of-expression-part-two/

Muncaster, P. (2020, May 15) Attacks on Banks Spike 238% During #COVID19 Crisis, Infosecurity Magazine. [online] https://www.infosecurity-magazine.com/news/attacks-on-banks-spike-238-during/

O'Donnell, L. (2020a, March 17) APT36 Taps Coronavirus as 'Golden Opportunity' to Spread Crimson RAT, ThreatPost.com. [online] https://threatpost.com/apt36-taps-coronavirus-as-golden-opportunity-to-spread-crimson-rat/153776/

O'Donnell, L. (2020b, March 23) Fake Coronavirus 'Vaccine' Website Busted in DoJ Takedown, ThreatPost.com. [online] https://threatpost.com/fake-coronavirus-vaccine-website-busted-in-doj-takedown/154031/

O'Donnell, L. (2020c, March 31) Covid-19 Poll Results: One in Four Prioritize Health Over Privacy, ThreatPost.com. [online] https://threatpost.com/covid-19-poll-results-one-in-four-prioritize-health-over-privacy/154218/

O'Donnell, L. (2020d, April 10) Compromised Zoom Credentials Swapped in Underground Forums, ThreatPost.com. [online] https://threatpost.com/compromised-zoom-credentials-underground-forums/154616/

O'Donnell, L. (2020e, April 17) Zoom Bombing Attack Hits U.S. Government Meeting, ThreatPost.com. [online] https://threatpost.com/zoom-bombing-attack-hits-u-s-government-meeting/154903/

O'Halloran, J. (2020, April 14) WHO wades into UK fake 5G Covid-19 links as regulator probes leading broadcaster, Computer Weekly. [online] https://www.computerweekly.com/news/252481569/WHO-wades-into-UK-fake-5G-Covid-19-links-as-regulator-probes-leading-broadcaster

O'Neill, P.H. (2020, March 12) Chinese hackers and others are exploiting coronavirus fears for cyber espionage, TechnologyReview.com. [online] https://www.technologyreview.com/s/615346/chinese-hackers-and-others-are-exploiting-coronavirus-fears-for-cyberespionage/

Olson, R. (2020, March 24) Don't Panic: COVID-19 Cyber Threats, Palo Alto Networks. [online] https://unit42.paloaltonetworks.com/covid19-cyber-threats/

Osborne, C. (2020, May 7) Major European private hospital operator struck by ransomware, Zero Day. [online] https://www.zdnet.com/article/europes-largest-private-hospital-chain-struck-by-ransomware-attack/

Palmer, D. (2020, April 8) Hackers are scanning for vulnerable VPNs in order to launch attacks against remote workers, ZDNet. [online] https://www.zdnet.com/article/hackers-are-scanning-for-vulnerable-vpns-in-order-to-launch-attacks-against-remote-workers/

Parker, D. B. (2002) Toward a New Framework for Information Security. In S. Bosworth, & M. E. Kabay (Eds.), Computer Security Handbook, 4th Edition (pp. 5·1-5·19). John Wiley and Sons.

Perrigo, B. (2020, April 16) Facebook Is Notifying Users Who Have Shared Coronavirus Misinformation. Could It Do the Same for Politics? Time. [online] https://time.com/5822372/facebook-coronavirus-misinformation/

Pfleeger, P., & Pfleeger, S. (2003) Security in Computing, 3rd Edition. Prentice Hall.

Poisel, R. A. (2004) Modern Communications Jamming Principles and Techniques. Artech House.

Prior, B. (2020, April 16) Hackers are selling Zoom zero-day exploits for over R9 million – Report, MyBroadband.com. [online] https://mybroadband.co.za/news/security/347907-hackers-are-selling-zoom-zero-day-exploits-for-over-r9-million-report.html

Ramluckan, T., and van Niekerk, B. (2009). The Terrorism/Mass Media Symbiosis, Journal of Information Warfare, 8(2), 1-12.

Samuels, S. (2020, March 22) NSFAS Warns Against Fake Social Media Posts, CareersPortal. [online] https://www.careersportal.co.za/finance/nsfas-warns-against-fake-social-media-posts

Scroxton, A. (2020a, April 14) Coronavirus: Zoom user credentials for sale on dark web, Computer Weekly. [online] https://www.computerweekly.com/news/252481427/Coronavirus-Zoom-user-credentials-for-sale-on-dark-web

Scroxton, A. (2020b, April 22) NCSC overwhelmed by response to coronavirus campaign, Computer Weekly. [online] https://www.computerweekly.com/news/252481999/NCSC-overwhelmed-by-response-to-coronavirus-campaign

Scroxton, A. (2020c, May 7) NCSC Covid-19 scam reporting service sees more than 160,000 reports, Computer Weekly. [online] https://www.computerweekly.com/news/252482790/NCSC-Covid-19-scam-reporting-service-sees-more-than-160000-reports

Scroxton, A. (2020d, May 7) Contact-tracing app fails to protect privacy and human rights, Computer Weekly. [online] https://www.computerweekly.com/news/252482805/Contact-tracing-app-fails-to-protect-privacy-and-human-rights

Scroxton, A. (2020e, May 19) GDPR wholly inappropriate to govern contact-tracing data, Computer Weekly. [online] https://www.computerweekly.com/news/252483355/GDPR-wholly-inappropriate-to-govern-contact-tracing-data

Scroxton, A. (2020f, May 20) NCSC discloses multiple vulnerabilities in contact-tracing app, Computer Weekly. [online] https://www.computerweekly.com/news/252483418/NCSC-discloses-multiple-vulnerabilities-in-contact-tracing-app

Seals, T. (2020, May 18) Ransomware Gang Arrested for Spreading Locky to Hospitals, ThreatPost.com. [online] https://threatpost.com/ransomware-gang-arrested-locky-hospitals/155842/

Seitz, A. (2020, May 11) Twitter to Label COVID-19 Tweets That Make Disputed or Misleading Claims, Time. [online] https://time.com/5835418/twitter-covid-19-misleading-tweets/

Selisho, K. (2020a, April 8) DA wants Lesufi's head for R30m cyber security tender, The Citizen. [online] https://citizen.co.za/news/south-africa/politics/2266849/da-wants-lesufis-head-for-r30m-cyber-security-tender/

Selisho, K. (2020b, May 7) Hacker's hurl racial abuse at Thandi Modise during virtual meeting, The Citizen. [online] https://citizen.co.za/news/south-africa/politics/2280325/hackers-hurl-racial-abuse-at-thandi-modise-during-virtual-meeting/

Sheridan, K. (2020, April 20) Stimulus Payments Are Popular Leverage for Cyberattacks, DarkReading.com. [online] https://www.darkreading.com/threat-intelligence/stimulus-payments-are-popular-leverage-for-cyberattacks/d/d-id/1337601

Singletary, M. (2015, November 19) After the Paris attacks, an opening for scam artists, Washington Post. [online] https://www.washingtonpost.com/news/get-there/wp/2015/11/19/an-attack-by-scam-artists-following-the-paris-attacks/.

Skelton, S.K., (2020, May 13) Government tells social media companies they must go further to address disinformation, Computer Weekly. [online] https://www.computerweekly.com/news/252483063/Government-tells-social-media-companies-they-must-do-more-to-address-disinformation

Staff Reporter. (2020, April 11) Criminals use names of popular social meeting applications to distribute cyber-threats, IOL. [online] https://www.iol.co.za/technology/software-and-internet/criminals-use-names-of-popular-social-meeting-applications-to-distribute-cyber-threats-46490802

Staff Writer. (2020, April 8) Here is all the personal information government is using to track South Africans during the lockdown, BusinessTech. [online] https://businesstech.co.za/news/technology/388391/here-is-all-the-personal-information-government-is-using-to-track-south-africans-during-the-lockdown/

Steinmetz, K. (2020, March 26) You've Tested Positive for COVID-19. Who Has a Right to Know? Time. [online] https://time.com/5810231/covid19-sharing-positive-result/

Stengel, R. (2019) Information Wars: How We Lost the Global Battle Against Disinformation and What We Can Do About It. Grove Press.

Swan, B.W. (2020, April 21) State report: Russian, Chinese and Iranian disinformation narratives echo one another, Politico. [online] https://www.politico.com/news/2020/04/21/russia-china-iran-disinformation-coronavirus-state-department-193107

Szurdi, J., Chen, Z., Starov, O., McCabe, A., and Duan, R. (2020, April 22) Studying How Cybercriminals Prey on the COVID-19 Pandemic, Palo Alto Networks. [online] https://unit42.paloaltonetworks.com/how-cybercriminals-prey-on-the-covid-19-pandemic/

The Economic Times. (2020, March 29) John Hopkins varsity disassociates from study on India's possible COVID-19 cases, India Times. [online] https://economictimes.indiatimes.com/news/politics-and-nation/john-hopkins-varsity-disassociates-from-study-on-indias-possible-covid-19-cases/articleshow/74872298.cms

United Nations. (1948, December 10) Universal Declaration of Human Rights, General Assembly resolution 217 A.

van der Merwe, P. (2020, March 26) Unprecedented spike in cyber attacks since declaration of national disaster, TimesLive. [online] https://www.timeslive.co.za/news/south-africa/2020-03-26-unprecedented-spike-in-cyber-attacks-since-declaration-of-national-disaster/

van Niekerk, B. (2018). Information Warfare as a Continuation of Politics: An Analysis of Cyber Incidents, 2018 Conference on Information Communications Technology and Society (ICTAS). [online] https://ieeexplore.ieee.org/document/8368758.

Vermeulen, J. (2021, July 19) Committing high treason using WhatsApp in South Africa — what the law says, MyBroadband.com. [online] https://mybroadband.co.za/news/security/406512-committing-high-treason-using-whatsapp-in-south-africa-what-the-law-says.html

Vijayan, J. (2020a, April 22) Domain Registrars Under Pressure to Combat COVID-19-Related Scams, DarkReading.com. [online] https://www.darkreading.com/vulnerabilities---threats/domain-registrars-under-pressure-to-combat-covid-19-related-scams/d/d-id/1337616

Vijayan, J. (2020b, April 24) WHO Confirms Email Credentials Leak, DarkReading.com. Retrieved from https://www.darkreading.com/attacks-breaches/who-confirms-email-credentials-leak/d/d-id/1337650

Walcott, J. (2020, April 9) Foreign Spies Are Targeting Americans on Zoom and Other Video Chat Platforms, U.S. Intel Officials Say, Time. [online] https://time.com/5818851/spies-target-americans-zoom-others/

Waldman, A. (2020a, April 3) Microsoft warns hospitals of impending ransomware attacks, TechTarget.com. [online] https://searchsecurity.techtarget.com/news/252481164/Microsoft-warns-hospitals-of-impending-ransomware-attacks

Waldman, A. (2020b, April 15) Malware found on 45 percent of home office networks, TechTarget.com. [online] https://searchsecurity.techtarget.com/news/252481642/Malware-found-on-45-percent-of-home-office-networks

Waldman, A. (2020c, May 11) Volunteers join forces to tackle COVID-19 security threats, TechTarget.com. [online] https://searchsecurity.techtarget.com/news/252482930/Volunteers-join-forces-to-tackle-COVID-19-security-threats

Waltz, E. (1998) Information Warfare: Principles and Operations. Artech House.

Wardle, C., and Derakhshan, H. (2018) Thinking about 'Information Disorder': Formats of Misinformation, Disinformation, and Mal-Information, In: Ireton, C. and Posetti, J., Journalism, 'Fake News' & Disinformation (pp. 44-56). United Nations Educational, Scientific and Cultural Organization.

Whittaker, Z. (2020, April 8) Zoom sued by shareholder for 'overstating' security claims, TechCrunch. [online] https://techcrunch.com/2020/04/08/zoom-sued-shareholder-security/

World Health Organization. (2020) Rolling updates on coronavirus disease (COVID-19) [online]. https://www.who.int/emergencies/diseases/novel-coronavirus-2019/events-as-they-happen.

Zetter, K. (2014, November 3) An Unprecedented Look at Stuxnet, the World's First Digital Weapon, Wired. [online] https://www.wired.com/2014/11/countdown-to-zero-day-stuxnet/

Author biographies

Dr Brett van Niekerk is a senior lecturer in IT at the Durban University of Technology in South Africa. He serves as chair for the International Federation of Information Processing Working Group on ICT in Peace and War, and is co-Editor-in-Chief of the International Journal of Cyber Warfare and Terrorism. He has numerous years of information/cyber-security experience in both academia and industry, and has contributed to the ISO/IEC information security standards. In 2012 he graduated with his PhD focusing on information operations and critical infrastructure protection. He also holds a MSC in electronic engineering and is CISM certified.

Dr Trishana Ramluckan is the Research Manager at Educor Holdings and an Honorary Research Fellow at the University of KwaZulu-Natal's School of Law in South Africa. Prior to this she was Postdoctoral Researcher in the School of Law and an Adjunct Lecturer in the Graduate School of Business at the University of KwaZulu-Natal. She is a member of the IFIP working group on ICT Uses in Peace and War and is an Academic Advocate for ISACA. She is also the Editor-in- Chief of the Educor Multidisciplinary Journal (EMJ). In 2017 she graduated with a Doctor of Administration specialising in IT and Public Governance and in 2020 she was listed in the Top 50 Women in Cybersecurity in Africa. Her current research areas include Cyber Law and Information Technology Governance.

Chapter Seven

Joint All-Domain Command and Control and Information Warfare: A Conceptual Model of Warfighting

Joshua Sipper

Air Force Cyber College, Air University, Montgomery, USA

jasipper@gmail.com

Abstract: A riot of change strategically and operationally has erupted within the joint force, drawing in two powerful concepts: joint all-domain operations (JADO) and information warfare (IW). With renewed emphasis on IW with the cyber-enabled construct including the consequential information related capabilities (IRC) of information operations (IO), intelligence, surveillance, and reconnaissance (ISR), and electromagnetic warfare (EW), and a cross-cutting requirement for joint all-domain command and control (JADC2), the joint force is on the cusp of a significant strategic shift. This chapter and its discussion explored linkages between IW and JADC2, explain how IW benefits and enables JADC2, and presents a conceptual model detailing how IW and JADC2 can work together to produce operational effects and advance US strategic interests now and into the future.

Keywords: cyber operations, information warfare, intelligence, information operations, electronic warfare

1 Introduction

The explosion of capabilities available through technology and the IRCs it drives has become a virtual juggernaut within the auspices of modern warfare theory and practice. IW as a strategic construct has emerged in the twenty-first century as an important way forward in the ongoing struggle of great power competition, especially between the US and China. The IW paradigm is characterized by its four IRCs: cyber operations (CO), ISR, IO, and EW, providing a power scaffold on which to hang and matrix multiple methods of interdisciplinary control methodologies for producing effects across domains and battlespaces. This ability to reach into and across capabilities and domains makes IW a strong foundational strategy for enacting, supporting, and driving the JADC2 operational structure.

The following analysis will begin with a structural examination and aggregation of JADC2 to get a clearer view of the strategic and operational concepts undergirding the construct. Following the JADC2 analysis, the elements of IW will be explored related to how IW affects and is affected by JADC2. The combinatory power of elements will be discussed as well as how each element provides C2 capability and functionality across the joint domains. Finally, a conceptual model will be introduced, detailing IW IRCs and JADC2 interoperability.

2 JADC2 structure and character

Over the centuries, the military profusion and might of the US has grown from a land-centric militia to an army of massive proportions, a privateer sea force to one of global, naval omnipresence, and from balloons used for simple intelligence collection to an air force that controls skies from the ionosphere to the ground. Now, out of the air force, a space force has emerged, furthering the US reach and capabilities beyond the horizon; indeed outside the Earth itself. Finally, with the elevation of cyberspace to domain status, all of the aforementioned domains have only increased in power, influence, and reach. This short history is a picture of the individual elements seen across the world today by enemies and allies alike, but it is not the end of the story. Now, the US military has embarked upon an historical fusion of these domains and the services that oversee and operate within them. "[W]e must integrate our advantages across these domains in new and dramatically effective ways. Linking operations moving at the speed of light with operations moving at the speed of sound requires we bring it all together" (Goldfein, 2018). Through the interleaving of these domains and the force power associated with them, capabilities can be leveraged to produce battlespace effects exponentially greater than they would be individually.

A great deal of the effects sought through JADC2 have to do with the fact that great power competitors like Russia and China have powerfully employed anti-access/area denial (A2/AD) strategies with significant effects. While Russia projects A2/AD into eastern European countries, historically known for Russian ties, China as extended its reach into Taiwan, North Korea, and numerous other Pacific theater regions. "The four Armed Services … agree that they must conduct operations in all domains, land, sea, air, space and cyber. They even are in general agreement on the initial objective for the Joint Force in such a conflict. This is to penetrate and disintegrate an adversary's layered and networked arrays of anti-access and area-denial (A2/AD) systems by conducting rapid and coordinated attacks across all domains" (Goure, 2019). Through the aggregation of capabilities amounted in the service elements and domains, effects to counter strategies like A2/AD can be vastly improved.

JADC2 efforts are progressing rapidly across the services with joint exercises underway. Major General Paul Chamberlain confirmed that the Army would be participating in the Air Force's second JADC2 exercise to be held in April but was still determining what their role would be. "[We are waiting for] the development of the Joint warfighting concept, and then we will figure out how we will plug into that" (Underwood, 2020). With training and joint doctrine development moving forward rapidly, the opportunity for bringing capabilities together across all domains is quickly becoming a reality. In fact, the army has already designed the concept (see Figure 1, TRADOC, 2018) with some interesting outcomes. Through the use of integrated capabilities across the domains, power projection of the joint force can drive farther into adversary physical and virtual battlespaces with 1. Competition, 2. Penetration, 3. Dis-integration, 4. Exploitation, and 5. Re-competition.

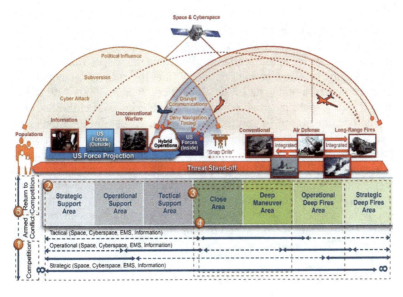

Figure 1: JADO Concept

Another vitally important consideration toward the development of a JADC2 strategy and capability is a system designed for the seamless integration of capabilities to enable and create battlefield effects. "The Air Force recently requested $US435 million for the Advanced Battle Management System

(ABMS), the leading technical solution to the problem of Joint All Domain Command and Control (JADC2)" (Dwyer, 2020). With systems being designed specifically for JADC2 implementation, the opportunity for bringing the domains together is even more of a reality. Of course, the integration of these systems is only possible through the use of IRCs and technical capabilities which include the IW construct to be discussed.

The recently signed Air Force JADO Doctrine Note 1-20 offers further advancement of the JADO/JADC2 concepts. As mentioned above, the Army is working closely with the Air Force concerning JADO and the joint concepts that will grow out of this ground-breaking strategic formula. "JADO requires an approach that evolves continuously to take advantage of opportunities as they arise and present a flexible, responsive defense" (Goldfein, 2020). Together, with the capabilities offered through IW, this flexibility and responsiveness can be leveraged to control all domains and exert joint force power at a level many orders of magnitude greater than each strategic concept alone.

General John Hyten gives a solid and penetrating look at what JADO is and what it can do for the US joint force. "All-Domain Operations…combines 'space, cyber, deterrent, transportation, electromagnetic spectrum operations, missile defense — all of these global capabilities together … to compete with a global competitor and at all levels of conflict'" (Clark, 2020). This kind of flexibility and capability, coupled with the capabilities and flexibilities of IW offer an even greater push into the physical and virtual, information spaces of adversaries, making it possible for the joint force to map out and control information and actions in increasingly contested and congested environments. "[I]f we figure that out, we'll have a significant advantage over everybody in the world for a long time" (Clark, 2020). JADO strategy is decidedly not a passing idea, but a persistent and necessary addition to the joint force arsenal of strategies and capabilities; one that can be further enabled through the use of IW and the combined effects (see Figure 2, Orye & Maennel, 2019) and strategies offered there.

3 IW IRC Elements and Interoperability

Although the IRCs of ISR, EW, and IO have been available and in use for most of the 20th century and forward, cyber is the latest on the scene and yet the capability that ties the rest of the IRCs together. This unusual placement of an IRC in the company and annals of traditional IRCs makes cyber not only an intriguing field, but a true icon in its classification.

Joshua Sipper

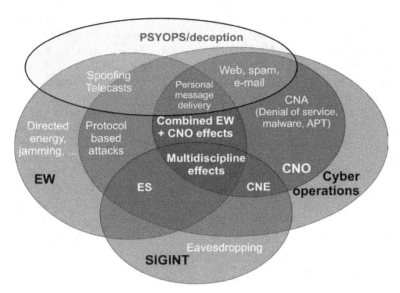

Figure 2: IW and Combined Effects

When it comes to capability maturity, cyber is definitely a candidate, yet also an ever-growing IRC. This fact simultaneously makes cyber a powerful tool, a dangerous weapon, and an unbridled and sometimes unpredictable IRC. With this image in mind, we must understand the power of such a tool and how, as it ties the other IRCs together through networks, communications, and other technological and infrastructure enablement, cyber is also a delicate and powerful tool.

Cyber, especially in the US collection of IRCs is a capability unmatched by any other power in the world. "US skills at cyberwar have no equal. US institutions lead the world in the commercialized arts of persuasion, and the collection and analysis of personal information for commercial and political purposes have proceeded farther in the United States than anywhere else. No country is more advanced in digitizing and networking things" (Libicki, 2017). This is also relevant in relation to cyber capability across the spectrum of not only warfare, but industry, banking and other important Critical Infrastructure (CI) umbrellas. "The use of cyber assets has been a form of force projection that helps initiate crises far ahead of and beyond the frontlines, creating forms of more complex crises that affect energy infrastructure, banking systems, and political leadership, and not solely the armed forces fighting on the frontlines. Again, the extension of traditional military conflict is not a new strategy, but new technologies have been able to provide both the means and vulnerabilities to allow such operations at a scale not often witnessed before, and with a smaller investment in resources on the part of the aggressor" (Danyk, et. al., 2017). It is evident that cyber has found its way into basically every area of life and it shows no sign of stopping. This is also evident in the fact that cyber has been established as a domain, specific to its own capabilities and effects within the greater military construct. "The allocation of 'domain' status to cyberspace (alongside maritime, land, air, and space) serves a bureaucratic purpose to ensure that cyber operations (CO) receives sufficient financial and material support" (Argles, 2018). Overall, cyber has grown exponentially within its own sphere, replicating itself into the fissures of practically all other areas of military strategy, operations, and TTPs. Within the superstructure of IW, cyber holds a special place, encompassing the production of effects regardless of the IRC combination (see Figure 3).

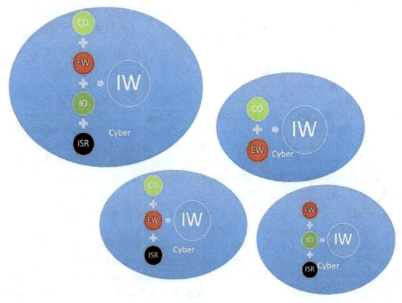

Figure 3: Combined IW Effects

The cognitive affect from such rapid growth has been enormous with cyber becoming not only a term at the tip of every tongue, but a capability of which every entity desires a part. "Few cyber phenomena have captured the fascination of the media and the general public more than information theft through cyber exploitation and data exfiltration" (Jabbour & Devendorf, 2017). The terror and splendor inflicted on the collective considerations of the public show just how powerful and mature cyber has become and just how much we still have to learn.

As an IRC, ISR is one of the oldest with roots in warfare back to the dawn of recorded time. However, with cyber capabilities introduced in the 20th and 21st centuries, especially within the last two decades, ISR has become even more capable and powerful. As a discipline, there has never seemed to be any question concerning the power and utmost necessity of ISR. This is evident in the amounts of money invested in this IRC from the highest echelons of government with organizations such as the NSA, CIA, and FBI, all of which depend on ISR operability and capability to function. The great enabler in much of the maturation of ISR has been technology, again an area of obvious importance from the top down. With technology comes the need and desire to integrate other IRCs, most notably cyber capabilities, into the ISR capability framework. With this integration has come a new way of conducting ISR operations including the kinds of information sought and the kinds of information environments accessed and used. After the breakdown of IW in the 90s, ISR and the other silos of IRCs continued on parallel paths. "The ISR community kept building and operating systems of greater acuity and range. Electronic warriors went back to mastering their magic in support of air operations, counter–improvised explosive devices, and other combat specialties. Psychological operators continued to refine the arts of persuasion and apply them to an increasing roster of disparate groups. Cyber warriors bounced through the space community before getting their own sub-unified command within which they could practice their craft" (Libicki, 2017). These parallel paths have characterized the ways in which ISR has expanded its own sphere of operational influence and continued to add to this important and versatile IRC. "A key component of such independent operability in both ISR and combat operations is the development and use of unmanned drones. The increasing use of drones for different functional areas (intelligence, electronic countermeasures, direct strikes, etc.) and different operational environments (land, sea, air, amphibious) is an important consideration for flexibility in dynamic conflict situations" (Danyk, et. al., 2017). With key capabilities like drone and other network-dependent operations has come the inescapable tie-in of cyber which has only served to abut these two fields even more closely. The recent merger of the Cyber 24th Numbered Air Force (NAF) and the ISR 25th NAF into a new 16th NAF, makes the objective clear; a combined capability bringing with it not only cyber and ISR, but other IRCs as well.

ISR as a capability is also growing across the globe. "Foreign intelligence services use cyber tools in information-gathering and espionage. Several nations are aggressively working to develop information warfare doctrine, programs, and capabilities to enable a single entity to have a significant and serious impact by disrupting the supply, communications, and economic infrastructures that support military power" (Jabbour & Devendorf, 2017). With this in mind, it is important to see the advantages of such constructs and how NATO and the U.S. are going to meet the challenges of other nation states and the capabilities they continue to develop. The continued development of ISR as a capability has kept pace with and now has even combined with cyber, leading to a continued technology and IRC arc that shows every sign of culminating in a combined IW construct.

As a shift and evolution of cyber and ISR capabilities has occurred, EW has followed a similar trajectory. As technology and cyber and ISR capabilities progress, EW as an IRC finds itself at a distinct advantage due to the peculiar niche it fills. EW is focused on controlling, disabling, and manipulating various signals and devices from and within multiple electronic environments. "[E]lectro[magnetic] warfare can … be carried out by controlling devices that emit radio-frequency (RF) energy. New forms of RF signals pervade homes and cities: Bluetooth, Wi-Fi, 5G, keyless entry systems, and Global Positioning System (GPS), to name a few. The coming Internet of Things (IoT) is essentially an Internet of RF-connected items. If software-defined radios (those capable of broadcasting or receiving signals over an arbitrarily selected frequency) become ubiquitous, they could be hijacked to jam or spoof targets hitherto inaccessible using traditional EW boxes" (Libicki, 2017). With this powerful reach into the RF spectrum, EW stands as an excellent, cyber enabled resource, capable of combining with other IRCs in many, powerful ways. Other nations such as China have recognized this powerful combination of capabilities for some time. "A 2004 White Paper on National Defense increased the PLA focus on "informationalization" and advocated the use of cyber and electro[magnetic] warfare in the early stages of a conflict" (Jabbour & Devendorf, 2017). Under these circumstances and with a full understanding of the scope of these capabilities, it is in the distinct interest of NATO and the U.S. to hone their own capabilities in this realm while leveraging the full power of other IRCs. Again, Russia is already moving forward with this philosophy: "Russia has … developed multiple capabilities for information warfare, such as computer network operations, electro[magnetic] warfare, psychological operations, deception activities, and the weaponization of social media, to enhance its influence campaigns" (Majir & Vailliant, 2018). China has pronounced provenance as well as is related to EW: "In early writings, Major General Dai

Qingmin stated, 'the destruction and control of the enemy's information infrastructure and strategic life blood, selecting key enemy targets, and launching effective network-electro[magnetic] attacks.' He argued that this integration of cyber and electronic warfare would be superior to the US military's approach at the time of network-centric warfare" (Kania & Costello, 2018).

EW is another IRC that has persisted for much of the 20th and 21st centuries. However, there has been a marked growth in capability with the advent of cyber and the continuing growth and expansion of ISR and IO that have led to a closer tracking of these capabilities, now seen from a holistic perspective. As these IRCs continue to cross streams and implement the others' precious proficiencies, the need for closer attention and support from NATO and the U.S. will be necessary.

Information Operations like ISR has been used in war for literally thousands of years. However, IO looks at information in a way distinct from the other IRCs, especially as it relates to psychological influence and the power of propaganda. "[T]he NATO Allied Joint Doctrine for Psychological Operations states that Information Operations are defined as 'a staff function that analyzes, plans, assesses and integrates information activities to create desired effects on the will, understanding and capability of adversaries, potential adversaries, and North Atlantic Council (NAC) approved audiences in support of Alliance mission objectives"(Bialy, 2017). With the creation and proliferation of social media, IO has become an extremely powerful tool in the world of cyber and ISR specifically. IO also draws power significantly from cyber as an enabling force. IO has been used for centuries as a way to influence, deter, and coerce through non-kinetic and generally non-lethal means. "Non-lethality and ambiguity, for their part, may be exploited to modulate the risk of reprisals—notably, violent reprisals—for having carried out information operations" (Libicki, 2017). This technique combined with other, non-lethal means such as cyber and EW can generate power across the battlespace at many levels. China has used such integration and should be expected to continue this strategy into future conflicts in peace and in war. "The SSF's cyber corps approach the cyber domain in a much more comprehensive way, reflecting a highly integrated approach to information operations that actualizes critical concepts from PLA strategic and doctrinal approaches" (Kania & Costello, 2018). Other nations recognize the flexibility and power of IO as well as other advantages, including scalability, portability, cost, and ambiguity. "Russia recognizes that information operations offers an opportunity to achieve a level of dominance… it provides a significantly less costly method of conducting operations since it replaces the need for conventional military forces" (Majir & Vailliant, 2018). It is difficult not to see how powerful IO is in regards to influence and dominance since information has become and remains a key to everything from business to commerce to military operations, especially as it relates to social media. "[A]part from its monetizing potential, social media has also become an excellent channel to mobilize support, disseminate narratives, wage information operations, or even coordinate military operations in the real world. States and non-state actors have started to extensively use social media to influence perception, beliefs, opinions and behaviors of their target audiences"(Bialy, 2017). The mature capability of IO across the globe and in and through organizational constructs lends itself well to the growth potential of IW, making it an undeniable asset in the combined scope of IW capabilities.

The mature capabilities manifested in and through cyber, ISR, EW, and IO respectively tend to culminate in a combined IW merger that can harness and exploit all of these competencies in myriad combinations. "[G]iven today's circumstances, in contrast to those that existed when information warfare was first mooted, the various elements of IW should now increasingly be considered elements of a larger whole rather than separate specialties that individually support kinetic military operations" (Libicki, 2017). This concept continues to build as U.S. military services continue to not only merge capabilities into unified commands, but even characterize those commands as IW-centric. This philosophy of IRC warfare prosecution follows the emerging and established trends of the Russian and Chinese military complexes while further combining critical IRCs in a manner that will enable current and future warfare for decades to come.

4   Characterizing IW interoperability

The IW strategic construct contains within it numerous operational potentialities capable of delivering pronounced effects through cyberspace, the electromagnetic spectrum (EMS), and the information environment (IE) individually and collectively. As noted in Figure 4, these capabilities and their combinations can be used to great effect for disruption, denial, and destruction across several battlespaces simultaneously. The following scenarios and cases depict how each of these combinations of IRCs have been used in real conflicts and can be applied in the future within the JADC2/JADO frameworks.

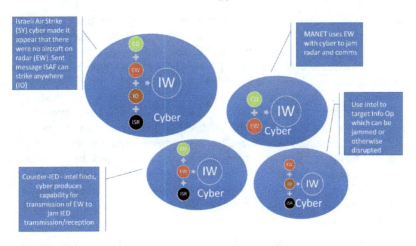

Figure 4. IW case examples

The four following cases are indicative of IW IRC combinations that either have been or could be used in operational circumstances. Each scenario will be explained and elaborated to show the full scope of the respective combinations and ramifications. Keep in mind that in each scenario, while Cyber Operations (CO) might not be present as an operational component, it nevertheless is present in the blue oval surrounding all aspects of each operation indicating that cyber must be present as the critical enabler for all operations within the IW construct.

4.1   Mobile Ad Hoc Networks

One of the most flexible system types within the IW framework for EW is the Mobile Ad Hoc Network (MANET). This type of network is useful in several important ways, especially within environments where flexibility and lack of infrastructure exist (e.g., in a battlefield or environmental disaster situation). MANETs are often used in deployable environments where a wireless, local network is necessary to establish and continue operations and may consist of multiple devices, vehicles, power sources, and other materials or technology necessary for ad hoc setup and operation. MANETs are also "self-healing" networks with multiple "mesh" connections that allow for continuous operational resilience in the event of loss or destruction. This is not only accomplished through redundant equipment, but through multiple, parallel interconnections which allow dynamic rerouting of communications, electromagnetic signals, and data.

MANETs are of extreme importance in the execution of EW in deployed battlefield situations as the communications, data, Electromagnetic Support (ES), Electromagnetic Protection, and Electromagnetic Attack (EA) systems used to prosecute EW and control the EMS are heavily dependent on the interconnections afforded through MANETs. For instance, in the Syrian conflict of recent years, MANETs provided land-based EW assets the connections necessary to connect to air, ground, sea, space, and cyber assets necessary for data associated with location, radar parametrics, cyber systems, intelligence, communications, and a host of other information sources. As the top, right oval in Figure 4 indicates, MANET systems and their associated EW linkages provided the EW capabilities which operated through and with the CO elements that afforded the network, communications, human, and data assets necessary to perpetuate EW operations in a congested and contested EMS.

Consider a scenario in which a MANET is deployed in a forward operating theatre. The MANET configuration would include multiple power sources, servers, communications antennae and units, and other equipment operated on a cyber foundation and operating with the intent to conduct and support kinetic and non-kinetic operations. If an unit in this configuration became non-operational, the interconnections established through wired and wireless ad hoc infrastructure within the MANET network could "fail over" to redundant equipment and continue operations. Only once all nodes became non-operational through failure, destruction, or degradation, would the MANET cease being operationally effective. In the unlikely event of such degradation, other similar deployable systems could ostensibly be deployed to undertake continuity or operations or EW operations could fallback to other air, sea, space, cyber, and potentially software defined radio (SDR) systems. The resilience and redundancy offered through this IW concept is substantial, if not insurmountable.

4.2   Disruption of Information Operations

In contrast to the wartime scenario detailed above, information operations (IO) are an ongoing, gray zone strategy perpetrated continuously by adversaries at every level. The purpose of IO are myriad, with roots in destabilization, cultural fracturing, societal upheaval, and even regime change. While these effects may not contribute directly to violence, destruction of physical property, or loss of human life, their second and third order effects indeed may contribute. In IW, controlling the narrative is an important and integral part of setting the stage in the IE. This is the case not only for nation states, but for criminal and terrorist organizations. IO as a

Joshua Sipper

strategic tool has a low entry point economically, technologically, and operationally, making it an enticing and often used strategy for almost anyone.

Perhaps the area most rife with instances of IO is social media. Literally anyone with an internet connection and interface can set up and use a social media account. While the amount of influence individuals and groups can exert through social media will differ widely, with the right tools and knowledge regarding how these assets work, a person or organization can create a viral disinformation, misinformation, or propaganda strain quite easily. For instance, numerous independent radical groups have used social media such as Twitter, Facebook, and Instagram to propagate their radical ideologies through the use of "bot" accounts that repost and promote their messaging to add an air of significance and legitimacy. After their disinformation efforts are dispersed, unwitting individuals will often repost the disinformation thus perpetuating and adding more credence to the information.

As depicted in the lower, right oval of Figure 4, IO can be prosecuted throughout the IE through numerous means. In the scenario detailed in this case, an adversary IO could be combatted through the use of ISR to identify the IO content, source, and other information and EW could be used to deny the transmission of this information through jamming of the electromagnetic signals used to send the information. This would be especially useful in situations where a local terrorist group in a contested area such as eastern Syria might have a cell phone or SDR network established that is used for communicating IO propaganda or disinformation to its adherents. Through the identification of the offending message sources an the frequencies on which they operate through intelligence collection, these frequencies can be jammed and the communications denied or otherwise disrupted.

4.3 Countering Improvised Explosive Devices

Improvised explosive devices (IEDs) are used during numerous conflicts the world over. However, their devastating effects were felt daily for sometime during the Operation Enduring Freedom (OEF) and Operation Iraqi Freedom (OIF) conflicts. As IEDs and the resulting deaths from their use continued to rise, commanders began to ask questions about how forces under their command might be able to detect and disable these devices. What became immediately evident was that there was not an easy or straightforward answer to this conundrum. No one capability would be able to mitigate these disasters, however the combination of several operational capabilities might be able to help.

Of course, as with any situation where information is a key to understanding an operational environment, ISR stood out as an initial vector for beginning to ascertain the particulars of the problem. As had been known for sometime, IEDs were often detonated using signals from devices such as cell phones or garage door openers; devices that operated in the EMS. With this information in hand, ISR analysts could begin collecting and making sense of the complex EMS environment. However, the amount of data and the often convoluted parametric data that was found in the IE made identifying and locating the devices difficult. This is where ISR signals intelligence (SIGINT) and electromagnetic intelligence (ELINT) operators turned to CO for assistance.

As with any signal or information rich environment, the massive amounts of data collected and parsed can become immediately overwhelming. Billions of signals riding a seemingly infinite prismatic display of frequencies are propagated through the firmament and space every second. Even with extraordinary, modern ELINT collection capabilities, the systems used to parse this data during the OEF/OIF era were inadequate for the task of sorting and identifying the IED signals used to set off these roadside bombs. However, with new applications of artificial intelligence (AI) and machine learning (ML), data sorting, filtering, and recognition could be sped up drastically, leading to rapid identification, reporting dissemination, and mitigation of IEDs. While the cyber capabilities enabled this advancement, EW accounted for the final stage of countering the IEDs.

The EMS is an extremely complicated and busy IE. Already contested and congested, the EM real estate continues to be in higher and higher demand and increasingly crowded. As a result, EW and spectrum management have become areas of extreme import to warfighters who depend on the EMS for communications, datalinks, and all the connections that make modern warfare possible. This has sparked a revolution in the design of new EW capabilities that can be used for numerous applications, especially when it comes to IEDs. Not only can jammers be mounted to vehicles or carried by personnel in dangerous environments, ordinance can actually be pre-detonated to remove threats prior to entering a contested area. Through the use of EW capabilities in the EMS, the danger can be removed and operations can continue.

4.4   IW in Total: Using All Four IRCs

While an IW operation does not have to use all four IRCs to be considered IW, there will invariably be operations in which all IRCs can be leveraged to deliver mass effects. Such is the case in the Israeli bombing of a joint Syrian and North Korean nuclear facility. The effort, code named OPERATION

ORCHARD , used Israel's significant IW capabilities to end a program that could have been significantly destabilizing to the region. Israel is a nation surrounded by aggressive actors and nation states, exerting constant pressure on its government and military. In this geopolitical crucible, Israel has refined its significant military and informational power, making it a formidable opponent to any adversary that might seek its destabilization or destruction. Syria is such a foe, armed with a gnawing desire to develop strike and counterstrike capabilities bent on domination of Israel and the entire Middle East region.

With its precise ISR capabilities, Israel constantly monitors its Middle Eastern neighbors, even as far as Iran, to maintain deep situational awareness concerning weapons and operations that could do grave harm to Israel and its people. These capabilities include advanced espionage techniques including SIGINT and its subcategories of ELINT, communications intelligence (COMINT), and cyber intelligence (CYBINT). Through thorough collection and analysis of the Syrian integrated air defense system (IADS) network, Israeli SIGINT analysts discovered the specific frequencies used by Syrian IADS as well as the communications channels used by the personnel, allowing them to detect patterns in communications in operational situations. However, it was CYBINT collection and analysis that yielded some of the most critical information for OPERATION ORCHARD.

Cyber capabilities were leveraged in at least two ways during OPERATION ORCHARD. The first was obviously through computer network exploitation (CNE) which allowed the collection of the various routes, information, and ports and protocols used in the Syrian IADS. But, it was the operational delivery of capabilities Israel brought to bear through CO that allowed an Israeli supreme IW and JADO victory. As Israeli fighter-bombers flew toward the Syrian nuclear facility on September 6, 2007, Israel conducted offensive cyber operations (OCO) within the already deeply penetrated Syrian IADS, sending spoofed signals to their radar interfaces to make it appear that aircraft were not present. This allowed the aircraft to fly in essentially undetected and successfully destroy the nuclear facility with zero casualties. In a photo originally reported by Al Jazeera (Figure 5) it is clear that the facility was completely cratered.

The significant cyber operation also included the EW component of allowing Israeli EW operators in concert with intelligence obtained through ISR and consequent manipulation through CO to completely dominate the EMS. While CO is an extremely important IRC, without the EMS, CO could not occur. Even the electrical and light waves propagated through electrical and fiber optic cables are considered part of the EMS, making CO utterly dependent on the EMS as a domain. Cyberspace is an established warfighting domain under US and NATO military doctrine, but the critical enabler for CO remains and will continue to be the EMS. This was evident from two angles during OPERATION ORCHARD as the EMS was used for both OCO and denial in the EMS through the inoperation of the Syrian IADS. Without the EMS at its disposal, Syrian radar operators were effectively blind, allowing Israeli aircraft and EW to gain supremacy in the EMS throughout the conflict.

Figure 5. Bombed Syrian Nuclear Facility

The final, and perhaps most important and lasting IRC as a result of OPERATION ORCHARD was the IO effects left in the wake of the operation. It does not take much to imagine the frustration, demoralization, and lasting psychological effects left by such an operation on a local, regional, and global scale. Firstly, Syria and its military were completely taken off guard and their defenses rendered useless, allowing Israel to crush their IADS and the nuclear facility. This also sends a signal to regional adversaries that Israel is willing and able to carry out complex IW operations with impunity. Finally, the North Korean scientists, engineers, and other personnel present would likely have been impressed upon by this operation, leading to additional global recognition of Israel's military power.

The cases detailed above are only a very few examples of the power brought to bear through the massing of IW and JADO capabilities. Within each case, multiple IRCs are used to project and operationalize power from varying directions. These kinds of operations not only add complexity to operations making them more difficult to defend against, they add confusion within the adversary's cognitive spaces, preventing them from making decisions quickly and decisively and giving the IW aggressor the strategic advantage.

5 JADC2 and IW: Enabling and Driving Joint All-Domain Operations

The fact that JADC2 and IW are both strategies growing in parallel and power makes right now a perfect time to interleave these concepts. Both scaffolds include multiple capabilities, integration of technology and communications, and combined battlespace effects making the ultimate confluence of the two intuitively practical. However, it is a given that this is no easy task; one fraught with extreme complexity, culture clash, and opportunity for miscommunication. These difficulties, however, only highlight the pronounced need to get underway with their integration and get out far ahead of our adversaries. "It's a bold approach, one that takes what the US military calls jointness to a new level" (Clark, 2020). This paradigm shift includes multiple levels of combinatory power and effects (see Figure 6). The concept of IW and JADC2 for JADO includes overlaying and matrixing the strategies, capabilities, and effects in myriad fashion.

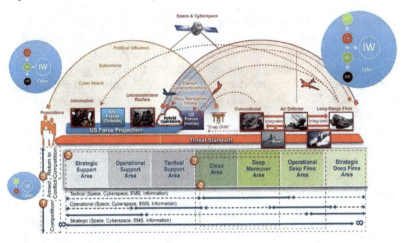

Figure 6: IW Enabled JADC2

In order to bring these concepts closer together, further ties will have to be created and reoriented between combatant commands and other structures. "For example, the commanders of Space Command and Cyber Command have authority over operations in the space and cyberspace domains. All-domain operations, however, will integrate space and cyberspace with operations in the air, land, and sea domains, where geographic commanders traditionally have authority. Therefore, to integrate all domains—including space and cyberspace—JADC2 will require new links between combatant commands" (Dwyer, 2020). This is another area where IW will need to be woven into the JADO concept. With cyber as an IRC along with IRS, IO, and EW, the combinatory power of these capabilities must be interspersed with JADC2 in order to ensure JADO is made possible. Without a strong tie to the information piece of warfare, JADO cannot become a reality.

Information is not just words, pictures, video, and other bits of communicative matter, but rich, processed data such as that used in IO, ISR, EW, and CO. "To the three traditional domains of warfare – land, sea and air – space and cyber have been added. Some strategists include information as its own domain" (Goure, 2019). The central importance of information for strategic and operational penetration and supremacy is the crux of IW. Through the use of IW, JADC2 is tied together and enabled to fully leverage all domains for JADO. The effects made possible through the use of IW and JADC2 for JADO can be seen in Figure 7. (Kasubaski, 2018) Combined JADO and IW Effects.

The growth and potential of JADC2 and IW together to enable JADO is recognized by the joint force and continues to permeate all areas of modernization and strategic development. "The Army leadership recognizes that changes in the character of warfare will take place, and that these changes are unpredictable. The goal of the modernization strategy is to set the conditions for the Army to adapt to those changes better than any possible rival" (Wille, 2019). This push combined with the previously mentioned Air Force and joint service commitment to establishing JADO makes the integration of JADC2 and IW all the more important. Nakasone and Lewis give a direct look into this possibility as they relate JADO to the IRC, IW combination of EW, CO, and IO: "The harnessing of the electromagnetic spectrum and the advent of modern communications technologies have allowed militaries with advanced warfighting capabilities to seize the advantage by engaging in multiple domain battle" (Nakasone & Lewis, 2017). This multi-level technologically potent combination across the all-domain spectrum makes for a potential game changing battlespace in which joint operations using IW will continuously overpower adversary capabilities.

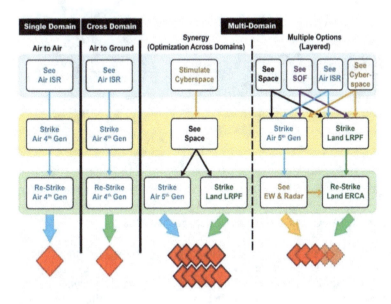

Figure 7: Combined JADO and IW Effects

6   JADC2 and IW for JADO Conceptual Model

The following is an explanation of the JADC2 and IW for JADO Conceptual Model (Figure 8) (Sipper, 2021). The model is built from the other referenced figures in this paper to depict how the strategic concepts can be flowed together in a way to create combined IW and JADC2 exponential effects. Rolfe, et. al., characterize the complexities of multi-domain conflict well when they state, "There are significant challenges in understanding a situation. First, there is a large amount of data relevant to a situation and it changes constantly. The topology of nodes, links, nodal equipment, architecture, protocols, and networks is always in flux. Also, network traffic is changing, together with software applications for the user and for the managers of the networks" (2014). The JADC2 and IW for JADO Conceptual Model is an effort to provide a high-level strategic view of these complexities and interconnections on which to further build operational capabilities and concepts.

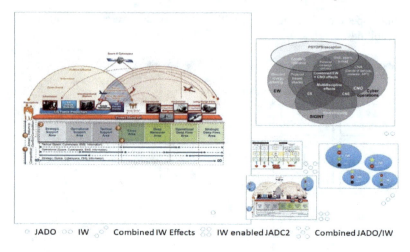

○ JADO ○○ IW ○○ Combined IW Effects ○○ IW enabled JADC2 ○○ Combined JADO/IW

Figure 8: JADC2 and IW for JADO Conceptual Model

The model begins with the overarching concept of JADO, recognizing that all domains must first be interlaced and integrated such that operations from a joint perspective are possible. The next level of the model includes a graphic representation of the IW IRCs, indicating how these capabilities overlap and interoperate to produce effects. The third level graphic explains how IW occurs at multiple levels. The concept is not an all-or-nothing proposition, but one of combined capabilities from many different IRC perspectives. However, regardless of the combination of IRCs, cyber is ubiquitous, providing the enabling domain capability for all of the associated IW components. IW enabled JADC2 basically takes the Combined IW Effects and overlays them onto the JADO concept to show how IW can be integrated to enable JADC2 for JADO. Finally, Combined JADO and IW Effects are presented in the fifth and last level of the model indicating the culmination of the JADC2/IW combinatory modalities. The conceptual model is ultimately a way to see how all of these strategic and operational concepts can be streamed in such a way to outstrip adversary strategy and power.

7 Conclusion

The collective supremacy of JADC2 and IW is a case involving a great deal of complex and ramified concepts. JADO is an area of recent, prolific, and profound expansion and will likely continue with theory, doctrine, and joint operations and exercises characterizing its definitive establishment. IW is growing and becoming ingrained in parallel with JADO, making the time for integration of these super strategies suitable. With the integration of JADC2 and IW for JADO, the relationships between IRCs and all-domain interoperability stands to benefit greatly and proliferate into strategy and operations prodigiously. The JADC2 and IW for JADO Conceptual Model is one way to look at these relationships and obtain a strategic and operational view of this potentially game changing combination. Through the use of IW, JADO can not only be made to work better, but to project joint force power deeper into all battlespaces now and far into the future.

References

Argles, C. (2018). A Conceptual Review of Cyber-Operations for the Royal Navy, *The Cyber Defense Review*, Vol. 3, No. 3 (FALL 2018), pp. 43-56.

Bialy,B. (2017). Social Media—From Social Exchange to Battlefield, *The Cyber Defense Review*, Vol. 2, No. 2 (SUMMER 2017), pp. 69-90.

Clark, C. (2020). Gen. Hyten On The New American Way of War: All-Domain Operations, *Breaking Defense*, Accessed 4/26/2020: https://breakingdefense.com/2020/02/gen-hyten-on-the-new-american-way-of-war-all-domain-operations/

Danyk, Y. Maliarchuk, T. and Briggs, C. (2017). Hybrid War: High-tech, Information and Cyber Conflicts, *Connections*, Vol. 16, No. 2 (Spring 2017), pp. 5-24.

Dwyer, M. (2020). Making the Most of the Air Force's Investment in Joint All Domain Command and Control, *Center for Strategic and International Studies*, Accessed 4/26/2020: https://www.csis.org/analysis/making-most-air-forces-investment-joint-all-domain-command-and-control

Goldfein, D. (2018). Enhancing Multi-Domain Command and Control: Tying it All Together, Air Force Chief of Staff Policy Letter, Accessed 4/26/2020: https://www.af.mil/Portals/1/documents/csaf/letter3/Enhancing_Multi-domain_CommandControl.pdf

Goure, D. (2019). A New Joint Doctrine for an Era of Multi-Domain Operations, *RealClear Defense*, Accessed 4/26/2020: https://www.tradoc.army.mil/Publications-and-Resources/Article-Display/Article/1987883/a-new-joint-doctrine-for-an-era-of-multi-domain-operations/

Jabbour, K. and Devendorf, E. (2017). Cyber Threat Characterization, *The Cyber Defense Review*, Vol. 2, No. 3 (FALL 2017), pp. 79-94.

Kania, E. and Costello, J. (2018). The Strategic Support Force and the Future of Chinese Information Operations, *The Cyber Defense Review*, Vol. 3, No. 1 (SPRING 2018), pp. 105-122.

Kasubaski, B. (2018). Exploring the Foundation of Multi-Domain Operations, Small Wars Journal, Accessed 5/4/2020: https://smallwarsjournal.com/jrnl/art/exploring-foundation-multi-domain-operations

Libicki, M. (2017). The Convergence of Information Warfare, *Strategic Studies Quarterly*, Vol. 11, No. 1 (SPRING 2017), pp. 49-65.

Majir, M. and Vailliant,B. (2018). Russian Information Warfare: Implications for Deterrence Theory, *Strategic Studies Quarterly*, Vol. 12, No. 3 (FALL 2018), pp. 70-89.

Nakasone, P. and Lewis, C. (2017). Cyberspace in Multi-Domain Battle, *The Cyber Defense Review*, Vol. 2, No. 1 (WINTER 2017), pp. 15-26.

Orye, E. and Maennel, O. (2019). Recommendations for Enhancing the Results of Cyber Effects, 2019 11th International Conference on Cyber Conflict

Rolfe, R., Louisa-Lamos, F., Odell, L., Agre, J., Gordon, K., Alspector, A., and Barth, T. (2014). 19th ICCRTS Cyber Operations Model for Multi-Domain Conflict, Institute for Defense Analyses.

TRADOC PAM 525-3-1 *2018, The US Army in Multi-Domain Operation 2028.

Underwood, K. (2020). U.S. Army Sets Aside Money for Joint All-Domain Operations, SIGNAL AFCEA, Accessed 4/26/2020: https://www.afcea.org/content/us-army-sets-aside-money-joint-all-domain-operations

Wille, D. (2019). A Summary of Multi-Domain Operations, New America.

Author biography

Dr Joshua Alton Sipper is a Professor of Cyberwarfare Studies at the Air Force Cyber College. He completed his Doctoral work at Trident University in September of 2012, earning a Ph.D. in educational Leadership (emphasis, E-Learning Leadership). Dr. Sipper's research interests include cyber ISR, policy, strategy, and warfare.

Chapter Eight

Mathematical Modeling in Cyberspace

Abderrahmane Sokri

DRDC CORA, Ottawa, Canada
Sokriab@gmail.com

Abstract: Cyberspace has become a new battlefield where attacks can be highly sophisticated and would-be challengers unspecified. While cyber-attacks are not directly lethal, they may result in significant damage to a country's critical infrastructure and reputation. Mathematical modeling has been recognized as a sound theoretical foundation for managing information security, allocating limited resources, and guiding defensive strategies in cyberspace. This chapter provides a comprehensive review of literature on the application of mathematical approaches in cyberspace. The main issues and open research questions associated with this application are also underlined. Three state-of-the-art mathematical models are presented and discussed to show how to inform and improve decision making in the cyber world. The first model uses the most common risks to demonstrate how a risk analysis can be conducted in cyberspace. The second uses a sequential game theoretic approach to determine the optimal defensive investment in information security. The third model uses a deception-based approach to show how deception as a force multiplier can be formulated in cyberspace. This exploration indicates that mathematical models should be combined with other potential tools and techniques to provide more detailed results and better support for decisions in cyberspace.

Keywords: Mathematical modeling, cyber-attacks, risk analysis, sequential games, defensive cyber deception.

1 Introduction

In addition to its long-term nature, the current strategic context is characterized by three main particularities (DND, 2019; Sokri and Ghanmi, 2021):

1. Simultaneity of military operations across multiple domains;

2. A persistent state of competition and potential conflicts;

3. A necessary coordination with multinational partners to develop and execute operations and to deter and defeat potential attacks.

In this new era, military strategies have changed from dealing with specified opponents to strategies coping with hypothetical threats from unspecified would-be challengers. They have also changed from strategies coping with limited threats of a particular area to strategies dealing with global ones (Morgan, 2003). Cyberspace has become a new battlefield with its own characteristics and a lot of challenging issues. This new domain is fundamentally different from the physical domains of land, sea, air, and space. Its attacks can be highly sophisticated overstepping all geographic and political boundaries (Moisan and Gonzalez, 2017).

Defenders and attackers in cyberspace can be individuals, devices, or software with conflicting objectives. Their weapons are malicious software ranging from upgraded viruses to advanced persistent threat (APTs) (Bernier et al., 2012; Aslanoglu and Tekir, 2012). Cyber weapons or threats present two main characteristics or paradoxes: (1) they are subject to time-decay and (2) their usage may shortly enhance the target's defence (Podins and Czosseck, 2012). They are designed to exploit unknown vulnerabilities in the target's defence. Without these vulnerabilities, cyber-attacks would be reduced to social engineering, flooding Denial-of-Service (DoS), and Distributed Denial-of-Service (DDoS) (Moore et al., 2010; Podins and Czosseck, 2012).

A vulnerability is a weakness in system security procedures that can be exploited by an attacker. The vulnerability can reside in the system design, its internal controls, or its implementation (NIST, 2002). A vulnerability is deemed to be exploitable if an attacker has the ability to exploit it. It may be caused by human behaviour (e.g., no password protection), technology (e.g. no firewall), and system settings (e.g., no proper privileges) (Martins et al., 2012; Sokri, 2019a). Vulnerabilities are inherently dynamic. When they are detected by the defender, the attacker's weapons exploiting them become useless and the target's defence turn out to be enhanced (Podins and Czosseck, 2012).

In the context of cyber security, risk appears when a threat meets a corresponding vulnerability (Bowen et al., 2006). Three elements are generally used to portray the overall shape of cyber risk: (1) the probability that the threat may become harmful, (2) the probability that the vulnerability may be exploited, and (3) the resulting impact (Schneidewind, 2009; Branagan, 2012; Abdel-Basset et al., 2019). The impact expresses the damage inflicted by a successful attack or an unwanted event in terms of harm, injury, disadvantage or loss (Standards Australia, 2009). A simple cyber-security attack on a critical infrastructure may result in immense effects on a country's safety and reputation (Aslanoglu and Tekir, 2012; Acquaviva, 2017).

While cyber-attacks are not directly lethal, they can cause many immediate and long term effects. They can, for instance cause loss of data availability (e.g., disruption of access), confidentiality (e.g., unauthorized disclosure of information), or integrity (e.g., unauthorized modification of information) (Bowen et al., 2006). They can not only compromise systems but can also destroy equipment (Ziolkowski, 2010; Podins and Czosseck, 2012). They may ultimately cause significant damage to networked and critical infrastructures such as water supply, flight control, and hospital management (Bier et al., 2009).

The unprecedented sophisticated Stuxnet worm that took place in 2010 is considered as the real start of cyber warfare (Adams et al., 2012). It is a virus that can spread from a computer to another without human interaction. This cyber-attack tried to destroy Iran's nuclear enrichment centrifuges by operating its motors at damaging speeds. It infected more than 30,000 computers in Iran and about 30,000 computers in other countries including the United States, China, Germany, and the United Kingdom. This attack has broken down a common idea affirming that information assets are covered if the used computers are not connected to the Internet and new memory sticks are used in exchanging data. It has also disproved a common belief stating that viruses are detectable by the unusual behaviour of computers (Aslanoglu and Tekir, 2012; Podins and Czosseck, 2012).

Mathematical modeling, as a multidisciplinary approach, has been viewed by many researchers as a sound theoretical foundation for managing information security, allocating limited resources, and guiding defensive strategies in cyberspace. Game theory, for example, is a common formalized way to to understand defence strategies in network security. Statistical techniques are widely used for cyber security risk modelling and assessment. Genetic algorithms are used in network mapping. Reliability modeling is used to predict the likelihood that a component or a system will function prior to its implementation. These techniques may be combined with other potential tools and techniques to provide more detailed modeling and better support for decisions in cyberspace.

The aim of this chapter is to discuss the use of mathematical modeling in cyberspace. It offers an intuitive understanding of its application focusing on both theoretical and applied dimensions of cyber security. Three models are presented and discussed to show how to inform and improve decision making in the cyber world. The first model demonstrates how a risk analysis can be conducted in cyberspace. The second shows how to optimally allocate resources in the cyber domain in a methodical manner. The third illustrate how to defend against digital attacks in a non-conventional way. The chapter also highlights the recognised challenges associated with the applicability of each model in the cyber world.

This chapter is the result of an invitation to expand a paper published in the proceedings of the European Conference on Cyber Warfare and Security (Sokri, 2021). It also incorporates some elements of other previously published work by the author (Sokri, 2019b; Sokri, 2021a). The chapter is organized into six sections. Following the introduction, section 2 provides a comprehensive review of literature on the application of mathematical approaches in the cyber domain. Section 3 provides a brief presentation of traditional and non-traditional defensive techniques. Section 4 presents and discusses three different models on cyber warfare and security. The main challenges surrounding the applicability of mathematical models in cyberspace are discussed in section 5. Some concluding remarks are indicated in section 6.

2 Literature review

The current literature on cyber-attack modeling follows three separate lines of thought: (1) Cyber security risk assessment, (2) resource allocation, and (3) defensive cyber deception.

2.1 Cyber security risk assessment

Cyber risk refers to the intersection of a threat and a vulnerability that allows it to manifest (Bowen et al., 2006). A cyber-security breach may lead to six main consequences if the threat does occur (Blyth and Kovacich, 2006; Bernier et al., 2012):

- **Interception:** unauthorised access to an asset,
- **Degradation:** slowdown in the rate of information delivery,
- **Interruption:** when an information asset becomes unavailable,
- **Modification:** when an attacker interferes with the asset,
- **Fabrication:** counterfeiting of an asset, and
- **Unauthorized use:** when an attacker uses an asset for his own purpose.

Methods for assessing cyber risk may be split into qualitative and quantitative methods, depending on data availability (Van Asselt, 2018). Qualitative methods use subjective reasoning to quickly and cost-effectively prioritize cyber risks. Quantitative methods are mostly probabilistic and seek to measure them numerically. Dreyer et al. (2018), for example, developed a methodology for estimating present and future costs of cyber risk. The authors used an input-output model to take the industry-level impacts and translate them into broader systemic economic impacts. They also provided a companion Excel-based modeling and simulation platform that allows users to alter assumptions and investigate a wide variety of research questions. To incorporate uncertainty into the model, many of the parameters are defined by probability distributions including uniform, triangular, and generalized beta distributions. Their results indicated that the resulting values are highly sensitive to input parameters.

More recently, Sokri (2019b) proposed a new cyber risk formulation combining the probability of exceedance and Monte Carlo simulation techniques. To illustrate the approach, the author presented and discussed a case study using the most common threats, vulnerabilities, and impacts. He used a Program Evaluation and Review Technique (PERT) distribution to represent the inherent risk curve and conducted a correlation analysis using stochastic simulation to determine which risk mitigation strategies would have the most impact. The model can assist civilian and military decision-makers in identifying critical risk drivers and the need for contingency plans.

2.2 Resource allocation

In the resource allocation problem, defenders seek to find the optimal resource allocation that minimizes their expected loss due to a successful attack. Attackers seek to maximize their expected benefit and minimize the risk of being traced back and punished (Acquaviva, 2017). Scarce resources in the cyber world are used to minimize the success probability of a potential attack. They may be:

- **Protective devices**: to cover a set of targets at risk of being attacked,
- **System administrator's time**: to be spent across different activities,
- **Defensive budget**: to be allocated over various components and systems, and
- **Investment**: to be made in critical infrastructures

Vanek et al. (2012), for example, examined the problem of optimal resource allocation to detect potential threats in large networks. The authors used a game where an attacker tries to harm multiple vulnerable computers by sending malicious packets. The defender seeks to optimally allocate the available resources to maximize the probability of malicious packet detection. The authors formulated the problem as a graph-based security game with multiple resources and propose a mathematical program for finding optimal solutions.

Bloem et al. (2006) developed an algorithm for optimal allocation of the system administrator's time available for responding to attacks. The authors modeled the interaction between a distributed Intrusion Detection Systems (IDS) and an attacker using a game theoretic approach. They assert that their approach is general enough to be applied to a variety of IDSs and computer networks. Assuming a limited available budget, Azaiez and Bier (2007) considered a security system to find the optimal defensive investment in strengthening its components. The authors characterize the optimal attack and defence strategies. They also solved the optimization problem for some important special cases.

Gordon and Loeb (2002) used an economic model that determines the optimal amount to invest in information security. Since extremely vulnerable information assets may be very expensive to protect, the authors indicate that defenders may be better off concentrating their efforts on information assets with midrange vulnerabilities. They showed that the investment should not exceed 37% of the expected loss. Hausken (2006) used an alternative class of security breach probability functions and showed that the optimal investment level may no longer be capped at 37% of the expected loss. More recently, Sokri (2021a) analyzed the defender's optimal security investment level as a cyber-deterrence strategy. His findings indicate that the investment in security should be formulated for the middle part of losses.

2.3   Defensive cyber deception

Deception-based information security is a very effective supplement that can enhance the established solutions and mechanisms (Fraunholz and Schotten, 2018). Deception can be defined as an active manipulation of reality (Almeshekah and Spafford, 2016) aiming to mislead attackers, increase their uncertainty, and push them to behave against their interests (Carroll and Grosu, 2011; Zhu, 2019). It has been widely seen as a force multiplier in war and military conflicts. Throughout history, deception has played a prominent role in warfare. Its foundations date back to ancient civilizations. But since the seminal book by the Chinese military strategist Sun Tzu, every military admits that warfare is the way of deception.

Deception has been extensively used within the military. The success of the Trojan horse in the capture of Troy is a well-known example (Davis, 2016). When the friendly forces (Blue Team) are able to attack, they must seem unable; when they are active, they must seem inactive; when they are near, they must make the adversary (Red Team) believe they are far away; when far away, they must make the enemy believe they are near (Tzu, 1994; Cohen, 1998; Heckman et al., 2015; Almeshekah, 2015). As the extensive use of information technology systems pervades into business transactions and military operations, deception finds new fertile ground (Chou and Zhou, 2012). Successful deception in cyberspace depends on the information asymmetry between the deceiver and the deceivee (Zhu, 2019).

Cyberspace created a unique opportunity for deception modeling. A growing body of literature recognizes it as a well-suited supplement solution to protect information systems. The existing literature seeks to show how mathematical modeling can guide defensive deception against cyber-attacks. Carroll and Grosu (2011), for example, used a signaling game to model the use of deception in network security. In their scenario, the defender deploys honeypots in the network and the attacker observes the system and decides whether or not to proceed compromising it. The authors characterized the perfect Bayesian equilibria of the game and discussed the benefits of employing deceptive equilibrium strategies in the defence of a computer network.

More recently, Sokri (2021b) used a game theoretic approach to show how deception as a defence strategy can be formulated in cyberspace. The author formulated the adversarial interaction between a defender and an attacker in cyberspace as a leader-follower game where the defender disguises honeypots to detect, prevent, and analyze cyber-attacks. Results showed that the game has multiple equilibria where the most valued system will be targeted, no matter what its state is. The interested reader is referred to Davis (2016) for further information on this deception modeling. The author provided a survey of the game theory models of deception, defined a quantitative measure of deceptive risk, and introduced a multi-objective model of deception.

3   Defensive techniques

To overcome these problems and enhance the target's defence, a variety of conventional measures have been employed. These techniques can be separated along methodological lines into two main categories: (1) Traditional and (2) deception-based techniques.

3.1   Defensive cyber deception

A number of techniques are employed to deter and defeat potential cyber-attacks. Traditional network security techniques include:

- **Antivirus programs:** Software used to scan devices, detect signs of malware presence, and remove them.
- **Firewalls:** Security controls used to limit access to private networks connected to the Internet.
- **IDS:** Algorithms used to detect suspected intrusions and alert the security specialists in real-time.
- **Attribution techniques:** Methods used to determine the physical or digital identity of an attacker.
- **Cryptography:** Techniques of authentication based on merging words with images to protect data.
- **Tamperproof techniques:** Methods of identification based on measurable physiological characteristics such as voice or fingerprints.

While these defensive techniques are still crucial mechanisms against casual attackers using well known techniques, they cannot be a panacea. There is an ongoing race between attackers and defenders in cyberspace. As soon as a new solution is proposed, a more sophisticated technique to bypass it is established (Roy et al. 2010). Combining these protective and reactive measures with other potential tools and techniques may enhance their effectiveness. Using them under solid theoretic formalisms will yield a greater improvement of their rigor. These formalisms include three interdisciplinary subfields of mathematical sciences: Statistics, operations research, and game theory.

Statistics are used to collect, organize, analyze, and interpret data. Statistical methods are used in risk assessment and are mostly probabilistic. They can be deductive or inductive. Deductive methods such as attack trees trace are backward search techniques that trace from undesired events to possible causes. Inductive methods such as event trees are forward search techniques that trace from possible causes to undesired events. Risk assessment methods are typically used to objectively derive the most likely cyber risk profile. After identifying, analyzing, mitigating cyber risks, these methods can also be used to quantitatively compare inherent risk (risk observed before any mitigation), tolerance risk (the maximum acceptable risk), and residual risk (risk after mitigation) to inform Security Assessment and Authorization (SA&A) programs.

Operations research or operational research uses optimization algorithms to find optimal or near-optimal solutions to complex problems. In operations research, analysts make single decisions in situations where "nature" is the only "opponent". This discipline benefits from advancement in computer science to investigate a wide range of decision making problems in cyberspace. These problems particularly include the determination of (1) the optimal investment level in security, (2) the optimal allocation of the total defensive budget over a number of systems, (3) the optimal allocation of limited resources over the set of targets, and (4) the optimal replacement of cyber hardware. It also provides a means for conducting what-if analysis to determine the key factors influencing each decision for further investigation.

Game theory has the ability to model the strategic interactions between multiple decision makers in different contexts. This discipline has been recognized by many researchers as well-suited to defensive cyber deception. It has been particularly applied to understand the information asymmetry between deceivers and deceivees in network security (Baston and Bostock, 1988). Its analytical setting can be non-cooperative (e.g., a game between defenders and attackers) or cooperative (e.g., sharing collective costs or rewards between allies). It can be discrete or continuous, static or dynamic, deterministic or stochastic, and linear or non-linear (Sokri, 2019a). In contrast to decision-theoretic techniques such as operations research, in game theory, it is the players who select their optimal strategies to maximize a benefit or to minimize a loss.

3.2 Deception-based techniques

Defenders can also use deception as a defence strategy to enhance the effectiveness of their security. Deceptive techniques can be divided into two main acts: (1) dissimulation and simulation (Bell and Whaley, 1991; Almeshekah, 2015). Dissimulation hides the existence, the nature, or the real value of targets. Simulation displays false information. As shown in Table 1, each act consists of three basic components where the deceiver manipulates reality by hiding it, altering it, or manufacturing it.

Table 7: Simulation and dissimulation techniques

Dissimulation		Simulation	
Components	Definition	Components	Definition
Masking	Making the real undetected	*Mimicking*	Making the real to look like something else
Repackaging	Making things appear different	*Inventing*	Creating a new reality
Dazzling	Confusing the target with others	*Decoying*	Driving attention away

There is a fundamental difference between deception-based mechanisms and traditional security tools such as anomaly-based IDS. Traditional techniques focus on the attacker's unwanted actions and try to detect and prevent them. Deception-based techniques focus on the attacker's perceptions and try to manipulate them.

These non-traditional techniques offer three significant advantages over the traditional tools: First, they induce the opponents to expose themselves and take actions that are useful to the defender. Second, in contrast to traditional tools such as IDS, they offer a clear line between normal user activities and abnormal ones. Third, in contrast to traditional techniques, the unavailability of objective data does not limit their applicability. They can be applied even when there are data gaps. These differences reduce the rate of false positive, generates less logging data (Almeshekah, 2016), and increases the trustworthiness of their results.

The deceiver can employ a honeypot as a normal system to increase the deceivee's uncertainty and effort to determine whether the system is true or fake (Cohen, 1998; Rowe et al., 2007; Carroll and Grosu, 2011, Sokri, 2019a). The captured data from the attacker's actions can also be used by the defender to better protect the network. (McCarty, 2003; Rowe et al., 2007; Carroll and Grosu, 2011; Pibil et al., 2012). Honeypots are totally independent systems with no valuable information. They give service providers the ability to disconnect and analyze the system after a given attack without any unwanted interruptions. As shown in Table 2, honeypot-based tools are generally designed to accomplish four main missions (Almeshekah, 2015): The detection, prevention, research and response to cyber-attacks.

Table 2: Security applications of honeypots

Mission	Strategic objectives
Detection	Detect and stop spams
Prevention	Slow down attacks Confuse attackers Transfer risk to the attacker's side Deter attacks
Research	Investigate the latest attacks Analyze new families of malware
Response	Preserve the attacked system's state Simplify the forensic work

4 Mathematical models of cyber warfare

There are several mathematical models in the existing literature for exploring cyber warfare and security problems. These models can be split into different categories: (1) Cyber security risk assessment, (2) resource allocation, and (3) defensive cyber deception. Our objective here is not to thoroughly explore this literature, but to offer for each category a representative model that we have developed recently. Each representative model is appropriate and general enough to solve many cybersecurity standard problems.

4.1 Modeling cyber security risk assessment

The suggested cyber security risk assessment approach is based on the most recent contributions in risk analysis. It will assist cyber analysts in conducting cyber risk analyses with more transparency and replicability. The approach involves six steps as summarized in the flow diagram in Figure 1.

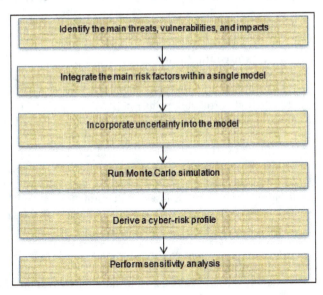

Figure 3: Schematic presentation of the cyber risk analysis steps

Identify the main threats, vulnerabilities, and impacts
In this step, risk threats that would have serious impact on the asset are listed. Examples of these threats include Trojan horses, viruses, and worms. Each

individual cyber-security breach is characterized by its probability of occurring and its impact range if the threat does occur.

Integrate the main risk factors within a single model
At least two elements should be used to derive the overall cyber risk against an information asset a:

- p_t which is the probability of a successful attack using threat t, and

- l_t which is a loss resulting from the successful attack.

The expect impact can be expressed in the form of a multiplicative factor and the inherent risk observed before any mitigation can be written as

$$R_a = \sum_{t=1}^{n} p_t l_t, \qquad (1)$$

where

- n is the number of threats on the list of the identified risks, and

- $p_t l_t$ is the defender's expected loss due to a successful attack using threat t.

Incorporate uncertainty into the model
Instead of using constant values for the probability and impact of a given threat, as is standard in the existing literature, we suggest assigning probability distributions. Probability distributions are used in this step to obtain the most likely impact and the corresponding probable spread. A probability distribution function can be assigned to each parameter and each variable to describe the range of their possible values. Two comprehensible and very practical probability distributions are particularly suitable for this assessment: Triangular and Program Evaluation and Review Technique (PERT) distributions. They use a three-point estimates (optimistic, most likely, and pessimistic) approach. PERT is more adequate than the Triangular distribution in case of skewness or asymmetry in the distribution (Sokri and Solomon, 2013).

Run Monte Carlo simulation
Stochastic simulation is a well-established method for evaluation of risk. In this step, this technique simulates the impacts of all possible threats that might occur, provides a single distribution of the outcome, and helps in conducting sensitivity analysis to determine key threat drivers for risk mitigation. In contrast to other techniques such as moment generating functions, characteristic functions, and manipulation of integrals, Monte Carlo simulation presents more flexibility and power for combining probability distributions.

Derive a cyber-risk profile

Risk profiling is a process for finding the level of risk the organization may be comfortable with. To determine an acceptable level of risk, let the random variable L be the cyber risk or the total expected loss, F its Cumulative Distribution Function (CDF), and G its Complementary Cumulative Distribution Function (CCDF). In mathematical terms, this function is expressed as

$$G_L(l) = 1 - F_L(l) = P(L > l), \text{ for all } l \geq 0. \qquad (2)$$

This mathematical function is commonly known as the Loss Exceedance Curve (LEC) or the probability of exceedance. It is assumed to be continuous, strictly decreasing, and bounded between 0 and 1. An example of its curve is provided in Figure 2. This curve identifies and graphically displays for each loss the likelihood of exceeding it. This curve has been particularly used in the areas of survival analysis, actuarial science, and nuclear power (Hubbard and Seiersen, 2016).

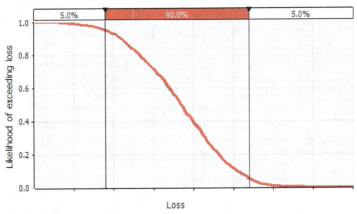

Figure 4: Example of a Loss Exceedance Curve

Perform sensitivity analysis

Sensitivity analysis provides a useful way to show what would happen to the overall risk if the major sources of uncertainty vary. It mainly shows how sensitive the overall risk is to the different threats. Sensitivity analysis can be conducted by varying more than one factor at the same time (multi-way sensitivity analysis) or by varying a single factor while all other parameters are held constant (one-way sensitivity analysis). It can also be performed using the outcome distributions (probabilistic sensitivity analysis).

Probabilistic sensitivity analysis can be carried out using different analytical techniques. Bivariate correlation and regression analyses are the most useful of them. These two techniques compute a pairwise association between the outcome and each of its simulated predictors. Bivariate correlation, for example, determines the strength and direction of the potential association. The higher its correlation coefficient, the more significant the threat is in affecting the overall risk. This what-if analysis objectively determines which risk mitigation strategies would have the most impact on the asset security (Sokri and Solomon, 2013; Sokri and Ghanmi, 2017). After analyzing and mitigating cyber risks, analysts can use this approach to profile and quantitatively compare inherent, tolerance, and residual risks.

4.2 Modeling cyber resource allocation

Determining the optimal investment level in security is one of the most challenging issues in cyberspace. As demonstrated in the first model, traditional risk analysis provides sound theoretical frameworks for assessing the risk associated with security breaches. This approach suffers, however, from two serious shortcomings that limit its usefulness: (1) It does not determine the optimal investment level in security and (2) it does not influence the attacker's behaviour. By investing in information security, the defender can (1) reduce the vulnerability of potential targets, (2) reduce the probability of successful attacks, and consequently (3) avoid significant potential costs. In this second model, we adopt a game-theoretical approach that offers two significant advantages over traditional risk analysis. It (1) determine the optimal security investment level and (2) deter would-be attackers.

Defender's loss and attacker's benefit
In this second model, we consider a sequential security game played between two adversarial agents: a strategic defender (the leader) and an attacker (the follower). The defender determines the security investment i to protect an information system. This investment may include (but are not limited to):

1. Procurement of detection and prevention tools such as Antivirus software, Firewalls, and IDS, and/or

2. Establishment of physical monitoring and inspection procedures.

The attacker reacts with a certain level of latent willingness-to-attack. Since the true willingness-to-attack is not directly observable, it is modeled as the effort t that the attacker exerts to compromise the system. This effort corresponds to the first activities of the cyber kill chain (Mihai et al., 2014). These activities particularly include (but are not limited to):

Abderrahmane Sokri

- **Reconnaissance** — Collecting information about the system,
- **Weaponization** — Analyzing the collected data, and
- **Delivery** — Transmitting the weapon to the targeted system.

Each successful attack can result in a possible benefit b to the attacker and a potential loss l to the defender and. The benefit and loss occurring can be tangible or intangible.

The system is characterized by an inherent vulnerability v_0. The probability of a successful attack $p(i, t)$ is expressed as a function of i and t. As in Sokri (2021a), the defender seeks to minimize the following total cost.

$$W_D = p(i,t)l + i, \qquad (3)$$

where $p(i,t)l$ is the defender's expected loss due to a successful attack. The attacker seeks to maximize the following payoff.

$$W_A = p(i,t)b - t, \qquad (4)$$

where $p(i,t)b$ is the attacker's expected benefit.

Game's equilibrium
To characterize the optimal solution to the deterrence game, we start by deriving the optimality conditions. Assuming an interior solution, the first-order optimality conditions for the attacker and the defender optimization problems can be respectively written as

$$\frac{\partial W_A}{\partial t} = \frac{\partial p(i,t)}{\partial t}b - 1 = 0, \qquad (5)$$

and

$$\frac{\partial W_D}{\partial i} = \frac{\partial p(i,t)}{\partial i}l + 1 = 0. \qquad (6)$$

Equations 5 and 6 lead to the following equilibrium condition.

$$\frac{\partial p(i,t)}{\partial t}b = -\frac{\partial p(i,t)}{\partial i}l. \qquad (7)$$

This equilibrium condition indicates that the reduction in the defender's expected loss attributable to one extra investment unit should be equal to the increase in the attacker's expected benefit due to one extra effort unit.

Probability of a successful attack
To find the outcome of this leader-follower interaction, we should specify the form of the probability of a successful attack. As in Wu et al. (2015) and Sokri (2021a), we consider that the defender can use security investment i to

reduce the probability that the vulnerability may be exploited. Therefore, the probability that the vulnerability may be exploited can be written as

$$v(i) = v_0 \, exp(-\alpha i),$$ (8)

where the parameter $\alpha > 0$ represents the rate at which vulnerability decreases with investment in security.

The probability $p(i,t)$ of a successful attack can be expressed as the product of the probability that the vulnerability may be exploited, $v(i)$, and the threat probability (i.e., the probability to receive an attack)

$$p(i,t) = v_0 \, exp(-\alpha i)\left(1 - exp\left(-\frac{t}{\mu}\right)\right).$$ (9)

The threat probability or the probability of attack, is written in equation 9 as the cumulative distribution function (CDF) of an exponentially distributed random variable evaluated at t. It provides the probability that the attacker's effort will be less than t. The parameter μ represents, at the same time, the mean effort required to attack and the standard deviation of the distribution.

Optimal strategies
Assuming an interior solution, the optimal effort of the attacker and the optimal security investment of the defender are respectively given by

$$t = -\alpha\mu i + \mu ln\left(\frac{bv_0}{\mu}\right),$$ (10)

and

$$i = \frac{1}{\alpha}ln(\alpha l v_0).$$ (11)

To prove this result, note that after substitution for $p(i,t)$, equation 4 becomes

$$W_A = v_0 \, exp(-\alpha i)\left(1 - exp\left(-\frac{t}{\mu}\right)\right)b - t.$$ (12)

Computing the derivative of W_A with respect to t, equating to zero, and solving leads to the expression of t as a function of i.

The derivative of the attacker's expected effort t in equation 10 with respect to the defender's investment i 9 indicates that the parameters α and μ and their interaction effect are the key factors in cyber warfare. An increase in these parameters will decrease the probability that the vulnerability may be exploited, lessen the probability of a successful attack and, therefore, result in a reduction in the attacker's level of effort. The parameter α represents the speed at which the security investment translates into a reduction of the system's vulnerability to attacks. The parameter μ splits cyber-attacks into targeted attacks and opportunistic attacks.

On the other hand, equations 3 and 9 imply that

$$W_D = v_0\, exp(-\alpha i)\left(1 - exp\left(-\frac{t}{\mu}\right)\right)l + i. \tag{13}$$

The expression of t in equation 10 is equivalent to

$$exp\left(-\frac{t}{\mu}\right) = \frac{\mu}{bv_0}\,exp(\alpha i). \tag{14}$$

Substituting for $exp\left(-\frac{t}{\mu}\right)$ from equation 14 in equation 13, computing the derivative of W_D with respect to i, equating to zero, and solving provides the equilibrium strategy. The expression of i in equation 11 relates the defender's strategy to three parameters: v_0, l, and α. Substituting for i from equation 11 in equation 10 provides the following attacker's optimal level of effort

$$t = \mu ln\left(\frac{b}{\alpha\mu l}\right). \tag{15}$$

Potential loss

To characterize the defender's optimal security investment level i as a function of the potential loss l, consider the expression of i in equation 11. It is straightforward to show that its first derivative with respect to l is positive and its second derivative is negative. Meaning that i is a concave function in l that increases at decreasing rate. In order to have a positive investment, we should have $\alpha l v_0 > 1$. This means that the defender should not invest in security (beyond best practices) until the potential loss reaches

$$l_0 = \frac{1}{\alpha v_0}. \tag{16}$$

The defender's optimal investment as a fraction of potential loss l is given by

$$r(l) = \frac{i}{l} = \frac{1}{\alpha l}ln(\alpha l v_0). \tag{17}$$

Using the l'Hopital rule, one can demonstrate that $\lim_{l\to\infty} r(l) = 0$, which shows that $r(l)$ has a horizontal asymptote at $y = 0$. This means that, for large potential losses, the optimal amount to spend on information security should be far smaller than the potential loss. All these findings are on par with the existing literature. They are particularly consistent with the study conducted by Gordon and Loeb (2002).

4.3 Modeling defensive cyber deception

Deception-based techniques use the information asymmetry between deceivees and the deceivers to manipulate the attacker's perceptions. This third model uses a game theoretic approach to show how deception as a force multiplier can be formulated in cyberspace. The adversarial interaction is formulated as a leader-follower game between an attacker a (the follower) and a defender d (the leader) in a computer network. In the concept of leader-follower equilibrium, also known as Stackelberg equilibrium, the leader anticipates the follower's reaction and determines and commits to a given strategy. The best reaction of the follower at the equilibrium will maximize the leader's objective function (Coniglio, 2013).

In the present model, the defender disguises honeypots to detect, prevent, and analyze cyber-attacks without any unwanted interruptions. This deception model provides at least two significant advantages over previous two models: (1) The used honeypots are totally independent with no valuable information at risk. (2) Instead of using data to conduct the analysis, honeypots give the defender the ability to collect data on the latest attacks without any interruptions.

Defender's loss and attacker's benefit
Following Rowe et al. (2007) and Carroll and Grosu (2011), we assume that the defender seeks to prevent attacks by disguising $k \leq n$ honeypots as normal systems. The purpose of this camouflage is to detect unauthorized access and record their methods of attack. Let $S = \{s_1, s_2, ..., s_n\}$ be a set of n systems that the attacker may choose to attack. The defender can use a fake target and get a reward $R_d(s_i)$, if the target is attacked. She can also leave the target normal and incur a cost $C_d(s_i)$, if it is attacked. The attacker can attack a target and get a reward $R_a(s_i)$, if the target is normal. If the target is a honeypot, she will incur a cost $C_a(s_i)$. Let X_i be the random variable taking the value 1 with probability δ_i, if the system i is a honeypot and the value 0 with probability $1 - \delta_i$, if the system is normal. Similarly, denote by Y_i another random variable taking value 1 with probability ρ_i, if the system i is attacked and the value 0 with probability $1 - \rho_i$, otherwise.

In this stochastic framework, the expected utilities of the attacker and the defender are respectively given by

$$E(U_a) = \sum_{i=1}^n \rho_i\big((1 - \delta_i)R_a(s_i) - \delta_i C_a(s_i)\big) \qquad (18)$$

and

$$E(U_d) = \sum_{i=1}^{n} p_i(\delta_i R_d(s_i) - (1 - \delta_i)C_d(s_i)). \tag{19}$$

The cost-benefit formulations in equations 18 and 19 depend simply on the attacked systems and their state (fake or normal).

Game's equilibria
Fixing the value of δ_i, the first problem to solve is to find the attacker's best response to δ_i. This optimization problem can be formulated as a linear program where the follower maximizes her expected utility given δ_i.

$$Max \sum_{i=1}^{n} p_i\big((1 - \delta_i)R_a(s_i) - \delta_i C_a(s_i)\big) \tag{20}$$

$$s.t. \sum_{i=1}^{n} p_i = 1 \tag{21}$$

$$p_i \geq 0, \forall i \tag{22}$$

The two constraints define the set of feasible solutions p.

Denoting by $p_i(\delta_i)$ the follower's best response to δ_i, the leader seeks to solve the following problem.

$$Max \sum_{i=1}^{n} p_i(\delta_i)(\delta_i R_d(s_i) - (1 - \delta_i)C_d(s_i)) \tag{23}$$

$$s.t. \sum_{i=1}^{n} \delta_i = k \tag{24}$$

$$\delta_i \in [0,1], \quad \forall i \tag{25}$$

The two constraints enforce the defender's mixed strategy to be feasible.

Assuming that the attacker will play only pure strategies and choose to attack a single target, it is clear that the optimal strategy for the follower is to attack the system s_i that maximizes her expected payoff $\big((1 - \delta_i)R_a(s_i) - \delta_i C_a(s_i)\big)$. This means that the attacker would target the most valued system no matter what its state is (fake or normal). The defender would seek to prevent this attack by employing a honeypot. If, for example, the first system has the highest expected payoff, this defender-attacker Stackelberg game will have multiple equilibria of the form

$$\langle \delta = (1, \delta_2, \delta_2 ..., \delta_n), \ p = (1, 0, ...,0, 0)\rangle. \tag{26}$$

This standard solution is in par with the existing literature. It is particularly consistent with the studies conducted by Jain et al. (2010) and An et al. (2011) in the physical world. Jain et al. (2010), for example, applied game theory to assign air marshals to protect flights in airports. In this model, we formulated deception as a defence multiplier in cyberspace where security is more complex than in physical domains.

5   Challenges and open research questions

Modeling cyber warfare has been an ongoing challenge for military forces. The models presented in the previous section are grounded enough that they could be repeated or extended using different assumptions. They present state-of-the-art methods for assessing cyber security risk, allocating limited resources as well as deception modeling. While their underlying mathematics is clear and conceptually based, their applicability is limited by the complexity and the dynamic nature of cyberspace. The trustworthiness of their results is reduced by the unavailability of objective data and the uncertainty of the cyber domain scenarios.

5.1   Modeling cyber security risk assessment

There is a wide range of powerful and long-established risk assessment methods that could be applied in cyberspace, but their applicability depends on the availability and quality of the needed data. Because of the unavailability of objective data, risk assessment methods in cyberspace are primarily qualitative. Qualitative methods use subjective reasoning to provide a high level judgment of cyber risk. They use ordinal scaling techniques to describe the risk probability and impact. While they are a quick and cost-effective way of prioritizing risks when there are data gaps, they are not able to conduct a detailed risk analysis.

In addition to the lack of historical data on cyber-attacks, many other challenges surround the applicability of mathematical models in cyberspace. These challenges include a lack of understanding of interdependencies between risk elements, inconsistency in the application of statistical methods, and lack of common quantitative risk taxonomy. To address this kind of gaps, it is essential that we define a standard risk management approach that provides analytical methods able to guide risk estimators and project managers in conducting an appropriate cyber risk analysis. The risk management process should be organized, comprehensive, and iterative including risk planning, identification, analysis, handling, and monitoring (Sokri and Ghanmi, 2017).

5.2   Modeling cyber resource allocation

Policy makers have a myriad of quantitative methods to analyze cyber-attacks. These methods vary from operations research to game theory. In these frameworks, the defender may want to find the optimal resource allocation that minimizes cyber security risk as well as the unnecessary associated cost (Acquaviva, 2017). The aim of this cost-benefit perspective is also to send a signal to potential challengers that they will be unsuccessful. If the cost of taking an unwanted action outweighs its potential benefit, they most likely would be deterred. This impenetrability strategy that subtracts from the attacker's perceived benefit is known in the literature as deterrence by denial. (Brantly, 2018; Wilner, 2017).

Deterrence is more complex in cyberspace than in the physical world. The most challenging problem in cyber deterrence is the attribution dilemma (Wilner, 2017). It is generally difficult and time-consuming to determine who to blame for cyber-attacks. Since deterrence by punishment requires the knowledge of potential attackers, it cannot be adequately used in digital space. While deterrence by denial manipulates the perceived benefits of potential attackers, deterrence by punishment manipulates their perceived cost. This tit for tat or equivalent retaliation strategy is still at its beginnings and needs further efforts to address the blame attribution problem.

5.3   Modeling defensive cyber deception

Throughout history, deception has been used as a force multiplier in military conflicts. More recently, deception has found a fertile ground in cyberspace. This defence strategy can enhance the established techniques by manipulating the information asymmetry between deceivers and deceivees. Since deception is an adversarial interaction between multiple self-interested agents, game theoretic reasoning has been widely seen as a sound theoretical foundation to analyze it. As for the resource allocation problem, the adversarial interaction between defenders and attackers in deception problems is formulated using a cost-benefit approach.

In addition to the complexity and the dynamic nature of cyberspace, the most challenging issues in in these security models is the problem of common knowledge. It is often assumed in these models that defenders and attackers are able to exactly evaluate their own payoffs and the payoffs of their opponents. This assumption is unfortunately not always true. Moreover, the costs and benefits occurring in cyber security problems are mainly intangible such as loss and gain in reputation. The valuation of such non-market elements remains an under-researched area and an ongoing challenge for future research. Using defensive cyber strategies with incorrect values of costs and benefits may make them ineffective.

The application of mathematical models in cyberspace faces many other challenges. In the real-world, cyberspace interactions are inherently dynamic where the system state changes with time. Defenders may face multiple unknown attackers, from multiple locations, and using different types of cyber weapons. Interactions may involve rational and irrational decision makers with unknown goals. Scaling up the models to take all these complexities into account would make them intractable. Applying them under idealized assumptions would make their findings less useful. To find a middle ground between these two extremes, it is highly recommended to combine mathematical models with other techniques and tools such as computer simulation, wargaming, and IDS. Shiva et al. (2012), for example, have already proposed a framework that combines game theory and traditional protective and reactive measures in cyberspace such as self-checking hardware and software components, built-in or bolt-on applications, and antivirus software.

6 Conclusion

Cyberspace has become a new battlefield where weapons are shaped on knowledge of targets' vulnerabilities. Their transmission can overstep all geographic and political boundaries. While they are not directly lethal, cyber-attacks can cause public or private institutions to lose important data, money, or their own reputations. Cyberspace offered many opportunities to civilian and military sectors, but also created a series of complex and challenging problems. Mathematical modeling, as a multidisciplinary approach, has been widely used to understand the ongoing race between attackers and defenders in this area. Decision-theoretic techniques such as operations research have been used to describe the complexity and the dynamic nature of this domain. Game theory has been used to model the strategic interactions between defenders and attacker in different contexts.

Three state-of-the-art mathematical approaches were presented and discussed in this chapter to show how mathematical modeling can be used to inform and improve decision making in the cyber world. The first used the most common risks to conduct a risk analysis in cyberspace. The model has the particularity to combine the probability of exceedance and simulation. The second used a sequential game theoretic approach to optimally allocate resources in cyberspace. An intuitive probability of a successful attack was used in the model to characterize the optimal solution. The third used a deception-based model to show how deception can enhance the effectiveness of traditional defensive measures in cyberspace. The adversarial interaction between a defender and an attacker is formulated as a leader-follower game. In this game, the deceiver employs honeypots as normal systems to increase the deceivee's uncertainty and effort.

While the underlying mathematics of these three models is clear and conceptually based, their analytical settings are still far from completely addressing all the known cybersecurity issues. The discussion of these models raised a wide variety of research questions on the use of mathematical modeling in the cyber world. These questions particularly include (but are not limited to):

- How to define a standard risk management approach that guides cyber risk analysis and solves the problem of data unavailability?

- How to solve the problem of the attribution dilemma and determine who to blame for cyber-attacks?

- How to quantify the intangible costs and benefits occurring in cyber security problems such as the value of reputation?

Scaling up the models to include the entire complexity of cyberspace would make them intractable. Using them under static scenarios and idealized assumptions would limit their applicability. To find a compromise between these two extremes, we recommend adopting a multidisciplinary approach where mathematical models are combined with other techniques and tools such as computer simulation, wargaming, and IDS.

References

Abdel-Basset M., Gu M., Mohamed M., and Chilamkurti, N. (2019) "A framework for risk assessment, management and evaluation: Economic tool for quantifying risks in supply chain", Future Generation Computer Systems, Vol. 90, pp 489-502.

Acquaviva JR. (2017). Optimal Cyber-Defence Strategies for Advanced Persistent Threats: A Game Theoretical Analysis. Master Thesis, the Pennsylvania State University.

Adams A, Reich P, and Weinstein S. (2012). A Non-Militarised Approach to Cyber-Security. Proceedings of the 11th European Conference on Information Warfare and Security. Filiol, E. and Erra, R. (eds). Laval, France, pp. 1-8.

Almeshekah, M. H. (2015). Using deception to enhance security: A Taxonomy, Model, and Novel Uses.

Almeshekah, M. H., and Spafford, E. H. (2016). Cyber security deception. In Cyber deception (pp. 23-50). Springer, Cham.

Aslanoglu R, Tekir S. (2012). Recent Cyberwar Spectrum and its Analysis. Proceedings of the 11th European Conference on Information Warfare and Security, Laval, France, p. 45-52.

Azaiez N. and Bier VM. Optimal Resource Allocation for Security in Reliability Systems. European Journal of Operational Research, Vol. 181 (2), 2007, pp. 773–786.

Baston, V.J. and Bostock, F.A. (1988). Deception Games. International Journal of Game Theory, Vol. 17 (2).

Bell, J.B. and Whaley, B. (1991). Cheating and Deception. Transaction Publishers, New Brunswick.

Bernier M, LeBlanc S, and Morton B. (2012). Metrics Framework of Cyber Operations on Command and Control. Proceedings of the 11th European Conference on Information Warfare and Security, Laval, France, p. 53-62.

Bier VM, Cox LA, and Azaiez MN. (2009). Why Both Game Theory And Reliability Theory Are Important in Defending Infrastructure Against Intelligent Attacks (Chapter 1). In: Game Theoretic Risk Analysis of Security Threats, Bier, V.M. and Azaiez, M.N. (eds) Springer: New York, pp. 1–11.

Bloem M., Alpcan, T., and Basar, T. (2006). Intrusion response as a resource allocation problem. IEEE Conference on Decision and Control.

Blyth A. and Kovacich G. (2006). What is Information Assurance?. In: Information Assurance. Computer Communications and Networks. Springer, London.

Bowen P. Hash J., and Wilson M. (2006). Information Security Handbook: A Guide for Managers. National Institute of Standards and Technology (NIST) Special Publication 800-100.

Branagan M. (2012). A risk simulation framework for information infrastructure protection. Ph.D. Dissertation, Queensland University of Technology, Australia.

Brantly, A.F. (2018). The cyber deterrence problem. 10th International Conference on Cyber Conflict (CyCon), IEEE, pp. 31-54.

Carroll TE and Grosu D. (2011). A Game Theoretic Investigation of Deception in Network Security. Security and Communication Networks, Vol. 4 (10), pp. 1162–1172.

Chou, H. M., and Zhou, L. (2012). A game theory approach to deception strategy in computer mediated communication. In 2012 IEEE International Conference on Intelligence and Security Informatics (pp. 7-11).

Cohen, F. (1998). A Note on the Role of Deception in Information Protection. Computers and Security, Vol. 17 (6).

Coniglio, S. (2013). Algorithms for Finding Leader-Follower Equilibrium with Multiple Followers. Ph.D. Thesis, Politecnico di Milano.

Davis, A. L. (2016). Deception in Game Theory: A Survey and Multiobjective Model. Air Force Institute of Technology Wright-Patterson, United States.

Department of National Defence (DND) (2019). Pan-domain Force Employment Concept, Ottawa, Canada.

Dreyer P, Jones T, Klima K, Oberholtzer J, Strong A, Welburn JW, and Winkelman Z. (2018). Estimating the Global Cost of Cyber Risk. RAND Corporation, Santa Monica, California.

Fraunholz, D., and Schotten, H.D. (2018). Strategic defense and attack in deception based network security. In 2018 International Conference on Information Networking (ICOIN), pp. 156-161. IEEE.

Gordon, L.A., and Loeb, M.P. (2002). The economics of information security investment. ACM Transactions on Information and System Security (TISSEC), Vol. 5, Issue 4, pp. 438-457.

Hausken, K. (2006). Returns to information security investment: The effect of alternative information security breach functions on optimal investment and

sensitivity to vulnerability. Information Systems Frontiers, Vol. 8, Issue 5, pp. 338-349.
Heckman, K. E., Stech, F. J., Thomas, R. K., Schmoker, B., and Tsow, A. W. (2015). Cyber denial, deception and counter deception. Springer.
Hubbard D.W. and Seiersen R. (2016). How to Measure Anything in Cybersecurity Risk. Wiley, New York.
Martins J., Santos H., Nunes P., and Silva, R. (2012). Information Security Model to Military Organizations in Environment of Information Warfare. Proceedings of the 11th European Conference on Information Warfare and Security, Laval, France, p. 172-179.
McCarty, B. (2003). The Honeynet Arms Race. IEEE Security Privacy, Vol. 1 (6):79–82.
Mihai, I.C., Pruna, S. and Barbu, I.D. (2014). Cyber Kill Chain Analysis. Int'l J. Info. Sec. & Cybercrime, Vol. 3.
Moisan, F. and Gonzalpez, C. (2017). Security under Uncertainty: Adaptive Attackers Are More Challenging to Human Defenders than Random Attackers. Frontiers in Psychology, Vol. 8:982.
Moore T, Friedman A, and Procaccia, A D. (2010). Would a 'Cyber Warrior' Protect Us? Exploring Trade-offs Between Attack and Defense of Information Systems. Proceedings of the 2010 Workshop on New Security Paradigms, p. 85–94.
Morgan, P. M. (2003). Deterrence now (Vol. 89). Cambridge University Press.
NIST. (2002). Risk Management Guide for Information Technology Systems. NIST Special Publication, p. 800-30.
Pibil R, Lisy V, Kiekintveld C, Bosansky B, Pechoucek M. (2012). Game Theoretic Model of Strategic Honeypot Selection in Computer Networks. In: Grossklags, J., Walrand, J. (eds.) Springer: Heidelberg, 2012, p. 201–220.
Podins K and Czosseck C. (2012). A Vulnerability-Based Model of Cyber Weapons and its Implications for Cyber Conflict. International Journal of Cyber Warfare and Terrorism, 2 (1), p. 14–26.
Rowe, N.C., Custy. E.J., and Duong. B.T. (2007). Defending Cyberspace with Fake Honeypots. Journal of Computers, Vol. 2 (2), p. 25–36.
Roy S, Ellis C, Shiva S, Dasgupta D, Shandilya V, and Wu Q. (2010). A Survey of Game Theory as Applied to Network Security. Proceedings of the 43rd Hawaii International Conference on System Sciences (HICSS).
Schneidewind, N. F. (2009). Models for Systems and Software Engineering. Wiley-IEEE Standards Association.
Sokri A. and Ghanmi A. (2017). Risk Analysis of Defence Acquisition Projects: Methods and Applications, DRDC Scientific Report DRDC-RDDC-2017-R124.
Sokri, A. (2019a). Game theory and cyber defence. In: Games in Management Sciences, Pineau, P.-O. and Taboubi, S. (eds) Springer International Series in Operations Research & Management Science.
Sokri, A. (2019b). Cyber Security Risk Modelling and Assessment: A Quantitative Approach. Proceedings of the 19th European Conference on Cyberwarfare and Security (ECCWS19), Coimbra University, Portugal.

213

Sokri, A. (2021a). Deterrence in Cyberspace: A Game-Theoretic Approach. Space & Defense, Vol. 12, No 1.

Sokri, A. (2021b). Defensive cyber deception: A Game Theoretic Approach. Proceedings of o the 20th European Conference on Cyber Warfare and Security: 24-25 Jun 2021.

Sokri, A. and Solomon, B. (2013). Cost Risk Analysis and Contingency for the NGFC DRDC CORA TM 2013-224.

Sokri, A., and Ghanmi, A. (2021). How game theory can enhance wargames? DRDC Scientific Report DRDC-RDDC-2021-R112.

Standards Australia (1999), Risk Management, Strathfield.

Tzu, S. (1994). The Art of War, trans. R. D. Sawyer, Boulder, CO: Westview Press.

Van Asselt E.D., Van der Fels-Klerx H.J., Raley M., Poulsen M., Korsgaard H., Bredsdorff L., et al. (2018). Critical review of methods for risk ranking of food-related hazards, based on risks for human health. Critical Reviews in Food Science and Nutrition, Vol. 58 (2), p. 178–193.

Vaneky O, Yin Z, Jain M, Boransky B, Tambe M, and Pechoucky M. (2012). Game-Theoretic Resource Allocation for Malicious Packet Detection in Computer Networks. Proceedings of the 11th International Joint Conference on Autonomous Agents and Multi-Agent Systems (AAMAS).

Wilner, A. (2017). Cyber deterrence and critical-infrastructure protection: Expectation, application, and limitation. Comparative Strategy, Vol. 36, Issue 4, pp. 309-318

Wu, Y., Feng, G., Wang, N., and Liang, H. (2015). Game of information security investment: Impact of attack types and network vulnerability. Expert Systems with Applications, Vol. 42, Issues 15-16, pp. 6132-6146.

Zhu, Q. (2019). Game theory for cyber deception: a tutorial. In Proceedings of the 6th Annual Symposium on Hot Topics in the Science of Security, pp. 1-3.

Ziolkowski K. (2010). Computer network operations and the law of armed conflict. Military Law and Law of War Review, Vol. 49 (2), pp. 47-94.

Author biography

Dr Abderrahmane Sokri has a Ph.D. in administration from HEC-Montreal. He is currently serving as economist for the Canadian Department of National Defence. His current research interest includes game theory applied to military operations. He has published in good international journals such as the European Journal of Operational Research.

Chapter Nine

Cybersecurity in Industrial Automation and Control Systems: The Recent Attack of the Colonial Pipeline

Christoph Lipps[1], Shaden Baradie[1], Jan Herbst[1], Leigh Armistead[3] and Hans Dieter Schotten[1,2]

[1]German Research Center for Artificial Intelligence, Intelligent Network Research Group, Kaiserslautern, Germany
[2]University of Kaiserslautern, Division of Wireless Communication and Radio Positioning, Kaiserslautern, Germany
[3]ArmisteadTEC LLC, Virginia Beach, United States
Christoph.Lipps@dfki.de
Shaden.Baradie@dfki.de
Jan.Herbst@dfki.de
leigh@armisteadtec.com
Hans_Dieter.Schotten@dfki.de

Abstract: Attacking networks and systems is (almost) as old as networks themselves, nonetheless, the tactics, nature and objectives of these attacks are currently changing significantly. It's no longer "script kiddies" trying their skills, using generalized Denial of Service (DoS) attacks to bring systems down, or attacks on Small and Medium Enterprises (SMEs); instead, this is about big money, high value and high-profile targets of Critical National Infrastructure (CNI) and large industrial facilities. These control systems and Operational Technology (OT) are often attacked in a very targeted manner, with greater danger for the future. Gartner (2021) forecasts that the damage caused by targeted hacker attacks will amount to more than $50 billion by 2023 and that by 2025 at the latest, people will be injured or killed by cyber attacks. In the first half of 2021 alone, the number of ransomware attacks as part of these attacks increased by more than 244%, and in the last two years by more than 800% (Oren, 2021). Although these attacks have been taking place for quite some time, they are moving into the media spotlight as their impact affects a larger segment of society. In May 2021 this happened to the East Cost of the United States (US) as hackers took down the largest fuel pipeline in the US and led to shortages in gasoline, diesel, etc. The cyber-criminal group DarkSide received $5 million of ransomware, as a result this attack. But, as the attack on the Colonial pipeline is just the beginning, this work highlights what Industrial Automation and Control Systems (IACSs) are, and why they are vulnerable. Furthermore, based on recent attacks on these systems and as it has already been shown in the past how easily individual targeted attacks can cause significant damage, in this chapter, a number of different attack vectors are described, with countermeasures referenced as the evidence is discussed, and the lessons learned are highlighted.

Keywords: Industrial Automation and Control Systems (IACS), Operational Technology (OT), Cybersecurity

1 Gasoline shortage and the attack on the Colonial Pipeline

In May 2021, the operators of the Colonial Pipeline were forced to proactively shut down operations and freeze Information Technology (IT) systems after becoming the victim of a ransomware attack. The 5,000+ mile pipeline supplies over 40 percent of the United States East Coast's fuel, including gasoline, diesel, home heating oil, jet fuel, and military supplies. The attack caused fuel shortages across several states lasting for days. Those affected included Florida, Alabama, Georgia, South Carolina, North Carolina, Tennessee, Virginia, and Maryland. The DarkSide group, a cyber-criminal organization believed to be based in Eastern Europe, claimed credit for the attack and on May 10, the FBI confirmed that DarkSide ransomware was responsible for the pipeline attack. On May 13, Bloomberg reported that the Colonial Pipeline company paid a ransom demand of close to $5.5 million in return for a decryption key that enabled it to regain control of its business networks and data.

All indications are that the Colonial Pipeline attack was a criminal operation; DarkSide operators targeted the company's business IT networks, rather than its IT and OT networks providing pipeline control. This is a strong indicator that the intent was financially-orientated rather than aimed at disrupting pipeline operations. In this respect, the company and indeed the entire country was extremely fortunate. An attack targeting the pipeline control systems could have potentially brought down the pipeline for months instead of days.

In the wake of the Colonial Pipeline incident, on May 28, the US Department of Homeland Security's Transportation Security Administration (TSA) issued new requirements for pipeline cybersecurity. The directive requires owners and operators to notify the Cybersecurity and Infrastructure Security Administration (CISA) within 12 hours of discovering a possible cybersecurity breach, even when the owner or operator is merely investigating the possibility of a security breach. It also requires owners and operators to designate a primary and alternate Cybersecurity Coordinator to be available 24 hours a day, seven days a week, to liaise with the TSA and CISA regarding possible cybersecurity breaches.

On 20 July 2021 the TSA issued a new cybersecurity directive requiring owners and operators of certain critical pipelines carrying hazardous liquids and natural gas to "implement a number of urgently needed protections against cyber intrusions" (Homeland Security, 2021). The July directive enhances the original directive released in May. The new confidential directive requires owners and operators of TSA-designated critical pipelines to:

- Implement specific mitigation measures and technical countermeasures to guard against ransomware attacks and similar cyberattacks,
- Develop and implement a cybersecurity recovery plan, and
- Review existing cybersecurity-architecture designs.

Moving forward, navigating cyber security risk management for critical infrastructure becomes even more important. While there is little information pertaining to how the Government will enforce these new TSA directives, rest assured that critical infrastructure protection, including the protection of civilian-owned infrastructures like petroleum pipelines and refineries, will receive increasing government scrutiny for the foreseeable future.

Government agencies as well as corporate organizations will need to provide cybersecurity risk management consulting and security engineering for both IT and OT systems, including the control systems and networks for pipelines, bridges, dams, locks, railroads, manufacturing, utilities, smart buildings and more. There is a need for organisations to assess their infrastructure risk management and work together to mitigate risks to their critical systems. A good cybersecurity risk effort includes from a US perspective:

- NIST Risk Management Framework (RMF)
- Federal Information System Modernization Act (FISMA) of 2014
- Payment Card Industry Data Security Standard (PCI DSS)
- USCG NVIC 01-20, Guidelines for Addressing Cyber Risks at Maritime Transportation Security Act (MTSA) Regulated Facilities
- UFC 04-010-06, Cybersecurity of Facility-Related Control Systems
- UFGS 25-05-11, Cybersecurity for Facility-Related Control Systems
- UFGS 25-08-11.0020, RMF for Facility-Related Control Systems
- International Maritime Organization (IMO) MSC-FAL.1/Circ. 3, Maritime Cyber Risk Management in Safety Management Systems

Obviously for European, NATO or other nations and international organizations, there will be additional and different criteria, but most nations still have a fundamental need to include designing and implementing cybersecurity risk management solutions, plus implementing a number of continuous monitoring solutions.

2 Industrial automation and control systems: The (vulnerable) backbone of industry

Industrial Control Systems (ICS) control the operations in the industrial sector by combining the existing hardware devices and machinery with suitable software services. Since the early 1960s, industrial process control has been applied by electric systems. In the mid-1970s, the term Supervisory Control and Data Acquisition (SCADA) emerged, describing the basics of automated control and data acquisition how we know them today.

2.1 Overview and architecture

Industrial control systems were introduced into various sectors that are responsible for essential services and facilities, such as power supply, telecommunication, water supply, food production, security services, etc. Being connected to such critical sectors with high dependency has made the ICSs a perfect target for attackers, who intend to blackmail certain authorities or perform destructive activities causing severe damages. This was witnessed through the countless attack incidents over the years and the continuously developed attack tools and techniques, that are presented in Section 4 (Duque Anton et al. 2021; Branquinho,2018).

Figure 1 illustrates how the architecture of a traditional industrial control system (Hassanzadeh et al., 2020; Quasim et al., 2021; Ahmed et al., 2017) is structured mainly into two levels:

- The lower level, which is a representation of the physical process, resides on the field site and consists of field elements, such as embedded computational devices, sensors, pumps and actuators. These elements require a control device, such as Programmable Logic Controllers (PLC) and Remote Terminal Units (RTU) to be properly operated and monitored. The control devices play an important role in controlling the field site elements, while at the same time performing as a connector to the control level over the network. This communication is made available using wired or wireless-type connections and with the help of protocols, such as Modbus, DNP3 EtherNet/IP, that lack authentication and encryption security precautions. The control devices then exchange information about the field site elements' parameters with a control server, like the Master Terminal Unit (MTU) taking part as the slave in a master-slave type communication.

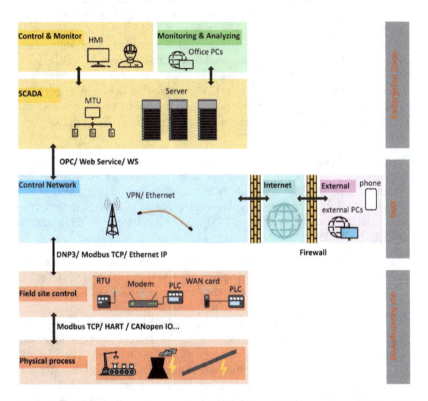

Figure 5: Schematic representation of an Industrial Automation and Control Systems

- The control center consists of a Human Machine Interface (HMI) that manages the operations of the field site remotely with the help of a control server, such as the MTU. Control engineers are able to reprogram/preview the logic controllers' content using an engineering workstation at the control level. The controllers' logs are also stored at the control center in a data historian for analysis and security development purposes.

Traditional ICS have been operational on the physical layer level and depend entirely on the OT networks alone, separated from the public network and lacking the connection to the IT networks. Therefore, security measures were not taken into account in their design or initial protocol versions, such as EtherCAT and Modbus. Later on, IT networks were integrated for purposes of development, cost efficiency, data collection, and automation. This integration introduced a new generation of ICS that uses automation technologies to control the industrial sector, known as Industrial Automation and Control Systems (IACS). With the incorporation of automation methodology, the industrial systems had better organization and administration between one another. However, new security challenges have appeared by exposing the control systems to the public network calling for more sophisticated security measures (Duque Anton et al. 2021; Branquinho, 2018).

As a way of facing the rising security challenges, IACS defined five different Security Levels (SL) and grouped the assets, devices, or elements of the system in three zones, each with different properties (Hassanzadeh et al., 2020) as illustrated in Figure 1. This characterization of the system forms the IACS security standard (ISA-62443) consisting of the different zones described as follows:

- **Enterprise Zone**: this zone resides on the IT network part of the IACS including the highest security levels; the 4th and 5th levels. It comprises the devices associated with business logistics, planning, monitoring, and the enterprise network.
- **Demilitarized Zone (DMZ)**: this zone forms a shield between the OT and IT networks supporting the OT devices from any incidents that may transverse from the IT side of the network. Therefore, it holds all the services that are responsible for accessing the OT network, such as web server, email services, etc.
- **Manufacturing and Control Zon**es: the manufacturing zone represents the entire OT domain including the physical process and basic control, while the control zone represents a part of the manufacturing zone that excludes the bridging connection to the control center.

2.2   Industrial control protocols

ICS protocols perform as a connecting bridge between different parts of the system's architecture; field site control, control network, and the control & monitoring layers. Efficiency and reliability were taken into consideration as number one priorities in designing these protocols. Besides, any additional features that may stall the real-time operations or cause inefficiency, such as security and authentication were excluded. Which has consequently created a source of vulnerability of the ICS protocols. Since ICSs were first known various requirements and services were incorporated demanding different protocols that serve every need. Modbus and DNP3 are two of the better known and used protocols in the industrial control systems' networks (Drias, Serhrouchni and Vogel, 2015; Drias, Serhrouchni and Vogel, 2015b):

- **Modbus**: the power of the Modbus protocol lies in its simplicity of implementation, which made it widely used for control and monitoring purposes. It was mainly developed to be used in the master/slave communications between the control server (MTU) and the field site controllers (PLC, RTU). With the integration of remote access and control, Modbus was extended from serial channels communication (Modbus serial) to communication over TCP/IP (Modbus TCP). The communication over Modbus is a one-directional commanded communication, where the master (control server) requests data from the slave (field site controllers) and the slave is only allowed to respond.

- **DNP3**: the reliability and efficiency of the Distributed Network Protocol while being at the same time compatible for real-time communications, have made it suitable for both cross-layer and inner-layer communications. Unlike Modbus, bidirectional communications are valid over DNP3, where both sides can request data and respond. DNP3 supports time-stamped and time-synchronized data transfer in the exchanged messages between devices and/or layers, which increases the level of reliability for real-time communications. Similarly to Modbus and most of the ICS protocols, DNP3 was developed later to work over IP and make remote access possible.

The lower part of Figure 1 represents the manufacturing site. Here, the field site control and the physical processes with the corresponding communication protocols are shown, for instance Modbus TCP, HART or CANopen IO. The middle part of the graphic shows the Demilitarized Zone (DMZ); the control network is separated from the Internet through a firewall. It exists off wireless or cable-based communication systems. External devices are able to communicate with the industrial network via VPN. The upper part of the graphic illustrates the Enterprise Zone. There, the controlling and the industry's own systems in the form of master terminal units (MTU), servers and corresponding communication paths are schematically shown. It also includes the sensitive control and monitoring of the industrial processes in form of human machine interfaces (HMI) and the organisation's own office department for monitoring and analysing.

3 Attack vectors: From wiretapping and spoofing to manipulating programmable logic controllers

Many organisations use external service providers for their IT mechanisms and they are also inclined to use external providers for any security they may apply. This means that the core knowledge and decision-making does not take place in the organisation at all, leading to a gap between decision-makers and mostly external experts.

Many organisations redesigned their communication protocols to work over IP (Slowik, 2019). Most protocols did not consider cyber security in advance and so they are at a much higher risk for cyber-attacks than traditional IT systems. In contrast to traditional IT systems most ICS do not fulfill the typical security conditions such as confidentiality, integrity and availability (Bonandir et al., 2021). Famous attacks like Stuxnet (Manohar et al., 2021) and BlackEnergy (Bonandir et al., 2021) have shown how easy it can be to infiltrate an organisation by simply spear-phishing emails or compromising USB drives. In case of an attack it is not only the economic efficiency of the organisation that suffers, but there can also be risk to human lives directly or indirectly.

The ransomware-attack at the Colonial Pipeline system in April of 2021 (Turton and Mehrotra, 2021) showed again the urgent need for action, and that cyber security is one of the most important aspects for an organisation to consider. In that case it was a compromised password for remotely accessing the company's computer network that led to the encryption of the company's infrastructure.

To obtain access to a company's ecosystem is not new. From the beginning of wireless communication hackers appeared. In 1903 at the presentation of a long-range wireless communication system by the physicist John Ambrose Fleming, which was developed by the Italian radio pioneer Guglielmo Marconi, the system was hacked and specific morse codes were printed out (Marks, 2021). Since then, a lot of different attack types have occured, and different infrastructures have been compromised. Hemsley and Fisher (2018) give a good overview of these early attacks.

Christoph Lipps et al

To access an organisation's computer network through phishing mails or compromised USB devices are popular types of attacks. Also very dangerous is the access to SCADA systems through open ports which can be passively detected through software like Shodan, well shown by Duque Anton (2021).

Often used Protocols in SCADA systems are DNP3, Modbus, IEC 60870-6-104, IEC 61850, IEC 61400-25 and IEEE C37.118 (Xu et al., 2017). Early versions of DNP3 or Modbus do not support encryption, which means if exposed to an open port it is easy to compromise a system. To appear as a receiving or sending device in the company's ecosystem is an easy task and can cause considerable damage to controlled PLCs and attached physical processes. By sitting in the middle between the compromised system and a control unit the hacker sends compromised commands to the control devices and sends normal behavior to an HMI. In this way the organisation does not know it has been compromised.

Examples of attacks that affect protocols include Man-In-The-Middle (MITM), Denial of Service (DoS), Replay, Injection, Spoofing, Eavesdropping, Modification or Reconnaissance attacks (Duque Anton et al., 2021). One point to consider when looking at the different attacks is the main intention. What was the purpose of an attack? Was it politically motivated to destabilize a country; was the attack aimed specifically at an important industry or was the attack financially motivated?

In the 2014/15 Ukraine Power Grid attack (Xu et al., 2017) the electricity was interrupted for around six hours and about 230 thousand people were affected. In 2016 the Ukraine Power Grid in the North of Kiev (Slowik, 2019) was compromised again. Another attack that took place in 2016 was the Kemuri Water Company attack (Hassanzadeh et al., 2020; Hemsley & Fischer, 2018b) where hackers gained access to the Programmable Logic Controllers (PLCs) and were able to manipulate the water treatment chemicals. Furthermore, the already known attack-typ of Shamoon, also in 2016, affected Saudi Arabia's civil aviation agency (Hemsley & Fischer, 2018b) and in 2017 the Triton attack impaired the Oil and Gas Plant in Saudi Arabia (Pinto, Dragoni and Carcano, 2018).

All these are highly systemically important attacks which affected the daily life of thousands of people. Most of the attacks mentioned were politically motivated, with the exception of the Colonial pipeline attack, where the main objective was purely financial.

In this case a specific software encrypted the host system. The attackers then claimed a ransom to decrypt the attacked system. Some other popular

223

examples mentioned by Branquinho (2018) include the Petya attack in 2016 and the WannaCry attack in 2017.

In the Colonial pipeline attack, after paying the ransom the attack ended and the company received a software application to restore their network, albeit very slow.

A well known politically motivated attack was the raid against the company Sony at the end of 2014 (Haggard & Lindsay, 2015). As a potential reaction against an upcoming movie the company's internal information was deleted and most internal emails of employees over the previous 10 years were leaked. This led to a sharp reaction from the US government which accused North Korea of the attack. Also, the US government received attention after the potential eavesdropping against the German chancellor and other German politicians (Lyons, 2013).

The various attacks described here show the importance of cyber security in the field of industrial environments. The following section considers what can be done to reduce the risk of a successful attack.

4   How to mitigate: Countermeasures, deception technology and turn the tables

After understanding the different existing protocols and familiarizing with the broad portfolio of attack vectors, the remaining question and tasks for industry and decision makers is how to mitigate or prevent attacks as well as how to initiate countermeasures. As mentioned above, one important requirement for owners and operators of TSA-designated critical pipelines is to implement mitigation and countermeasure techniques, and then to ensure that they are enforced.

For a countermeasure to be effective it is necessary to be able to detect the attack: without knowing an attack is taking place, no countermeasures can be initiated. Intrusion Detection Systems (IDSs) monitor network traffic both on the software and on the hardware side. Once it is evident that systems are under attack, there are different methods of "interacting" with the attacker. Deception Technology is an emerging area of cyber security, and includes methods to analyze and defeat attacks. The most famous representative are probably honeypots. The traditional approach to system security is to deny access to attackers, for example by providing adequate protection via passwords, tokens, or preventing physical access. Closely related to this is the authentication of accesses, since without knowing who is the one who wants access, no access can/should be granted. However, even if the best security mechanisms are in place, all of them are useless if they are not properly appropriated, so it is important that as much information as possible is carried to the decision-makers and users of the systems. This makes it possible to avoid wrong decisions and incorrect application with little effort.

4.1 Intrusion detection systems and deception technology

The first line of defence, and thus the keystone of a targeted security strategy, is the knowledge of an attack. Without the awareness that there is an ongoing attack, it is quite impossible to initiate the appropriate countermeasures. For this purpose, IDSs and Intrusion Protection Systems (IPSs) are installed to detect and identify attacks on networks and individual systems. Here, three main types of IDSs are distinguished: i) host-based IDS (HIDS). These are installed on each individual system to be monitored, and they must be compatible with the system operating system. Through the installation on each device, a comprehensive and dedicated monitoring of a system is achieved, in which specific statements and analyses can be deduced. ii) Network-based IDS (NIDS). These are particularly suitable to monitor the data traffic at the network level, for analysing suspicious activities and detecting attack patterns. Thus, a complete network can be monitored via one central node. With high data volumes and distributed applications, however, there are disadvantages, as there are with encrypted communication. iii) hybrid IDSs are also used which combine the principles in order to achieve a higher coverage. In this case, the system must be extended through management functionality.

There are different approaches to the operation principle of IDSs. For example, the comparison with known attack patterns in the form of a statistical analysis whereby filters and signatures are used to describe specific attack patterns. Obviously, this will only work if the attack is known in advance, which is why Deception Technology approaches can be combined with IDSs.

As the attack vectors are becoming increasingly complex and in order to detect both known and unknown attacks, a corresponding understanding of the functioning of the system and of an attack is required. This is based on heuristic methods which, starting from known attacks, are supposed to infer similar attacks and detect a deviation from the normal state. What is problematic is that either many false warnings (false-positives) are issued, or attacks are not detected (false-negatives). This can be supported by Deception Technology (DT) methods. These rather proactive methods are aimed at detecting, analyzing and defending against cyber attacks and deceiving attackers. By the targeted distribution of traps and decoys through the whole systems infrastructure the attacker is distracted and lured onto false tracks. This allows several objectives to be pursued at the same time: i) information about the attack is collected, aggregated and analyzed in so-called research honeypots; ii) production honeypots by contrast help to reveal compromise; iii) attackers can be slowed down by deliberately stalling them; iv) attackers can be led astray and the critical network elements can be protected.

In addition, this creates a false sense of security for the attackers (Fraunholz et al. 2016).

An important aspect of any attack is the collection of attacker information. Here it is of particular interest how an attacker proceeds; what steps or sequence of steps an attack contains, and what is the strategy? Since on the one hand hardware clones are relatively expensive and complex, and on the other hand the virtualization of networks towards Digital Twins is advancing, digital honeypots and DT methods are simple and straightforward to implement.

4.2 Limiting access, encrypting the content and authenticating the entities

One of the most traditional methods of preventing unauthorized third parties from accessing a system is the use of encryption and the application of secret and/or complex information. In addition to concepts such as secrecy through obscurity (assurance of security through non-disclosure of the mode of operation), and security through disclosure (broadest of possible transparency or full disclosure) (cf. Kerckhoffs' principle (Kerckhoffs, 1883)), the active and strong encryption of content is one of the most important security principles. Without stepping too deeply into the subject of cryptography at this point, a distinction is made between symmetric and asymmetric cryptography (the number of keys is important), the security of cryptography is based on the principles mentioned, secrecy of the key, secrecy of the way the key is generated and the complexity of generating a key (Schneier, 2015).

In addition to encryption alone, another aspect is also of key importance: identification and authentication of users and accesses (whether they are humans or machines). Without knowing who would like to have access to a system, and without verifying the claim, no reliable security can be provided. This is, though, becoming increasingly complex due to the ongoing globalization and interconnectedness of systems. To access a system it is no longer necessary to have physical access, it is possible to connect remotely from anywhere around the globe. In addition to authentication by *possession, knowledge* and *inherence* (Lipps, Herbst and Schotten, 2021c), there are approaches to integrate supplementary context information (Duqué et al. 2018) as a plausibility check in the process. For this purpose, data such as the time of an access, the outgoing IP address or the country of origin of the request are taken into account.

However, since the Industrial Internet of Things (IIoT) is packed with resource-limited devices (sensors, actuators, etc.), and the lifetime of industrial equipment is often many years (usually more than 20 years), complex cryptographic methods are not always effective or successful. Therefore, a promising approach for IIoT environments is Physical Layer Security (PhySec): the utilization of inherently given, characteristic, physical properties in systems in order to derive cryptographic primitives therefrom. Basically, these are divided into the three areas *of electiric/solicon* PUFs (Lipps et al. 2018), *Human PUFs* (Lipps, Bergkemper and Schotten, 2021) and *Channel PUFs* (Lipps et al. 2020). These lightweight security applications offer a major advantage to decision-makers: they are cheap, they do not require a major rebuild of equipment, and they are fast to integrate. One of the most important criteria for the operation of industrial facilities is that they are in operation. Every downtime causes financial losses. Unfortunately, this is one reason why systems security are often given a low priority by many operators. Against this background, PhySec's approaches are a great starting point for mastering this security issue.

4.3 How artificial intelligence can impact security

For all the countermeasures mentioned, one factor is crucial: the database. Without an appropriate amount of data, intrusion detection systems, for example, will not function effectively (both statistical and heuristic). This is precisely where the methods and algorithms of Artificial Intelligence (AI) can step in. AI systems, in combination with appropriate computing power, have advantages in handling large amounts of information and recognizing patterns. Based on appropriate data sets, the AI algorithms can not only support the analysis, but also draw appropriate conclusions and thus contribute to faster and more accurate detection of attacks and new vulnerabilities than conventional systems are able to do (Belani, 2021). As AI methods have the ability to learn (autonomously), these systems assist in predicting attacks and bring themselves up to date in an iterative and self-learning manner (Martin, 2021).

In terms of the PhySec approaches mentioned, AI offers several advantages: in particular, in the prediction of characteristics of the radio channel, AI helps to provide better and more secure keys with the Channel-PUFs; along with the development of Sixth Generation (6G) Wireless Systems, AI will have a major impact on the PhySec topic and serve as a catalyst for applications (Lipps et al. 2021b).

On the other hand, AI is not restricted to the defenders, as the algorithms are freely available and can be used in the hands of attackers quite easily for harming systems. Especially in the domain of dedicated AI-based attacks, there will be more attacks on networks and critical infrastructures in the (near) future. Not only because computing power has become cheaper and cheaper and the corresponding data on vulnerabilities and attack vectors is increasingly disseminated, but also because targeted attacks on infrastructures through cyber warfare are gaining strategic importance, the attackers are difficult to identify and the impact is tremendous.

5 Taking notes on the colonial pipeline attack

The history of attacks and in particular the attack against the colonial pipeline proved the need to rethink the importance of security in industrial environments. With further development of 5G and Beyond 5G (Jiang et al., 2021), the IIoT is moving ever more into focus. This means that the subject of security will become more important than ever with the continual development of interconnections and smart systems.

5.1 Timeline and impacts

The Colonial Pipeline Attack began on 6th May 2021 with a compromised password that was discovered in a data breach for another location, resulting in the intruders getting access into the corporate network (Kerner, 2021). Within a small timeframe they stole gigabytes of data and infected the IT network with ransomware which affected different systems, including the systems for billing and accounting. This ransomware attack was part of a series of attacks by the hacking group called DarkSide (Reeder and Hall, 2021). One day later the company becomes aware of the breach and the attack begins. To prevent the Pipeline´s operational network bing exposed, the whole 5,500 mile long pipeline system was shut down by the company. Only a couple of hours after learning of the attack the company pays the requested ransom of 75 bitcoin (Shear, Perlroth and Krauss, 2021). The attackers delivered a decryption tool which worked very slowly. On 12th of May the pipeline was restarted and was back on operation. During the process of recovering the pipeline system the president of the US declared a state of emergency because of the potential shortage of oil. On 7th of June 2021 the Department of Justice was able to recover 63.7 bitcoins from the attackers (Bing, Menn and Lynch, 2021).

The impact of this attack goes in different directions; the most evident is the ransom paid and the outage of transported gasoline and the loss of money due to the shutdown. The other side is the impact on people, which resulted in panic and over purchasing at gas stations due to the uncertainty of the situation and the lack of assurance as to when stations will be out of gas. The availability of gas is systemically relevant and a loss of it would create a failure in public transportation, ambulance service, air transport, emergency power supply and many more highly important fields. The panic of consumers created a sharp rise in the price of gas, which in turn resulted in destabilizing the already fragile economic system due to the ongoing pandemic situation, which could consequently lead to a rising inflation.

5.2 Lessons learned

One lesson learned from this attack is the importance of the interconnections of the whole system, since the attacker didn't need a complicated hacking tool or a special system to get access into the company's network. A compromised password for accessing a VPN to the network was enough entry for one of the biggest downtimes of a pipeline system in America. In reference to Figure 1 the breach went through the Demilitarized Zone into the control Network and affected the Monitoring and Analyzing-part of the Enterprise Zone. To prevent further spread the whole system including the Manufacturing Side was shut down by the company itself. To prevent the need to shut down the whole system in the future, the different subsystems should be further separated to be able to exchange compromised parts with backups. In addition, the need for rapid backup systems for critical infrastructures like the Colonial Pipeline is another important point (even if it seems to be obvious) to take into consideration. This attack brought out the vulnerability of the system in that a small open window can be enough for the right attacker to initiate a significant breach. Because of the size of the private sector, the need for secure standards is another of the other lessons learned. If the well-being of society is dependent on these companies, then high security standards are required to prevent the failure of these systems due to attacks.

On another note, it is crucial how the identification is handled in these organizations, in particular when passwords are included, as it is well-known how safety critical it is to use a password for multiple system authentication. Needless to say that the selection of the password itself plays an effective role as a safety measure. It has to meet a certain criteria of being memorable and complex enough at the same time, so that it will not contribute to compromising the system's security. Enhancing the level of authentication is also essential to protect the environment from possible attacks at all times. A way to achieve this is incorporating multi-factor authentication as a stronger safeguard against attacks. Therefore in addition to known methods of verification through a mobile phone, for highly critical systems where it is important to be sure of the user's identity, precise characteristics are required. One way of achieving this is by deploying the benefits of Internet of Things (IoT) devices, that can identify a person by its intrinsic characteristics, which are used in modern Biometrics such as fingerprints or facial recognition. Some examples of this are provided in Lipps, Herbst and Schotten, (2021c) and Lipps, Bergkemper and Schotten, (2021).

In addition, one remaining point of vulnerability for the hackers to take advantage of is the attentiveness of the Employees themselves, which makes periodic audits and examination of the network's state and users' privileges a possible countermeasure to prevent sudden attacks from exploiting the organization's network (Reeder and Hall, 2021).

The cyber activities over the years show that the attackers are making sure to choose the right time to attack, when an organization is at its most vulnerable and least attentive. Therefore it should be the goal to defend the network systems at all times against intruders and rely on backups with redundant systems in case a weak point breaks.

All of these different kinds of attacks (malware attacks, encrypted threats, intrusion attempts, cryptojacking attacks, ransomware attacks, IoT attacks) (Reeder and Hall, 2021) vary in their attack vectors, techniques, damages caused, and consequences, providing a wide scope of data that can be deployed towards better protection and recovery.

As the systems as a whole become more and more complex, and the attacks are increasingly specialized, specific knowledge of an appropriate defense is required. Artificial intelligence, deception technology and modern encryption that includes post-quantum cryptography are important and powerful tools in the "fight" for the upper hand, but the most powerful means are ineffective without the knowledge of how to use them. Therefore, it is not enough for computer and security specialists to address the issue of cyber security, the awareness, knowledge and teaching about it needs to be brought to decision- and policymakers.

6   Conclusion and future work

In this chapter the authors have demonstrated not only the dangers of what cyber attacks can do, but also how and when they happen, every day and with more frequency. Particularly over the last decade, not only the number but also the impact of such attacks has increased significantly. We believe that the effects will become even more noticeable than in the past, but we are also concerned that the focus of the attackers has changed. Whereas in the past it was the so-called script kiddies who tried out their skills, today cyber attacks are targeted actions by groups, organizations and nation states, even as a kind of modern (cyber) warfare. The more valuable the target, the more motivated someone is to attack it. And how profitable an attack on an infrastructure can be has been demonstrated by the recent attacks on the Colonial pipeline.

The good news is that there is still hope: There are solutions which can help to include security techniques such as intrusion detection, active encryption and the powerful methods of artificial intelligence. Each alone may not be the solution to the problem, but used in combination and with targeted expertise, these approaches are not only promising but provide a toolbox with which attacks can be detected, mitigated and prevented. However, it is essential to establish a corresponding awareness of the vulnerabilities in the systems in industry, in small and medium-sized enterprises, and above all among the decision and policymakers. The awareness of cyber security, but also a more in depth knowledge about it and the teaching of it throughout an organisation needs to be emphasized. Only through targeted and strategic coordination is it possible to make things as difficult as possible for the well-organized attackers and (hopefully) prevent a further attack on another important infrastructure. We hope that this work adds to that dialogue.

References

Ahmed, I., Obermeier, S., Sudhakaran, S. and Roussev, V., *"Programmable Logic Controller Forensics"*, *IEEE Security & Privacy, vol.* 15, no. 6, pp. 18–24, 2017, doi: 10.1109/MSP.2017.4251102.

Belani, G., "The Use of Artificial Intelligence in Cybersecruity: A Review", *IEEE*, November 2021, [Online], Available at: https://www.computer.org/publications/tech-news/trends/the-use-of-artificial-intelligence-in-cybersecurity

Bing, C., Menn, J., and Lynch, S.N., "U.S. seizes \$2.3 mln in bitcoin paid tp Colonial Pipeline hackers", *Reuters*, June 2021, [Online], Available at: https://www.reuters.com/business/energy/us-announce-recovery-millions-colonial-pipeline-ransomware-attack-2021-06-07/

Bonandir, N.A., Jamil, N., Nawawi, M.N.A., Jidin, R. Rusli, M.E., Yan, L.K. and Maudau, L.L.A.D., „A Review of Cyber Security Assessment (CSA) for Industrial Control Systems (ICS) and Their Impact on the Availability of the ICS Operation", *Journal of Physics: Conference Series, vol.* 1860, International Conference on Applied and Practical Sciences (ICAPS) no. 1, 2021, DOI: 10.1088/1742-6596/1860/1/012015.

Branquinho, M.A., "*Ransomware in industrial control systems. What comes after Wannacry and Petya global attacks?*", *WIT Trans. Built Environ.*, Bd. 174, S. 329–334, 2018, doi: 10.2495/SAFE170301.

Di Pinto, A., Dragoni, Y. And Carcano, A., "TRITON: The First ICS Cyber Attack on Safety Instrument Systems Understanding the Malware, Its Communications and Its OT Payload", *Black Hat USA*, 2018.

Drias, Z., Serhrouchni, A. and Vogel, O., "*Analysis of cyber security for industrial control systems*", International Conference on Cyber Security of Smart Cities, Industrial Control System and Communications (SSIC), *IEEE*, 2015, DOI: 10.1109/SSIC.2015.7245330.

Drias, Z., Serhrouchni, A. and Vogel, O., "Taxonomy of attacks on industrial control protocols", International Conference on Protocol Engineering (ICPE) and International Conference on New Technologies of Distributed Systems (NTDS),IEEE, 2015b, DOI: 10.1109/NOTERE.2015.7293513.

Duque Anton, S., Fraunholz, D., Krohmer, D., Reti, D., Schneider, D., and Schotten H.D., "*The Global State of Security in Industrial Control Systems: An Empirical Analysis of Vulnerabilities around the World*", *IEEE Internet Things Journal*, May 2021, DOI: 10.1109/JIOT.2021.3081741.

Duque Anton, S., Fraunholz, D., Lipps, C., Alam, K. and Schotten, H.D., "Putting Things in Context: Securing Industrial Authentication with Context Information", *Int. J. Cyber Situational Aware.*, vol. 4, no. 1, pp. 98–120, Dez. 2018, DOI: 10.22619/IJCSA.2018.100122.

Duque Anton, D., Fraunholz, D., Lipps, C., Pohl, F., Zimmermann, M. and Schotten, H.D., "Two decades of SCADA exploitation: A brief history", *2017 IEEE Conference on Applications, Information and Network Security (AINS) 2017*, pp. 98–104, 2017, DOI: 10.1109/AINS.2017.8270432.

Fraunholz, D., Schneider, J., Duque Antón, D., Lipps, C. and Schotten, H.D., "Honeypots for Industrial IoT Applications", Kleinheubacher Tagung (KH-2016), Miltenberg, Germany, 2016.

Gartner, "Gartner Predicts By 2025 Cyber Attackers Will Have Weaponized Operational Technology Environments to Successfully Harm or Kill Humans", 2021/07 [online] available at: "https://www.gartner.com/en/newsroom/press-releases/2021-07-21-gartner-predicts-by-2025-cyber-attackers-will-have-we"

Hassanzadeh, A., Rasekh, A., Galelli, S., Aghashahi, M., Taorima, R., Ostfeld, A. and Banks, K., "*A Review of Cybersecurity Incidents in the Water Sector*", *Journal of Environmental Engineering, vol.* 146, no. 5, 2020,   DOI: 10.1061/(asce)ee.1943-7870.0001686.

Haggard, S. and Lindsay, J.R., "North Korea and the Sony Hack: Exporting Instability Through Cyberspace", 2015. https://scholarspace.manoa.hawaii.edu/bitstream/10125/36444/1/api117.pdf

Hemsley, K.E. and Fisher, R.E., "History of Industrial Control System Cyber Incidents", *INL/CON-18-44411-Revision-2*, Nr. December 2018, [Online]. Availbale at: https://www.osti.gov/servlets/purl/1505628   DOI: 10.2172/1505628

Hemsley, K.E. and Fisher, R.E., "A History of Cyber Incidents and Threats Involving Industrial Control Systems To cite this version : HAL Id : hal-02076302 AND THREATS INVOLVING", 2019.

Homeland Security, "DHS Announces New Cybersecurity Requirements for Critical Pipeline Owners and Operators", 2021/07/20, [online] available at: https://www.dhs.gov/news/2021/07/20/dhs-announces-new-cybersecurity-requirements-critical-pipeline-owners-and-operators

Jiang, W., Han, B., Habibi, M.A., and Schotten, H.D., "The Road Towards 6G: A Comprehensive Survey", *IEEE Open Journal of the Communications Society,* vol. 2, pp. 334-366, 2021, DOI: 10.1109/OJCOMS.2021.3057679

Kerckhoffs, A., "La cryptographie militaire", *Journal des science militairs*, vol IX, pp. 5-38, 1883

Kerner, S.M., "Colonial Pipeline hack explained: Everything you need to know", *TechTarget Network*, July 2021, [Online], Available at: https://whatis.techtarget.com/feature/Colonial-Pipeline-hack-explained-Everything-you-need-to-know

Lipps, C., Weinand, A., Krummacker, D., Fischer, C. and Schotten, H.D., "Proof of Concept for IoT Device Authentication Based on SRAM PUFs Using ATMEGA 2560-MCU", in *2018 1st International Conference on Data Intelligence and Security (ICDIS)*, Apr. 2018, S. 36–42. doi: 10.1109/ICDIS.2018.00013.

Lipps, C., Krummacker, D. and Schotten, H.D., "Securing Industrial Wireless Networks: Enhancing SDN with PhySec", in *2019 Conference on Next Generation Computing Applications (NextComp)*, Sep. 2019, pp. 1–7. DOI: 10.1109/NEXTCOMP.2019.8883600.

Lipps, C., Mallikarjun, S.B., Strufe, M., Heinz, C., Grimm, C. and Schotten, H.D., "Keep Private Networks Private: Secure Channel-PUFs, and Physical Layer Security by Linear Regression enhanced Channel Profiles", *2020, 3rd International Conference on Data Intelligence and Security (ICDIS 2020)*, pp. 93–100, 2020, DOI: 10.1109/ICDIS50059.2020.00019.

Lipps, C., Bergkemper, L. and Schotten, H.D., "Distinguishiing Hearts: How Machine Learning identifies People based on their Heartbeat", *Sixth International Conference on Advances in Biomedical Engineering (ICABME),* Islamic University of Lebanon, Werdanyeh Campus, Lebanon, 2021, DOI:10.1109/ICABME53305.2021.9604855.

Lipps, C., Baradie, S., Noushinfar, M., Herbst, J., Weinand, A. and Schotten, H.D., "Towards the Sixth Generation (6G) Wireless Systems: Thoughts on Physical Layer Security", *Mobile Communication – Technologies and Applications – 25. VDE/VDI Fachtagung Mobilkommunikcation"*, Osnabrück, Germany, 2021b.

Lipps, C., Herbst, J., and Schotten, H.D., "How to Dance your Passwords: A Biometric MFA-Scheme for Identification and Authentication of Individuals in IIoT Environments", 16th International Conference on Cyber Warfare and Security, Cookeville, TN, USA, 2021c, DOI: 10.34190/IWS.21.016

Lyons, J., "Angela Merkel's phone ‚hacked by American spies': German Chancellor confronts Barack Obama over claims". https://www.mirror.co.uk/news/world-news/angela-merkels-phone-hacked-american-2485433

Martin, D., "8 Benefits of Using AI for Cybersecurity", *Cyber Management Alliance*, Mai 2021, [Online], Available at: https://www.cm-alliance.com/cybersecurity-blog/8-benefits-of-using-ai-for-cybersecurity

Manohar, M., Hiriyannaiah, S., Siddesh, G.M., and Srinivasa, K.G., "Risk Measurement and Cyber security in Industrial Control Systems", IOP Conference Series Materials Science and Engineering vol. 1110, no. 1, pp. 012014, 2021, doi: 10.1088/1757-899x/1110/1/012014.

Marks, P., "Dot-dash-diss: The gentleman hacker's 1903 lulz", 2011., *NewScientist,* 2011, [Online], Available at: https://www.newscientist.com/article/mg21228440-700-dot-dash-diss-the-gentleman-hackers-1903-lulz/ Access on Sep. 30, 2021).

Qasim, S.A., Ayub, A., Johnson, J.A. and Ahmed, I., *"Attacking the IEC-61131 Logic Engine in Programmable Logic Controllers in Industrial Control Systems"*, Fifteenth Annual IFIP WG 11.10 International Conference on Critical Infrastructure Protection (ICCIP), Arlington, VA, USA, 2020/03.

Reeder, J.R. and Hall, T., "Cybersecurity's Pearl Harbor Moment: Lessons Learned from the Colonial Pipeline Ransomware Attack", *GreenbergTraurig*, Summer 2021, [Online], Available at: https://www.gtlaw.com/en/insights/2021/8/published-articles/cybersecuritys-pearl-harbor-moment

Schneier, B., "Applied Cryptography: Protocols, Algorithms and Source Code in C", 20th Anniversary Edition, Wiley and Sons, 2015, ISBN: 978-1-11-09682-6

Shear, M.D., Perlroth, N., and Krauss, C., "Colonial Pipeline Paid Roughly $5 Million in Ransom to Hackers", *The New York Times*, Published May 13, 2021, Updated June 7, 2021.

Shimon Noam Oren, "2021 Mid-Year Cyber Threat Landscape Report" 2021/07 [online] available at: https://www.deepinstinct.com/blog/2021-mid-year-cyber-threat-landscape-report

Slowik, J., "Crashoverride: Reassessing the 2016 ukraine electric power event as a protection-focused attack", *Dragos Inc.*, 2019, [Online]. Available at: https://www.dragos.com/wp-content/uploads/CRASHOVERRIDE.pdf

Turton, W. and Mehrotra, K. "Hackers Breached Colonial Pipeline Using Compromised Password", *Bloomberg Cybersecurity*, 2021, [Online]. Available at: https://www.bloomberg.com/news/articles/2021-06-04/hackers-breached-colonial-pipeline-using-compromised-password

Xu, Y., Yang, Y., Li, T., Ju, J. and Wang, Q., "Review on cyber vulnerabilities of communication protocols in industrial control systems", in *2017 IEEE Conference on Energy Internet and Energy System Integration (EI2)*, Nov. 2017, vol., no. 1, pp. 1–6. DOI: 10.1109/EI2.2017.8245509.

Author biographies

Christoph Lipps graduated in Electrical and Computer Engineering at the University of Kaiserslautern in Germany where he lectures as well. He is the Lead of the *Cyber Resilience & Security* Team of the Intelligent Networks Department and a Researcher and Ph.D. candidate at the German Research Center for Artificial Intelligence (DFKI) in Kaiserslautern. His research focuses on Physical Layer Security (PhySec), Physically Unclonable Functions (PUFs), Artificial Intelligence (AI), entity authentication, Security in the Sixth Generation (6G) Wireless Systems and all aspects of network and cyber security.

Shaden Baradie graduated in Electrical Engineering specializing in Multimedia Systems and Services from Budapest University of Technology and Economics (BME). She is a Researcher at the German Research Center for Artificial Intelligence (DFKI) in Kaiserslautern. Her research is focused on wireless communication systems, network management, security, and Artificial Intelligence (AI).

Jan Herbst graduated with the diploma of physics at the University of Kaiserslautern. There he worked in the fields of molecular beam epitaxy, quantum dot growth and control programming. As a Researcher and Ph.D. candidate he is working at the German Research Center for Artificial Intelligence (DFKI) in Kaiserslautern. His fields of research are in Human-Physically Unclonable Functions (HPUFs), entity authentication, Artificial Intelligence as well as network and cyber security.

Dr Edwin "Leigh" Armistead is the President of Peregrine Technical Solutions, a certified 8(a) small business that specializes in Cyber Security. A retired United States Naval Officer, he has significant Information Operations academic credentials having written his PhD on the conduct of Cyber Warfare by the federal government and has published three books, in an unclassified format in 2004, 2007 and 2010, all focusing on Information Warfare. He is also the Chief Editor of the Journal of Information Warfare (JIW) https://www.jinfowar.com/; the Program Director of the International Conference of Cyber Warfare and

Security and the Secretary of Working Group 9.10, ICT Uses in Peace and War.

 Hans Dieter Schotten is a full professor and head of the chair for Wireless Communications and Navigation at the University of Kaiserslautern. In addition he is Scientific Director of the Intelligent Networks Research Group of the German Research Center for Artificial Intelligence (DFKI). He received his Ph.D. in Electrical Engineering from the RWTH Aachen in 1997. He was a research group leader there before moving into industry. He held the position of Senior Researcher at Ericsson and was Director of Technical Standards at Qualcomm. His topics of interest are wireless communication, 5G, Beyond 5G as well as the Sixth Generation (6G) Wireless Systems.